Crime in Ireland

CRIME IN IRELAND
A Sociological Introduction

CIARAN MC CULLAGH

CORK
UNIVERSITY
PRESS

First published in 1996 by
Cork University Press
University College
Cork
Ireland

British Library Cataloguing in Publication Data
A CIP catalogue record for this book is available from the British Library.

ISBN 1 85918 034 5 paperback
ISBN 1 85918 096 5 hardback
Typeset by Seton Music Graphics, Bantry, Co. Cork
Printed by ColourBooks, Baldoyle, Co. Dublin

CONTENTS

Acknowledgements   vii
Introduction   ix

1   Facts: Victims and Offenders   1

2   Explaining Crime in Ireland   30

3   The Crimes of the Middle Class   59

4   Women and Crime   86

5   Back to Explanations   117

6   Policing Irish Society   145

7   Punishing Criminals – Irish Style   177

     Conclusion: How to Reduce Crime   212

     Bibliography   224
     Index   238

ACKNOWLEDGEMENTS

A number of people contributed invaluable assistance and encouragement during the writing of this book. David Rottman, formerly of the Economic and Social Research Institute and now with the National Center for State Courts in Williamsburg, Virginia, USA, commented extensively on the first draft and provided a space in his home during which the second draft was planned. Mary Daly may be surprised to find herself mentioned here but she was a constant source of encouragement during the leave I spent in the European University Institute in Florence. Patrick O'Mahony, Piet Strydom and the staff of the Centre for European Social Research Institute in Cork provided me with the space in which to write the first draft of the text. Teresa Mc Cullagh read the early chapters and convinced me of their readability. Niamh Mc Cullagh checked the bibliography. To all of these my thanks.

The book is dedicated to Teresa, Niamh and Damian whose love and support are so important to me.

Introduction

One of the most significant changes in Irish society over the past thirty years has been the increase in crime coupled with the increasing realisation that it is a problem that must be responded to. However much of the debate about crime often appears to be driven by the anxieties of the particular moment rather than by a fuller understanding of the dimensions of the problem.

The aim of this book is to provide the material and the tools out of which a deeper understanding of crime can be constructed. It does this through a presentation of available material on crime in Ireland and through the introduction of a range of perspectives through which this material can be interpreted. It also presents a specific argument about the causes of crime in Ireland. There is a problem in approaching the topic of crime from this perspective. This lies in the lack of published research material on all aspects of the Irish criminal justice system, accompanied by the inadequate character of many of the official statistics on crime and especially on the courts and on the prisons. As a result there are significant gaps in our knowledge about many aspects of crime in Ireland and indeed an urgent need to fill them. It has meant that at important stages in the book informed speculation must take the place of empirically based argumentation.

The book begins with a consideration of the facts and figures of crime and with what they tell us about the nature of the crime problem in Ireland. How the problem might be explained is the subject of chapter two which outlines a range of sociological theories on the causes of crime and speculates on their applicability in the Irish context. In chapter three we take up the issue of one of the main kinds of crime which is under-represented in official statistics, that of a corporate or a white-collar nature. We discuss the significance of this type of crime, its importance in Ireland and what its existence and its extent mean for attempts to explain crime. The fact that most crime, whether of a conventional or of a corporate nature, is committed by males is taken up in chapter four. This outlines the range of theories that have been utilised to explain the low participation of women in crime, the experiences of women in the criminal justice system and, in a detailed consideration of the crime of rape, it looks at what may be the more typical criminal experience of women, namely that of crime victims.

In chapter five an attempt is made to construct an explanation for crime in Ireland that encompasses conventional crime, corporate or white-collar crime and the low participation rates of females in crime. While this may be the most contentious chapter in the book – and to the non-sociologist the most difficult – nonetheless it provides the basis on which the proposals to reduce crime in the final section of the book are built. Chapter six deals with the policing of Irish society through an examination of the forms that policing takes and in particular it deals with the role of the Garda Síochána. Chapter seven considers how the courts and the prison system function and looks at how effective both are in dealing with crime and criminals. Finally the conclusion looks at the question of how crime in Ireland might be reduced.

One concluding point needs to be made. The international literature on criminology and the sociology of deviance that this book draws on is a large one and it is not feasible to provide a comprehensive list of references to support every point and argument. Instead the procedure has been adopted of using the most recent, or what the author considers the most appropriate, reference to substantiate the point being made.

Ciaran Mc Cullagh

1 FACTS: VICTIMS AND OFFENDERS

Introduction

The purpose of this book is to shed light on crime in Ireland. A necessary prologue is to assemble the basic information on the nature of the problem. In this chapter we use the available official statistics to answer a number of the key questions about crime – how much there is, who commits it and who are the victims? We also examine a range of associated issues such as the seriousness of crime, the social backgrounds of offenders and the groups who are most at risk of becoming crime victims. Finally we draw this information together to see what kind of overall picture of crime it gives us. As we shall see, the nature of crime and the manner of its reporting and recording place important limitations on the information available to us and thus limit the comprehensiveness of the account that we can present.

I Crime: Facts and Figures

The major source of information on crime in Ireland is the statistics contained in the *Reports on Crime* produced by the garda commissioner. These reports have been published annually since 1947.[1] They record the number of offences that, in the phraseology used in the reports, 'Became known to the gardaí' in the particular year. The statistics are assembled around a distinction between indictable and non-indictable offences. This distinction is drawn from British legal statutes of 1849 and 1851. Indictable offences are serious and can or should be dealt with by a judge and jury. Non-indictable offences are fairly minor and can be dealt with by a judge acting alone (see Rottman, 1984: 60). The total figure for indictable offences is the one that is emphasised in the annual reports and is used as the measure of the level of crime in the country. As we shall see below the contemporary relevance of the distinction is open to question.

Table 1.1 is drawn from these reports for various years from 1961 to 1991. It shows the number of indictable offences reported to the gardaí and the number and percentage of offences in which, to use the phraseology of the reports again, either 'criminal proceedings were commenced' or 'the perpetrators were detected but for which no proceedings are shown'. This latter figure is used in the reports as the detection rate.

The Overall Level of Crime

The first point to be drawn from the table is the huge increases in crime that it documents. The first garda report on crime in 1947 recorded just over 15,000 indictable offences, a figure which is broadly similar to that in 1961. Since then there has been a six-fold increase in the amount of recorded crime over the thirty-year period. In effect the 1960s represented the end of the era of low levels of crime in Ireland. The key period of change in the table is 1966 to 1971 when the number of offences doubled. The size of the increases between 1971 and 1981 was less dramatic but still very substantial. By 1981 the level of crime was five times higher than what it had been in 1961. The highest number of offences

Table 1.1 Number of indictable offences reported to gardaí and number and percentage detected, in various years, from 1961–1991

		1961	1966	1971	1976	1981	1986	1991	Changes (%)
Offences against the person	No. reported	701	1,132	1,256	1,714	2,478	1,883	1,435	+104
	No. detected	646	1,060	1,128	1,546	2,174	1,487	1,162	+79
	No. detected (%)	92	94	90	90	88	79	81	
Offences against property with violence	No. reported	3,186	4,957	10,654	20,903	28,916	35,146	40,676	+1,176
	No. detected	2,439	3,624	5,444	9,152	11,181	9,287	12,530	+413
	No. detected (%)	77	73	51	44	39	26	31	
Larcenies etc.	No. reported	10,623	12,631	24,929	31,540	57,642	49,226	51,990	+389
	No. detected	6,473	7,535	10,103	11,583	19,089	16,344	12,668	+95
	No. detected (%)	61	60	41	37	33	33	34	
Other indictable offences	No reported	308	309	942	225	364	319	305	-1
	No. detected	280	291	825	201	310	304	293	+4
	No. detected (%)	91	94	88	89	85	76	96	
Total	No. reported	14,818	19,029	37,781	54,382	89,400	86,574	94,406	+537
	No. detected	9,838	12,510	17,518	22,482	32,754	32,795	31,653	+153
	No. detected (%)	66	66	46	41	37	33	34	

Source: Annual reports on crime, various years

Note: Offence categories are those used in garda statistics. Category (1) includes murder, manslaughter and assault; (2) includes burglary, house-breaking and robbery; (3) includes larceny from the person, of cars and from shops; (4) includes miscellaneous offences such as perjury and indecency.

in the history of the state was recorded in 1983. The level of crime fell in the following four years. It rose again at the end of the 1980s and it is currently (the figures for 1993 are the most recent available) just under 99,000 offences. So overall we had a period of low and stable crime levels in the 1940s, 1950s and early 1960s. This was ended by the rapid and substantial increases of the late 1960s, the 1970s and the early 1980s. There was a period of small but significant declines in the mid-1980s and the period ends with the level of crime beginning to rise again, much more slowly this time but none the less perceptibly. The figure for 1993 is the highest since 1984.

The Falling Detection Rate

The second point from the table relates to the number of detections, which has also risen in absolute terms. But it has done so at a considerably slower pace and so has failed to keep up with the rate of increase in crime. This means that the detection rate is declining. We can illustrate this by looking at the percentage of offences in which a detection was recorded. This has been in continuous decline since 1966. Then two-thirds of offences were detected. In 1991 it was 34 per cent. Again the key period of change is 1966–1971. The rate declined from 66 per cent in 1966 to 46 per cent in 1971, a level of decline that it has not undergone in any period since. The detection rate rose slightly in 1993 to 36 per cent but this is more of a minor fluctuation than an indication of a major reversal of the dominant trend.

Different Offences, Different Rates

Table 1.1 shows the total figures for indictable offences. The annual reports also divide these offences into four separate categories. The first is 'offences against the person': this includes murder, attempted murder, assault, rape and indecent assault. The second is 'offences against property with violence', made up primarily by the offence of burglary but it also includes armed robbery, malicious damage to property and interference with the railway. The third category is 'larcenies etc.', which covers a range of offences, including larcenies from the person, larcenies of motor cars and larcenies from unattended vehicles. The fourth is 'other indictable offences'. This covers a small number of offences including treason, riot, public mischief, and offences under the Official Secrets Act. As there have been no shortage of leaks to the press and only one offence recorded under the Official Secrets Act in the last ten years it raises intriguing questions about what qualities information has to have in Ireland to achieve the status of a state secret.

If we look at the specific categories of offences when looking at the overall increase in crime, we find significant differences in the size of the increases and in the pattern of detection. The main contrast is between offences against the person and offences against property. The number of offences against the person doubled between 1961 and 1991. The most serious of these offences is murder. While the number of murders fluctuates on a year-to-year basis to a greater extent than other kinds of serious crime, we can say that there has been a three-fold increase from eight recorded murders in 1961 to twenty-three in 1991. By contrast the number of offences against property with violence increased thirteen-fold, from just over 3,000 offences in 1961 to over 40,000 in 1991. The most common of these is burglary. The number of burglaries rose from just over 2,000 in 1961 to just under 31,000 in 1991. In this way the increase in the level of offences against property has been far more significant than the rise in offences against the person.

Similar trends are evident in detection rates. The detection rate for offences against the person has fallen somewhat, from 92 per cent in 1961 to 81 per cent in 1991 but it still remains high. That for offences against property by contrast has fallen dramatically and substantially, from 77 per cent of offences in 1961 to 31 per cent in 1991. We can highlight this again by contrasting murder and burglary. The detection rate for murder in 1961 was 62.5 per cent . This was unusually low for that period. In 1991 it was 87 per cent.[2] With burglary, by contrast, the detection rate has fallen dramatically, from 70 per cent in 1961 to 28 per cent in 1991. The lowest detection rates are recorded for particular forms of larceny, such as larceny from the person (14 per cent), larceny of motor vehicles (10 per cent) and larceny from unattended vehicles (20 per cent). One of the highest detection rates – 96 per cent in 1991 – is for the assault or wounding of a garda on duty. This suggests that the offence and its detection take place at around the same time and, one assumes, in much the same order.

The Significance of Property Crime

These figures show that the bulk of crime in Ireland falls into either 'offences against property with violence' or 'larcenies'. If we reduce these to the generic category of property crime, in that they both involve the illegal acquisition of property, then it accounts for 93 per cent of all indictable crime in 1961 and 98 per cent in 1991. In 1993 it also accounted for 98 per cent of all indictable crime. In this sense at least there is nothing new about the nature of the crime problem in Ireland. Now, as then, it is primarily one of property crime. What is new is that there is now far more of it about. Property crimes have shown the largest increases in incidence over the past thirty years and the largest declines in detection rates.

The Geographical Distribution of Crime

Overall the increase in crime has been a national one with both urban and rural areas experiencing significant increases.

But underlying this has been a notable regularity. This is the striking degree to which crime and in particular property crime is concentrated in the Dublin metropolitan area. This area contains about 35 per cent of the total population of the country. In 1961 it accounted for 52 per cent of indictable crime; in 1991 it was 55 per cent.

The Seriousness of Crime – The Victims

Crime in Irish society has, as we have shown, increased considerably but how serious is the kind of crime that is going on? Is it mainly irritating but generally minor forms of crime, is it dangerous and violent crime or is it both? This question is an important one but it is a difficult one to answer. It raises complex questions of definition and of measurement. The seriousness of crime must in some way be related to the harm that crime causes in society but what kinds of harm does it cause? In order to answer this question, it is useful, for presentation purposes, to distinguish between the harm or damage caused to victims and the seriousness to society.

Crime harms victims in four ways. The first is the direct physical harm of being assaulted or injured either as an offence in itself or in the course of a robbery or burglary. Consideration of this raises the question of whether Ireland is now a more violent society than it was in the 1960s. Unfortunately the available indicators do not provide us with a clear-cut answer. If we look at the kinds of crimes in which the intention is to do physical damage to the victim, then the evidence appears reassuring. The number of 'crimes against the person' has risen considerably. But the rate of increase has been much slower than for other kinds of crime. Moreover 'crimes against the person' constitute only a small proportion of the total of indictable crime and their proportion is now much lower than it was in the 1960s. In 1961 5 per cent of indictable crime consisted of offences against the person. In

1971 and 1981 the proportion was 3 per cent and in 1991 it had fallen to 1.5 per cent. However we need to counterbalance this with the argument that the viciousness of particular 'crimes against the person' has increased. The Director of Public Prosecutions (*Garda Review*, Sept., 1992: 16), for example, has said that 'there has been an appalling increase in the nastiness of the crimes of violence that are perpetrated'. But he went on to say 'this is not something that yields to statistical analysis'.

If we consider those crimes where the use of violence or the threat of violence is a means to an end rather than an end in itself, it is fairly clear that the level of violence being used in crime has increased. We can see this if we look at the increase in the number of offences involving the use of what the gardaí call 'firearms', but which are better known by their more colloquial title of guns. They were used in a total of 452 offences in 1991 – 76 cases of robbery and 376 cases of aggravated burglary. This is up somewhat on the 1981 total of 387 crimes – 306 robberies and 81 aggravated burglaries. Overall though these figures are of a different order of magnitude to those which show that firearms were used in only two robberies in 1961.

The second kind of damage suffered by victims of crime is psychological. The experience of being a crime victim creates anxiety, disbelief and insecurity. It can be particularly shocking for victims to find that their homes have been ransacked in their absence or to realise that they have been at home when a burglary had taken place. An important aspect of this is that the level of subsequent distress is often unrelated to the material value of what has been stolen.

The third and most easily quantifiable kind of damage, and the only one on which we have readily available information, is the financial loss that victims of certain kinds of crime suffer. Garda statistics record the monetary value of what has been stolen each year in crimes against property. These figures have a significant limitation. They take no account of the 'ability' of people to be victims of crime in the very specific sense that the loss of £20 may be a minor irritant to a professional white-collar worker but it is a major disaster for an unemployed one. So the figures need to be inter- preted with considerable caution. The average amount taken in offences against property with violence in 1991 was £601 and in larcenies it was £328.³ This compares to averages in 1961 of £215 (in 1991 values) and £101 respectively. These suggest that from the victim's point of view, the average property crime is now more serious than it was thirty years ago. We can also see this if we break the figures down in more detail. In 1961 75 per cent of property crimes involved amounts of £100 or less. In 1991 this was down to 44 per cent.

It is probably some consolation to the victim if the stolen property is later recovered. If so then there was more of this kind of consolation about in 1961 when 55 per cent of stolen property was recovered than in 1991 when only 8 per cent was recovered. Thus from the victim's viewpoint the average crime is now more serious in monetary terms than used to be the case and the chances of having the stolen property returned are considerably less.

The fourth kind is the indirect harm that crime causes. A criminal act has at least two sets of victims, the direct and the indirect ones. Direct victims are the people who have been attacked or robbed. Indirect victims are those who restrict their lifestyle or who alter their behaviour and their use of pub- lic space to avoid becoming a crime victim. The Irish victim survey (Breen and Rottman, 1985: 84), for example, concluded that 'the elderly have, contrary to popular belief, a low risk of victimisation'. But it is possible that they achieve this by imposing significant restrictions on the way they live. If this is so then their lower risk levels are acquired at a considerable cost and may exacerbate the levels of social isolation to which the elderly are susceptible. It would certainly appear to be the case that the elderly suffer to a greater extent from a fear of crime than do others in our society. This can hardly be con- sidered to be one of the consolations of old age. In this sense the elderly constitute the major group of indirect victims of crime.⁴

The precise relationship between the fear of crime and the actual risk of being a victim is currently a matter of considerable contention among criminologists (for a discussion, see Sparks, 1992). For some the level of fear is a direct reflection of the distribution of the risk of being a crime victim. Those with the highest levels of fear are those with the highest levels of risk of becoming victims. In this sense their fears are rational. For others fear is indirectly related to the actual incidence of crime in society. The knowledge of crime from which people's fears are constructed is, the argument goes, partly a product of their own experiences and of the discussions about crime they have with their friends and acquaintances. But it is also based on the knowledge and information about crime that is carried to them through the mass media. Media coverage gives a higher level of coverage to crime than it warrants and tends to emphasise crimes of violence rather than the more common crimes against property (see Mc Cullagh, 1986a). As a result levels of fear of crime are higher than they should be and people have particularly high levels of fear of being victims of violent crime. Yet their chances of being crime victims are relatively low overall and the chances of being victims of property crime are far greater than for violent crime.

In that sense then it can be argued that the crime problem has two separate dimensions, each of which requires a different kind of response. One dimension is the incidence of crime in society. The other is the level of fear of crime. The failure to distinguish between the two has meant that policies designed to deal with one problem have often made the other one worse. Some surveys have found that raising the level of policing in an attempt to reduce the level of crime can increase levels of anxiety about crime (see Mc Cullagh, 1983). Why, people think, would there be so many police around if there was not some danger? In much the same way programmes such as RTE's *Crimeline*, which according to the gardaí are of assistance in solving crime, can through their emphasis on the more dramatic, violent and atypical crimes increase anxiety about the level of crime in society. There is, as Mirrlees-Black and Maung (1994: 6) remark, 'an obvious tension between increasing awareness of risks and fuelling excessive anxiety'.

The evidence on levels of fear of crime in Ireland is based mainly on the results of opinion polls. This means that, for the most part, it is sketchy and unreliable (see Breen and Rottman, 1983). However these surveys suggest that the fear of being a victim and the perception that crime is now a major problem have increased substantially. A survey in early 1977 found low levels of concern about crime. Six years later, in 1983, an Irish Marketing Survey poll found substantially increased levels of concern, levels which it claimed were as high as comparable figures for major American cities (the results of these surveys are in Breen and Rottman, 1985: 18–20). Breen and Rottman (1985: 95) concluded from their survey of crime victims that 'the risk of crime victimisation in most areas of Ireland remains low' and that 'to an extent . . . some of that fear [of crime] is excessive'. Unfortunately this survey is the only national one done in Ireland and so we are deprived of the beneficial insights that can be gained from the kinds of information that a series of these surveys can provide. The British Crime Survey has found, for example, that the fear of crime has not increased in England and Wales since 1982 despite the high increases in recorded crime over the same period (Mirrlees-Black and Maung, 1994).[5]

The Seriousness of Crime – Society's View

From the point of view of society the seriousness of crime can be assessed in a number of ways; the most typical is through the use of international comparisons. These tell us how crime in Ireland compares to that in other countries and thus provide some measure against which we can assess the seriousness of our level of crime. The most recent comprehensive figures for Europe are from 1979 and so are very much out of date. They show that Ireland had the lowest crime rate of the countries used in the comparison (see Council of Europe, 1983: 28) and, along with England and Wales, it had the highest detection rate. More recent comparisons are available for specific countries. For example, if we look at the Federal Republic of Germany (as it then was) for 1987, we find crime rates considerably in excess of those in Ireland. The rate of burglary, for example, was 2,829 offences per 100,000 compared to the Irish one of 813 per 100,000. Comparisons with the jurisdictions nearest us also confirm the lower crime rates. The overall Irish crime rate of 2,600 offences per 100,000 in 1991 compares favourably with those given by O'Mahony (1993: 29) for Scotland (11,600 per 100,000), Northern Ireland (4,000 per 100,000) and England and Wales (10,500 per 100,000).

These comparisons suggest that while the level of violent crime and the amount of violence used in the commission of crime may have risen, Ireland is still a country with a low crime rate. However there are important limitations on the level of reassurance that such figures can provide. The main one is that they are burdened with a variety of statistical problems. The crime statistics of particular countries are not directly comparable because of differences in the content of their criminal law, in the procedures they use to count offences and in the willingness of their populations to report offences to the police. There is also the issue of the countries that we pick for comparative purposes. Our crime rate in 1987 was considerably lower than that for Germany. Yet for the same year it was greatly in excess of that for Japan. The overall crime rate there was 1,292 offences per 100,000 compared to 2,411 per 100,000 in Ireland (figures for Japan in Heiland, Shelly and Katoh, 1992: 69–72). This means that these kinds of comparative data need to be interpreted with considerable caution.

Two Kinds of Property Crime?

If we bear in mind the differential ability of people to be crime victims, it can be argued that the available data shows that a large percentage of property crime in Ireland at present involves, what could be considered, relatively small amounts of money. In 1991, 60 per cent of property crimes offences involved amounts of less than £200 while only 1.5 per cent involved amounts of £5,000 and over. This suggests that there are two distinct types of crime in Ireland. The first is a small amount of what might be regarded as professional crime involving relatively large amounts of money. This kind of crime attracts a lot of media coverage because of its dramatic nature and the flamboyant character of some of its perpetrators such as the recently deceased 'General', Martin Cahill. He was believed to be responsible for the single largest robbery in the history of the state, that of the Beit paintings in 1974, valued at around £7 million, and for the kidnapping of a Dublin banker. It is also the type of crime where some of those involved have, in the past at least, claimed a political motivation. These crimes most typically are comprised of bank robberies but there have also been suggestions of involvement in drug-smuggling and drug-selling. They are justified as fund-raising for a political cause though in many cases the difference between a political and a personal motivation can be difficult to disentangle. It may be, as Martin Cahill is reputed to have said, that political criminals are 'simply ordinary criminals with airs'.

The second type of crime is a large amount of relatively minor crime, the kind described by the garda commissioner (*Annual Report on Crime*, 1985: 2) as being of 'a random and opportunist nature'. This distinction has implications for the manner in which we respond to crime. Petty crimes may, for example, be felt by the public to be more irritating and upsetting than major crimes like bank robberies and they may contribute more to the sense of unease that people have about a decline in the quality of civility in society. This means that the potential is there for discrepancies to emerge between the police's notion of what the priorities in the struggle with crime should be – catching 'professional' criminals has obviously a higher status than catching petty thieves – and those of the general public.

The Facts on Crime – A Summary

We can summarise the results of our analysis of official crime statistics in the following manner. There have been dramatic increases in the amount of crime in the last thirty years in Ireland. In the late 1960s and in the 1970s the increases were particularly large. There was some decline in the 1980s but a pattern of slow but significant annual increases seems to have re-established itself in the 1990s. There has been some increase in crimes against the person but the most significant increases have been in the various forms of property crime. These increases have been accompanied by increases in the seriousness of individual crimes as measured by the amounts of violence used and by the monetary value of stolen property. Nonetheless we can distinguish usefully between two different kinds of property crime. There is a small amount of sophisticated crime involving large sums of money and a large amount of relatively minor crime involving small sums of money.

The increases have also been accompanied by significant declines in the detection rate. These reductions have been concentrated in property crime. The detection rates for violent crime against the person remains high. There may also have been increases in the level of fear of crime in Ireland though the evidence for this is not definitive and the precise relationship between levels of fear and levels of risk has not been the subject of consistent research.

Despite these changes three things have remained fairly constant. The major proportion of crime continues to be concentrated in the Dublin area. Ireland continues to be, by international standards, a low-crime country. Property crime continues to be the most important kind of crime in Ireland.

The Limitations of Official Crime Statistics

The picture of crime in Ireland that we have just outlined is one produced by an analysis of crime statistics. But if the international experience is anything to go by, it may be incomplete in certain significant respects. There is an extensive literature in criminology to suggest that there are important limitations on the degree to which crime statistics reflect accurately the level of crime in society. These limitations become evident if we follow the stages an incident must go through to be established as a crime and to become a crime statistic. The first stage is that there must be some criminal law to prohibit it. Many would argue that although the criminal law is presented to us as covering all of the more serious kinds of anti-social behaviour its reach is in fact uneven (see, for example, Hagan, 1994). There are many kinds of behaviour that cause individual injury and social harm but which are not dealt with by and through the procedures of the criminal justice system (see chapter three). As a result these kinds of incidents never make it into crime statistics and the people involved in them are deprived of inclusion in studies of the social background of the criminal population. This point is developed further in chapter three which looks at white-collar crime.

The second stage is that the offending incident must be reported to the police. This is not automatic or inevitable and it produces what criminologists refer to as 'the dark figure of crime'. This is the difference between crimes that victims feel have happened to them and the crimes that are recorded by the police. We have two sources of information that suggest that this difference may be considerable. The first source is victim surveys. In these, samples of the population are asked if they have been victims of crime and if so whether they have reported it to the police. Their answers are then compared to the totals found in police statistics. Large discrepancies have been discovered between the two in studies conducted in many cities in the United States, in England and Wales, in Holland and in Germany. The discrepancies are at their highest in crimes of violence but they are also substantial for crimes like burglary and car-theft. Overall the results suggest that the level of crime is about three times as high as that recorded in official statistics.

Richard Breen and David Rottman (1985) carried out a survey of crime victims in Ireland in 1982 and 1983. A national sample of 8,902 individuals were asked if they had been the victims of any of six criminal offences. These included burglary, car theft, larceny from a vehicle and vandalism, offences which between them account for over half the recorded crime in Ireland. The results suggested that there was more property crime reported to the researchers by victims than was being recorded in garda statistics. For example, garda statistics record just under 17,000 domestic burglaries for the calendar year which approximates most closely to that in which the victim survey was done. Yet the results of the victim survey suggest that the figure should be in the region of 35,000. These kinds of results have been confirmed by a recent crime survey in Dublin (O'Connell and Whelan, 1994).

The second source that we have on the under-reporting of crime is the figures produced by agencies that deal with child abuse and with rape victims. The data on rape is considered in chapter four. Here we confine our attention to that on child abuse. A study for the Eastern Health Board (Mc Keown, Brannick, Riordan, Gilligan, McGuane and Fitzgerald, 1993) found that 990 alleged cases were reported to the board in 1988 and 512 of these were confirmed. The gardaí were notified in 507 of these. They referred 162 (32 per cent) of them to the Director of Public Prosecutions (DPP). The DPP prosecuted in 55 of these. Thus only 11 per cent of confirmed cases of child abuse in the Dublin area made it into crime statistics. This is by any standards a massive fall-out. If it is replicated on a nation-wide scale it suggests that the true figure for the extent of child sexual abuse is as much as ten times higher than that recorded by the gardaí. There is no directly comparable offence in garda statistics but if we add together all of these that could imply some form of sexual abuse the total recorded by the gardaí in 1988 for the entire country is 105.[6] A more accurate figure may be in excess of 1,000 offences.

The third stage in the path to becoming a crime statistic is the manner in which the police respond to crime reports and the classification systems they use to record them. Research shows that the police often make judgements about whether the incidents reported to them are to be considered as crimes on the basis of their assessment of the credibility of the individuals who make the complaints. With personal assault, for example, an individual's appearance, and what it is presumed to indicate about his or her social class, can be a factor in whether the complaint is acted on.

The Irish victim survey had the effect of making the recording practices of the gardaí an issue of some contention. Where victim surveys had been done in other countries the results suggested that discrepancies between victim reports and police statistics could be explained in terms of non-reporting by victims. By contrast the results of Breen and Rottman's survey suggest that this is not a significant problem in the Irish context (see also Whelan and Murphy, 1994). Most victims (88 per cent of the total) said that they had reported the offence to the gardaí. This means that out of 35,000 burglaries, 31,000 were reported to the gardaí. As only 17,000 of them are recorded in garda statistics, the problem appears to be the failure of the gardaí to record all the reported offences. This is, of course, an explanation that the gardaí strenuously reject.

Once the gardaí decide to record an offence, they then must decide what kind of offence they will classify it as. The choice is between indictable and non-indictable. The former are, as we have seen, believed to be the more serious type of offence and so the official crime rate is based on them. The latter are believed to be relatively minor and so tend to be much less publicised. However it is no longer clear that this distinction reflects what it was intended to reflect. For example, under the statutes of 1849 and 1851 indictable offences are ones that can or must be tried before a jury. Yet the current reality is that over 90 per cent of indictable offences are not tried by a judge and jury (Rottman, 1984: 140). They are dealt with summarily before a judge in the district court. Also as this distinction is based on judgements of the seriousness of offences in the mid-nineteenth century, it fails to account for changes in public perceptions of the seriousness of various types of crime and the creation of new offences since then. The issue of crimes relating to drugs, either in the form of their distribution or their consumption, illustrates both of these points. Drug offences are widely regarded as serious but as they were created in the recent past, most notably by the Misuse of Drugs Act 1977 and its subsequent amendment in 1984, they are not recorded as indictable offences. As a result they are classified as non-indictable, a distinction they share with offences like having no light on a bicycle and 'driving or attempting to drive or being in charge of animal-drawn vehicles while drunk'.

Their classification may be unsatisfactory but at least drug offences find their way into crime statistics in some form or other. The offence of car-theft is not so lucky. Currently car-theft comes into crime statistics in two ways. One is in the figures given for the theft of motor vehicles and the other is the figure for the taking of motor propelled vehicles 'without authority' or what are often called 'unauthorised takings'. The former refers to incidents where the car was stolen and not found. The latter refer to incidents where the car was taken but, as its purpose was for joy-riding, there was no intention to permanently deprive the owner of its use. The first kind of offence is recorded as indictable and the second as non-indictable. To complicate the issue even more the second figure does not include all 'unauthorised takings' but only those where someone has been charged with taking the car. The gardaí collect, but do not publish, figures on the total number of cars stolen, whether either the car or the offender has been found. According to Paul O'Mahony (1993: 52–3) in 1991 these were almost five times higher than those recorded in the published statistics for indictable offences. So while it may be fairly easy to have your car stolen in certain parts of our major cities, it is a more substantial achievement to get the theft into Irish crime statistics.

These limitations suggest that police statistics have major shortcomings as a guide to the extent and the pattern of criminality. They may understate the level of crime and, as certain kinds of crime are more prone to under-reporting than others, they may also provide distorted information on the pattern of crime in society.

The Increase in Crime: A Statistical Illusion?

A number of implications follow from the limitations of official crime statistics. Two are worthy of particular note. The first is that the 'real' level of crime in Ireland is unknown. Garda statistics suggest one set of figures; victim surveys and the figures collected by other agencies suggest other and higher sets of figures. The second implication is more important for our discussion of rising crime. When police statistics show an increase in the level of crime there can be a number of possible reasons for it.

The first reason is that the statistical changes reflect a real increase in the level of crime in society. The second is that the increase represents a change in the reporting of offences by the public rather than any increase in offensive behaviour as such. One of the ironies of an increase in the level of public confidence in the police is that it can lead to an increase in the level of reported crime in society rather than a decrease. If people feel that the police are now more efficient and capable they may be more willing to report offences to them. This will lead to changes in the level of recorded offences without any 'real' increase in the level of such offences. The third reason may be changes in the recording practices of the police. These can have the effect of either increasing or reducing the level of recorded crime. Séamus Breathnach (unpublished: 16), for example, has argued that the increases in crime in Ireland can be explained partly in terms of the greater willingness of the police to record reported offences, a willingness that was energised by the decision in 1970 to pay them for overtime work.

In the current state of our knowledge about crime in Ireland it is difficult, when confronted with recorded increases in the level of crime, to choose between these three explanations. But it is not impossible. Given the scale of the increases in crime over the past thirty years it is doubtful if these can be fully accounted for by non-reporting and non-recording. It has been suggested (see *Garda Review*, March, 1985: 4) that 'the public are even more zealous now in reporting crime'. As support for this the *Garda Review* points to the increased willingness of people to report property crime in which nothing has been taken. The number went up from 342 in 1961 to 6,713 in 1991, an increase of 6,371. Yet over the same period the overall number of property crimes rose from 12,701 to over 92,000 in 1991, an increase of almost 80,000 offences. This suggests that while a change in reporting may be a factor there is more going on than that.

Similarly the increase in crime can hardly be explained in terms of changes in recording practices of the gardaí. It would have required an enormous feat of under-recording in the past to conceal increases of this scale and even in Ireland someone was bound to notice. Finally it may be true that many offences are both unreported and unrecorded, but the inclusion of these in garda statistics is unlikely to change the relative proportion of the different offences in the overall crime figures. Thus while it is true that there is substantial under-reporting and under-recording of acts of violence, particularly those against women and children, there may also be significant under-reporting of many kinds of property crime. So if the levels of all of these crimes were more accurately reflected in crime statistics it would be unlikely to change the view that the most crime in Ireland is property crime.

II Victims and Offenders

In marked contrast to the amount of detail garda statistics provide about the level of crime, they give us no data concerning either the victims of crime or the offenders. Garda annual reports used to contain some limited material on the social backgrounds of juvenile offenders but this practice was discontinued in 1958. No other state agency collects this information either. As a result our information in this area is limited to a number of research studies.

Who are the Victims?

There are three research studies on the victims of crime. The first is on the victims of homicide. This is a combination of the offences of murder and manslaughter. In the course of his study of crime from the 1950s to the 1970s, David Rottman (1980: 117–40) analysed homicide statistics for two separate periods, 1951–60 and 1970–74. The amount of information this revealed about victims is fairly basic. We can summarise the results as indicating in very broad terms that murders in the 1950s tended to be rural and intra-generational, with an older male victim and a younger male offender. In the 1970s they increasingly became urban and inter-generational,

mostly involving younger working class males as both victims and offenders. To the extent to which women were
victims in both periods it tended to be in family homicides in
rural areas and the women at risk were the wives.

Rottman's analysis is revealing but it is limited to one crime
only and this crime does not constitute a significant proportion
of the offences reported to the gardaí in any one year. The
second study of victims is more widely based. This is the
national survey, discussed above, by Richard Breen and David
Rottman (1985). The information they collected enabled them
to identify the factors that influence the risk of being a crime
victim. It varies by where you live – people in urban areas,
especially Dublin, are more at risk than people living in rural
areas; by the size of the households you reside in – smaller
household are more vulnerable to crime than larger ones; by
the age of the household head – households where the head is
young, i.e. under thirty, are at greater risk than those where the
head of the household is old, and by the social-class background of the head of the household – the households most at
risk are those headed by a white-collar or self-employed
worker, those least at risk are those where the head of the
household is either a farmer or a manual worker. Thus it
appears that the typical victim of property crime is a young,
middle-class urbanite.

The recent Dublin Crime Survey (O'Connell and Whelan,
1994) confirmed that class is an important factor in crime victimisation and that, contrary to the pattern in Britain, the higher
one's social class the more likely one is to be a victim of property crime. However the survey found a more nuanced pattern
in relation to age. Property crime victimisation in Dublin was,
as Breen and Rottman found on a national level, lowest among
households headed by the over sixty-fives but Whelan and
O'Connell found that property crime victimisation was highest
among thirty-five to fifty-five year-old individuals. Unlike that
of Breen and Rottman their research also looked at personal
offences such as assault and found that in Dublin women are

more vulnerable to such offences than men. However they add the significant qualification that there were important gender and class differences in the reporting of crime – both to researchers and to the police – with women more likely to report than men and higher socio-economic groups more likely to report than lower ones. This means that their results may be a reflection of differential willingness to report offences rather than of differential vulnerability to being a victim.

Who are the Offenders?

The results of a number of studies suggest that the background of the typical criminal in Ireland is very different from that of the typical victim. This information comes from two sources. The first is from studies of the prison population. A number of these were done in the late 1960s and the 1970s on the backgrounds of offenders in reformatories and industrial schools, of juveniles on probation and on the social background of adult prisoners (for a summary, see Burke, Carney and Cook, 1981: 20–50). They show that, typically, prisoners were from socially deprived backgrounds, from families where poverty, alcoholism and unemployment were routine experiences and their level of education was generally low. These findings have been confirmed and amplified in the recently published, and more comprehensive, research by Paul O'Mahony (1993). On the basis of a survey of male prisoners in Mountjoy jail, he concluded that the 'typical Mountjoy male prisoner' (1993: 224) was in his early to mid-twenties, from a large family and from an urban area. If this was Dublin, he was from the inner city or from one or other of the poorer suburban areas such as Crumlin or Ballymun. He was likely to have been an early school-leaver, having dropped out before the legal minimum age of fifteen. He had limited experience of the world of work – generally in poorly paid and unskilled or menial work – and a considerably longer experience of unemployment. This was an experience he was likely to have in common with his father who typically was either a semi-skilled or unskilled manual worker, an indication of the working-class nature of the social background. Finally he was likely to have 'serious personal and emotional problems' (O'Mahony, 1993: 205) in addition to his criminal behaviour such as drug abuse and psychiatric problems. The Council for Social Welfare (1983: 14–15) summarised the results of these kinds of studies by saying that the prison population contains 'a disproportionate number of those who are poor, uneducated and unskilled'.

With the exception of age, these results are broadly in line with those found by Rottman in his 1984 study of the socio-economic characteristics of those who were arrested for an indictable offence in the Dublin area in 1981. The number involved was 20,712: 16,539 (84 per cent) males and 3,173 (16 per cent) females. The majority were either unemployed or in marginal employment. Eight out of ten males over seventeen and almost seven out of every ten females aged under twenty-one, for example, were unemployed. One-third of them were from inner-city areas in Dublin. The major difference between males and females was the younger age of the apprehended females. Thirty-one per cent of females arrested and 25 per cent of males were aged sixteen or less. A particularly striking feature of their circumstances, according to Rottman, was the number who were both young and from the inner city. At the time of the survey the inner city was home to only 15 per cent of the population of Dublin yet one-third of those apprehended were from inner city areas. Just under a third of these were less than seventeen and just over a third were aged between seventeen and twenty.[7]

A comparison of the two sets of results suggests that the typical offender is a young, under-educated, unemployed male from a working class background and that the major difference between arrest and imprisonment is age. Younger criminals do not get sent to prison; older ones do. In this rather depressing sense at least, persistence appears to pay off. If you start young and commit crime long enough, eventually you will get sent to prison. However before we can conclude that we have identified the key characteristics of offenders there is one other issue that needs to be addressed.

It is difficult to know if those who are arrested are a representative cross-section of those who commit crime. It is possible, for example, that those criminals who get arrested are either the less intelligent or less talented ones or those whom the gardaí are most skilled at catching. If this is the case then studies based on police or prison records are open to very different interpretations. The fact that many of those in prison have substantial problems of alcohol and drug abuse may not indicate that such people are more prone to crime or that such kinds of abuse are causal factors in crime. Instead it may just indicate that drunken or drugged offenders are easier to apprehend.

Equally the fact that those apprehended by the gardaí are mainly from working-class backgrounds may not reflect their greater criminal propensities as much as it reflects the level of policing of working-class areas and the underdevelopment of the policing of the kinds of criminal offences that would produce more middle-class offenders such as financial fraud and tax evasion. As we shall see in chapter three these offences are probably significant and fairly widespread in Ireland. Yet they are dealt with mainly through administrative procedures and offenders tend to be deprived of the status of a place in garda arrest records. This means that the arrest records, from which the prison population is subsequently drawn, may be more a reflection of the way the legal system and the gardaí treat different kinds of offences and offenders than they are of the distribution of criminal propensities in the population as a whole. As a result they cannot be considered a comprehensive guide to the characteristics that criminals have in common.

Self-Report Studies

The over-representation of working-class people in offender statistics is not peculiar to Ireland or to Irish police or prison records. The analysis of such records from cities, countries and regions as diverse as London, Paris, Florida, Boston, Tokyo, Israel, the former Yugoslavia, Australia, Denmark and Uganda shows a preponderance of working-class offenders (see Box, 1981). In many of these places the issue of the adequacy of police records has also been raised. Given its importance, criminologists have devised a research strategy to try to resolve the problem. This is the use of self-report studies.

The methodology of such studies is straightforward. Lists of criminal offences are prepared. They are shown to samples of the population who are then asked to indicate if they have ever committed any of the listed offences and if so, whether they were caught for them. In this way they 'self-report' on their own criminal activities. They are also asked to provide information on their social and demographic characteristics. The researchers then check the reporting of offences against the information available in police records and against the social background of the reporting 'offenders'.

These studies have the potential to answer two questions. They can give some indication of the level of unrecorded crime and also provide a definitive answer to the question of the relationship between social class and criminal involvement. Their success has not, however, been unqualified. A number of questions have been raised about their validity.[8] These include the accuracy with which people fill in these questionnaires, the range of offences covered in the surveys and the groups on which they have been used (see Beirne and Messerschmidt, 1991: 47–50). Many of these surveys have been done on populations of school pupils and so do not include the more serious delinquents in these age groups as they have either dropped out of school or have a pattern of regular absenteeism. It is also the case that few self-report studies have been done on the adult population. However for our purposes these studies present two major difficulties. The first is that their results are often mutually contradictory. In an extensive review of self-report studies, Hindelang, Hirschi and Weis (1979) concluded that there were few reliable differences between the results of these studies and the results of those based on police statistics, thus suggesting that crime is predominantly a working-class activity. Steven Box (1981: 75–84), on the other hand, concluded from his review of the relevant studies that while the older ones (those of the late 1940s and the 1950s) show a slight negative relationship between class and delinquency the more recent studies (those from the 1960s and 1970s) have found none. He argued that while social class is not a significant variable in the commission of criminal offences, it is a significant variable in getting offences into police statistics. In the last few years, according to Beirne and Messerschmidt (1991: 49), the results of more carefully designed self-report studies are beginning to move towards a more nuanced view of the social background of the offender. These studies make a clear distinction between minor delinquent acts and serious crimes. As a result the picture they give of the serious young delinquent is fairly close to that derived from police arrest records. The results of Elliott and Huizinga's 1983 study in the United States are a case in point. They argue that while there are few class differences in the reporting of minor delinquent offences, 'there are substantial class differences in both the prevalence and incidence of serious crime' (Elliott and Huizinga, 1983: 165).

The second problem is that in Ireland we do not have the kind of self-reported information that is available for other societies. However there are no immediately obvious reasons why the results of the more recent self-report studies should not be applicable in Ireland as long as we maintain our awareness of their limitations. If this is so then we can suggest that there is a clear relationship between social class and serious delinquent behaviour. Young people from working-class backgrounds are more likely than young people from middle-class backgrounds to engage in acts of serious delinquent behaviour. But these kinds of conclusions cannot be extended automatically to adults or to the kinds of crimes that are not dealt with by the police. As we shall see in chapter three this qualification is crucial.

Conclusion

We have set out in this chapter to provide basic data on the nature of the crime problem in Ireland. To do this we showed the kinds of information that can be gleaned from official garda statistics and from the limited number of research studies that have been done. We also pointed to the considerable limitations and shortcomings that these sources have. The account of crime that we end up with can be summarised as follows. Crime has increased dramatically over the past thirty years. There have been large increases in all kinds of crime, but the largest increases have been in the various forms of property crime. The increases have been accompanied by increases in the seriousness of individual crimes and in the level of violence involved in them. They have also been accompanied by significant declines in the detection rate for all kinds of offences but particularly for property crimes. Crime is primarily an urban phenomenon with almost 60 per cent of it occurring in the Dublin area. If we add to this the information we have about victims and offenders we end up with a view of the Irish crime problem as primarily one of property crime committed by young urban working-class males against what are mainly middle-class urban households. At the level of offenders at least, this is very much in line with international experience yet despite this, and despite the increases in crime outlined here, the level of crime in Ireland is still lower than that of most of the industrialised world.

Notes

1. From 1927 to 1946 crime statistics were published in the volumes of statistical abstracts produced by the Central Statistics Office.
2. The high detection rate for murder, and for offences against the person generally, is related to the circumstances of the crime. David Rottman's (1980) analysis of Irish homicide (that is murder plus manslaughter) for the 1950s and the 1970s shows that half the murders were committed by acquaintances of the victim, about 20 per cent by kin of the victim and 6 per cent by the spouse of the victim. This means that in effect the perpetrator is easily identified and quickly detected. There is some evidence that this may be changing as witnessed by the number of recent drug-related murders which remain unsolved.
3. These calculations are made by including the number of burglaries in which no property is taken with the number in which property is taken. Garda statistics do not follow this procedure.
4. The other group who are indirect victims of crime are the families of offenders who undergo the range of humiliations that accompany police investigations and court appearances. They are not normally considered among the victims of crime thus illustrating the ideological and political uses to which the term victim can be put.
5. It is not entirely clear why this survey is referred to as the British Crime Survey as it only covers England and Wales.
6. The offences are unnatural offences, indecent assault, defilement of girls under fifteen years, defilement of girls between fifteen and seventeen and incest. It is unfortunately a fairly crude indicator.
7. One final point from this survey is worthy of mention. The data analysed by Rottman shows that just over 1 per cent of the total number of arrested males could be classified as members of the travelling community. The comparison of this with their proportion in the general population is difficult to determine. But crude calculations based on a travelling population of 14,000 for the country as a whole and a population in Dublin of 1.5 million gives them as 1 per cent of the capital's population. This suggests that their crime rate is not out of line with that of the settled population.
8. Monica Walker (1983), for example, has concluded that 'it is very uncertain whether any valid conclusions can be drawn regarding the relationship between offence behaviour and sex, age and social class' from these kinds of studies.

2   EXPLAINING CRIME IN IRELAND

Introduction

The previous chapter set out the key characteristics of crime in Ireland as these are revealed to us in official crime statistics. They constitute the material that any proposed explanations for crime must account for. Thus we must be able to explain why crime is increasing, why it is primarily a problem of property crime, why it is committed largely by young working-class males and why crime in Ireland remains relatively low by international standards. For the most part these are features that we share with industrialised and other industrialising countries. So it is appropriate that we should look at the kinds of theories that have been offered by sociologists for crime in these countries and then look at the extent to which these have been, or might be, applied to crime in Irish society. This is what this chapter sets out to do.

Before we go on to the individual theories, it is necessary to clarify a number of points about the nature of theories in general and sociological theories in particular. Given the complexity of the issues involved here the comments can only be of a preliminary and provisional nature. In general terms it may be said that a theory is an attempt to identify factors that explain regularly observed and regularly occurring events. In this sense we are all theorists when we try to make sense of the range of mysterious social phenomena that we encounter in our society whether it is the inability of the Irish soccer team to score goals, the popularity of Daniel O'Donnell or the persistence of high unemployment. Because of this, a distinction is often made between 'lay' or common-sense theories and scientific ones. The latter tend to be more rigorous in their construction and are required to meet higher standards of evidence or proof than 'lay' theories are. So while it may be acceptable at the level of lay theory to say, for example, that most crime is caused by travellers, the proponent of this as a scientific theory would be required to show through a detailed analysis of the background of offenders whether this is true or not. The relevant evidence, it should be added, does not exist.

Sociological theories explain the occurrences of phenomena like crime by looking at the range of social forces that act on and constrain individuals and groups in society. They also aspire to scientific status through their commitment to the provision of empirical evidence through which the theoretical propositions they advance can either be accepted or rejected. Sociologists have two types of theories to offer for crime in society. The first is explanations of why the crime rate in one country is changing or why crime rates differ between countries. The second is explanations of why particular groups in a society have a greater propensity to commit crime than others. The first are theories of crime rates and the second are theories of motivation.

I Theories of Crime Rates

In this section we address two separate issues raised in theories of crime rates. Both are comparative. The first compares the crime rate in Ireland at present with that in the past and asks why has it increased? The second asks why the crime rate in Ireland is low by comparison with other countries. Central to these theories is the link between social and economic changes and increases in crime. The key questions they ask is what social and economic changes are related to changes in the crime rate and what is the nature of the link between them? If we begin with the issue of rising crime, we can identify two sets of explanations that have been proposed for it – those who argue from a perspective of social disorganisation and those who argue from a perspective of structural change, a group whom for the sake of convenience we can term 'structuralists' (see Rottman, 1980: 21–4).

Social Disorganisation

Social disorganisation theorists argue that the process of social change erodes the control and authority of the institutions that guarantee the stability of the society such as the neighbourhood, the community, the family and religion (see, for example, Park, 1967). When alternative ideas and attitudes begin to circulate in a society, religion, for example, can lose its control of moral regulation. If the mass media show alternative ways of life in which affluence is a routine and taken-for-granted aspect of people's lives, it can generate aspirations and expectations that are inconsistent with, or difficult to accommodate within, traditional religion. The family can also be disrupted by change. In traditional societies it is both the centre of production and of consumption. The power of parents, and especially of fathers, lies in their control over the resources, like money, that is available to family members. However one of the effects of economic change is to increase the number of employment opportunities available off the land and outside the home. This creates a new channel to resources which is not easily controlled through the power structure of the family. In these circumstances a decline in the centrality of parental authority is inevitable. If these changes erode the authority of the controlling institutions then, according to social disorganisation theorists, the moral binds on individuals are loosened and they are freed to engage in what was previously prohibited behaviour. When this happens forms of anti-social behaviour like crime increase.

A version of the social disorganisation argument has been put forward as the explanation for the increases in crime in Ireland. In 1982 one of the bodies representing the gardaí, the Association of Garda Sergeants and Inspectors (AGSI), published a document entitled 'A Discussion Paper Containing Proposals for a Scheme of Community Policing'. According to it,

> [T]he difficulties now being encountered in our cities and major towns arise from a breakdown of the social control that was effectively exercised in the small-town environment, both urban and rural. . . . Added to this are other changes in our society that have weakened community stability: high unemployment, urban decay, migration, industrial strife, the loosening of family structures and social values. (AGSI,1982: 6)

In other words the source of increased crime is in the decline of the community life found in small Irish towns and in rural environments and the consequent breakdown of the systems of social control, such as that in the family, found in these communities and on which their particular character depended. This argument taps into a common public sentiment that 'things are getting out of control' and that the solution is a return to old days and old ways. Given its nostalgia for the past it is perhaps odd that one of the main difficulties with this argument is that it lacks a sense of history. The notion of social breakdown implies the existence at some time in the past of an integrated and relatively trouble-free society. The precise historical location of this society is, at least in an Irish context, difficult to identify.

The nineteenth century is not a good place to start. It is generally accepted that even then, Dublin was, as O'Brien (1982: 184) puts it, 'one of the foremost centres of crime in

the United Kingdom' (as it was then constituted). It remained so into the early twentieth century. In 1910 Liverpool was
the only major city in these islands with a higher crime rate.
Furthermore, rural Ireland was not all that much different. It
was in many cases disorderly and violent (see Lampson, 1907:
250–4; O'Donnell, 1975; and Townshend, 1983: 11). Acts of
interpersonal assault were commonplace and many recreational pursuits, such as faction fighting, involved levels of
violence that in today's terms would be regarded as large scale
public disorder. Twenty people were killed in a faction fight in
Kerry in 1834. The fight itself involved, it is claimed, at least
two thousand combatants. The number of casualties was
untypical for such fights but the numbers involved were not
(O'Donnell, 1975: 133–74). The mythology of rural orderliness is also dispelled by the knowledge that at the end of the
century the more rural towns of Waterford and Limerick had
higher arrest records for drunkenness than Dublin.

If we move forward into the twentieth century, there are also
problems in finding the idyllic crime-free community in rural
areas. For example, there was considerable unrest throughout
the country in the 1930s associated with the Blueshirts.[1] In the
1940s, particularly during the Emergency, there were increases
in crime in Ireland (Rottman, 1980) while the low crime rates in
the 1950s must be considered against the background of the
demoralisation and massive emigration of the period. So there is
little evidence to suggest that rural Ireland was always a notably
harmonious and orderly place and when it was it was due to
conditions like emigration that nobody would be anxious to
promote as crime prevention measures.

If we cannot find the society that is supposed to have
broken down then these kinds of ideas are of limited utility
in explaining increases in crime. Integrated societies tend by
their nature to be difficult to find and crime-free periods tend
by their nature to be always in the past. They are, as Pearson
(1983: 48) puts it, 'glimmering in the distance, just out of
sight, back over the hill, twenty years ago, before the war'.

The choice of a period from which Irish society is supposed to have disintegrated is in practice not a precise historical calculation but a matter of rhetoric and ideological convenience. Moreover even if we could identify this period it would be difficult to recreate the conditions on which social control was built as the economic and social conditions that underpinned it are now a thing of the past. A mass movement by children to have the power of parents returned to its previous level of authoritarianism may be a comforting illusion but it is difficult to envisage in late twentieth-century Ireland.

Structural Arguments

The argument of the structuralists does not depend on the existence of a crime-free past nor indeed on any reified notions of Ireland's past. The claim here is that social change alters the manner in which a society is organised and one of the effects of this is to change the amount and the pattern of crime. Social change does not create the structure of opportunities for crime; it simply alters the existing one. What change does is to open the society to the possibility of more and different kinds of crime.

David Rottman's (1980) analysis of crime in Ireland is very much within this tradition. The concurrence of increases in crime with other major social changes constitutes his point of departure. If crime began to increase in the late 1960s what other changes were going on that might explain it? For him two are important. The first is a change in the criminal opportunity structure. The industrialisation process that began in the late 1960s produced two other changes – an increase in the level of affluence and an increase in the number and range of objects that could be stolen – televisions, motor-cars, money. It also produced, through a rise in the number of private dwellings, an increase in the number of locations from which they could be stolen. The effects of the concentration of housing produced by urbanisation was to increase the convenience and the accessibility of the new targets for crime, thereby creating the conditions for more efficiency in the criminal sector.

The increase in potential targets can be documented. It can be seen in the increased availability of consumer goods. In 1962, the first year they were introduced in Ireland, there were just over 127,000 television licences in the country. The number trebled to just under 475,000 in 1971 and rose again, more slowly this time, to 648,000 in 1981 and to 806,055 in 1990. While the number of licences bears an uncertain relationship to the number of television sets, it gives some indication of the scale of the increase in television ownership, the most rapid period for which it will be noted was between 1962 and 1971. If this meant there were more televisions to rob there were also more private cars to take as well. In 1961 there were 186,302 private cars in the country. By 1971 the number had risen to just over 414,000. By 1981 it was 710,334 and by 1991 it had reached 796,408, an increase since 1961 of over 400 per cent. Again, the most rapid period of increase was between 1961 and 1971. These increases in what might be described as mobile goods were accompanied by an increase in the number of locations from which they could be stolen. The number of private households rose from 676,402 in 1961 to 964,882 in 1986 (the most recent year for which such figures are available). The growing concentration of the population in urban areas can be indicated by the fact that by 1991 over half the population could be classified as living in urban areas.

The other change that coincided with and was related to industrialisation was a change in the age structure of the population. This is important because, according to criminologists, the age-group fifteen to twenty-four is the one that is most prone to crime and it is the age-group in which most criminals are found (see, for example, Wilson, 1975). Any increase in the size of this group and any change in its proportion in the population has the effect of increasing the supply of potential criminals in the society. This is what happened in Ireland. In 1961 the age-group fifteen to twenty-four constituted 14 per cent of the population. In 1986 it was up to 18 per cent, an increase in numbers from 200,767 to 617,524.

The explanation for the increased crime rate lies in the association between these two sets of changes. The combination of increased opportunities for crime and an increase in the supply of potential criminals produced, according to this argument, an inevitable increase in crime. Increased affluence, increased industrialisation and increased urbanisation conspired, as it were, with demographic changes to produce increases in crime.

There are a number of problems with this as an explanation for rising crime. The first is that the structuralist explanation as applied to Ireland appears to ignore two significant processes that occurred during this period and which might be presumed to have had a major impact on crime in Ireland. The first process has been the emergence or re-emergence of conflict in Northern Ireland. While the precise term used to describe the events may be a matter for political and historical analysis, there can be little argument but that the period since 1969 has been the most violent one in the history of the Northern state. It must obviously have had some spill-over effect on crime in the Republic but the precise nature of the influence and the amount of weight to give it are matters of some contention.

Clearly the conflict in Northern Ireland has contributed to the increase in the number of serious crimes such as armed robbery and kidnapping as paramilitary groups resorted to some fairly spectacular and sophisticated feats of fund-raising. However these activities have declined considerably in the late 1980s and early 1990s. Although rumours persist about paramilitary groups' involvement in the drug business, their level of involvement in serious armed robbery does not at present appear to be significant. What might be seen to be a more significant long-term contribution to the increase in crime has been the introduction of guns into the crime equation. They now seem to be freely available to criminals in many parts of Dublin and a profitable enterprise exists in the hiring of weapons for particular crimes.

However, while these contributions have been important, it is unlikely that crime in the Republic would have remained unchanged if conflict had not broken out in Northern Ireland. It is true that serious crime in the Republic may not have reached the levels that it did but the same cannot be said of the more common forms of crime. These, as we have seen in chapter one, are property crimes which involve relatively small amounts of money. As such they are unlikely to be attractive for paramilitary groups given the scale of their perceived financial needs. Moreover some of the most rapid increases in crime were recorded in the period 1966 to 1971 and so occurred at a time when the Northern conflict was still relatively underdeveloped. Thus the conflict may have compounded the problem of crime in the Republic but it does not appear to be one of its fundamental causes.

The second process of some significance for crime has been the development of an economy built around the importation, sale and consumption of illegal drugs. This has had spill-over effects through its influence on the level of crime by addicts as they struggle to meet their financial commitments to drug-dealers and through the unique way in which murder is used as a method of regulation of entry to and exit from the drugs business. The exact size of this economy is difficult to estimate. Garda statistics are not particularly useful here. They give some indication of the numbers arrested for drug-related offences. But they cannot tell us the amount of drugs in circulation or the numbers involved in the drugs business. This is because crimes relating to illegal drug use do not come to police attention in the way that most other crimes do – through complaints from victims. Drug-users have little incentive to report their own criminal activities so the offences are generally uncovered by pro-active policing, that is by the police targeting drug crime and devoting resources to its detection and control. Thus the number of such offences recorded is not an indication of the level of the crime but of police activity against it.

However it is increasingly the case that discussions of crime in Ireland focus almost exclusively on drug-related crimes. So it is important to introduce two relevant factors into the debate. One is that drugs have always played a part in crime. What we are witnessing now is the substitution of one abused drug for another. In the 1960s and the 1970s the abused drug was alcohol. Surveys of prisoners showed that the majority of them had serious alcohol problems (see O'Mahony, 1993: 198). In the present period the abused drugs are heroin and cocaine. The other point is that while these drugs have undoubtedly exacerbated the crime problem they are not its major cause. Crime began to increase prior to the emergence of the current drug problem and it was firmly established as an issue before drugs achieved their present level of prominence.

A more crucial problem for the structuralist argument is that while it points to the importance of new opportunities for crime, it leaves, as Rottman (1980: 77) puts it, 'a vital question unanswered: why do people take advantages of the new opportunities for criminal activity'. This question has particular significance in an Irish context. Many commentators (see Lee, 1989) have argued that taking advantage of new opportunities is not a distinctive characteristic of the Irish personality. If we have failed to take advantage of opportunities in political and economic areas why should they be availed of when they are of a criminal nature? To answer this we need to consider the second kind of explanations offered by sociologists: theories of criminal motivation. These are concerned with locating the sources of motivations to take advantage of criminal opportunities.

II Theories of Criminal Motivation

What these theories do is to look at the way in which the
workings of a society can produce or generate criminal motivations in certain sections of the population and not in others.
Within this general type there is a variety of theories. We shall
consider five of these – that of Robert Merton, that of radical
criminologists, that of the left realists, that of control theorists,
and that of labelling theorists. We begin by setting out the arguments of these theories and considering what their strengths
and weaknesses are. We then ask whether they have been or
indeed whether they can be applied in the Irish context.

Robert Merton and Social Disjunction

Robert Merton's argument is that certain kinds of society
systematically generate pressures that lead to crime and
deviance. To arrive at this conclusion he isolates two central
elements in a society. The first is the cultural structure, and
here the most important feature (for the analysis of deviance)
is the culturally defined goals of a society. These goals are
shared, initially at least, by all members of a society. They are
implanted in the socialisation process through the family and
through the education system and are reinforced by the
media. As a result people behave in ways that are likely to
lead to the achievement of these goals.

   The second element that Merton emphasises is the social
structure. The most pertinent aspect of this is the institution-
alised means by which the goals of a society are to be achieved.
Not only are there goals in a society that people are expected to
strive for but there are also proper and socially acceptable ways
through which these goals are to be achieved. Social status and
social esteem depends on attaining success as it is defined in a
particular society but also on doing so in the manner that is
socially acceptable.

Merton argues that in a well-regulated society, goals and means are integrated in that they are accepted by, and available to, all in the society. In such a society if an individual wishes to achieve success the means are available to do so. However, in many societies the legitimate means of achieving the goals are not accessible to all. Those who wish to achieve the goals, but who are denied access to the means, adapt to this situation. The most significant adaptation is what Merton calls the innovatory one. It is primarily one found among the working-class. They have internalised and accepted the cultural goals of the society but are denied access to legitimate means of achieving success. They are cut off, for example, from the upper reaches of the educational system and as a result find themselves faced with a future of low status and low-paying work. Crime represents for them an alternative means of achieving the goals of society. In a society where the possession of property is the primary aim this inevitably produces high rates of property crime among those with little access to the legitimate means of obtaining it. As Merton puts it:

> of those located in the lower reaches of the social structure, the culture makes incompatible demands. On one hand, they are asked to orient their conduct toward the prospect of large wealth . . . and on the other, they are largely denied effective opportunities to do so institutionally. The consequence of this structural inconsistency is a high rate of deviant behaviour. (1968: 200)

Crime, however, is not the only form of adaptation. People may react in a ritualistic fashion by rejecting the goals but continuing to live by the rules of society. They may also adapt by rejecting both the goals and the rules: this is what Merton calls the 'retreatist' solution. This is the response of drug addicts, vagrants, suicides and alcoholics. Finally, people may reject the rules and the goals and try to create a new kind of society with new cultural and social structures, a response that Merton terms as 'rebellion'.

Radical Criminology

Merton's analysis has been criticised on many grounds (see, for example, Clinard, 1964). One important criticism (see Taylor, 1971) is that while Merton can tell us what the consequences are when the goals and means in a society become disconnected he does not tell us why and how this happens. This does not constitute a notable difficulty for radical criminologists, who adopt a Marxist perspective. They argue that the origins of crime and deviance are to be found in the nature and contradictions of capitalist societies. Taylor, Walton and Young (1973) have developed this proposition. They claim that social problems can be divided into two kinds. The first kind is those that spring from human diversity such as prostitution, drug-taking and homosexuality. Capitalist society cannot tolerate these forms of diversity because their hedonistic overtones threaten to undermine the work ethic on which the society depends. So it designates them as crimes. The second kind of social problems are those caused by the material inequalities that are intrinsic to capitalist societies. The sources of most forms of conventional property crime are the inequalities of income, wealth and opportunity. Because of its nature as a social and economic system capitalism systematically and inevitably generates inequality and as a consequence systematically generates crime. The disjunction between ends and means is not an accidental or transient feature of capitalist society but an essential part of it.

For these criminologists it is capitalist society that is crimogenic. It is the kind of society that promotes the right to own property while simultaneously depriving an entire class of the possibility of having any. Jock Young (1975) suggests that people who are 'victims' of capitalism in this way have a number of options. They can allow themselves to be brutalised by the system and in the process become submerged in drink and drugs. They can play the capitalist game and enter the struggle for material accumulation. They can steal from the rich which, while seen as a crime by capitalist society, is in the context of that society a political act. It is a challenge, though a primitive and inarticulate one, to the current established order and to the current distribution of income and wealth. Their final option is to join the more self-consciously political struggle for a socialist society.

There are important similarities between the arguments of Taylor, Walton and Young and of Robert Merton. They see the nature of society as facilitating crime and deviance. They also see a range of possible responses to inequality in society, one of which is crime. However there is a crucial difference between the two. For Merton the disjunction between ends and means in a society is one that can be rectified. Social reforms which widen the opportunities available to the working-class but which do not fundamentally alter the nature of the society are the solution to crime. For radical criminologists however, major social transformation is necessary in order to create the kinds of equitable social and productive arrangements that will result in the abolition of crime.

New Realism

In the last decade a new criminology has emerged which challenges the claims of Marxist theory. According to the 'new realists' it is difficult to maintain that crime is a political act when its victims are not the rich and the well off but – as many victim surveys show – other working-class people. In addition, the related impacts of crime are disproportionately borne by working-class communities in terms of the demoralising effects that crime has on their already fragile way of life. Equally, the new realists argue, the fact that much crime is committed by unemployed and exploited people does not imply that it is a direct response to the experience of being unemployed or being exploited. Poor and exploited people have been around for generations without the high levels of crime that we have at the moment. So deprivation as such is not the key to crime. What is important, they argue, is the perception of deprivation, or what sociologists call 'the sense of relative deprivation'.

This means that the sense of deprivation that people have comes not from their absolute level of deprivation but from the sense they have of how badly off they are in comparison to other people. If poor people only compare their situation with that of other equally poor people then their sense of deprivation will not be as great or as strong a motivating factor than if they compare themselves to the rich and the well off. The first response is 'I'm not badly off because everyone else I see also is'. The second is 'Why can't I be as rich as them?'

Ironically, new realists argue, the capitalist system encourages the development of a sense of deprivation in the second and more extended sense of the term. It encourages everyone to get on and to do well but this encouragement exists within an economic system that generates significant levels of material inequality. The values of that system encourage people to compete and to compare themselves to others to see how well they are doing. The system however operates to ensure that some are better off than others so that when people make comparisons a sense of relative deprivation is inevitable among certain sections of the population. People who suffer from poor housing, from unemployment, from poor schooling compare themselves to others who are doing well and as a result they experience a sense of deprivation. In this way capitalism produces a sense of relative deprivation and this is one that people must come to terms with. The means through which they do so are what Lea and Young (1984) call 'survival strategies'.

Survival strategies include dejection and fatalism, the passive acceptance of life as it is. Some who try to live in these terms do not succeed and succumb to the strain through mental illness and alcoholism. The reality of deprivation can also be transcended through religious commitment with its promise of better things to come in an afterlife. Religious cults in Britain are an example of this. They offer people credible alternatives to their present deprivation. For others the syndrome of deprivation and inequality leads to discontent and in the absence of a political movement to mobilise and channel this discontent, crime is the outcome. According to Lea and Young (1984: 88), 'the equation is simple: relative deprivation equals discontent; discontent plus lack of political solution equals crime.'

It is difficult to see what is particularly different about this kind of argument. It has important similarities to the positions of both Robert Merton and radical criminologists in that it also locates the motivations for crime in the inequalities created by society and in the means through which people respond and accommodate to these inequalities. What is perhaps different is the new realist attitude that while the motivation to commit crime may be socially generated, if it leads to behaviour which harms those in similar living conditions to the criminal then it is not a just or defensible response (Lea and Young, 1984: 97).

Control Theories

Control theories do not fit easily into the category of theories of motivation. Even though they include the work of a wide variety of theorists the assumptions they have in common can be summarised in these terms. Human nature is such that people are inherently predisposed to crime so motivation is not an issue. Criminal motivations are not something a society must work to produce. They are some-thing it must work to prevent. Cultural and social controls on behaviour are important here. If they are strong in a society, deviant impulses are restrained. If they are weak, delinquency and crime are inevitable consequences.

Michael Gottfredson and Travis Hirschi (1990) are two of the foremost control theorists. They argue that there are no significant social class differences in crime so we do not need to look to the wider social context to find the impulse towards crime and delinquency. This impulse is universal and ubiq-uitous. What is crucial is the degree to which individuals succeed in controlling it. High levels of individual self-control reduce the possibilities of anti-social behaviour; low levels encourage it. In this sense then crime is a manifestation 'of an underlying tendency to pursue short-term, immediate pleasure' (Gottfredson and Hirschi, 1990: 93).

According to control theorists, the sources of self-control lie in child-rearing practices. If these are to be effective a number of conditions must be met. Parental concern for children is basic. Children cannot be successfully reared by parents who are indifferent, uncaring or hostile to them. Parents must consistently monitor their children's behaviour to prevent them from getting involved in delinquent acts and to enable them to develop the ability to avoid such acts without their parents being present. Poor conduct and deviant behaviour must also be recognised for what it is and parents must do something about it. The examples Gottfredson and Hirschi give include excessive television viewing, uncompleted homework, truancy from school, and smoking. If child-rearing is to produce the appropriate sense of self-control these must be sanctioned. The sanctions do not have to be physical or violent but they must indicate a clear disapproval of the behaviour involved.

From this Gottfredson and Hirschi identify the factors that prevent effective child-rearing. One is parental criminality. Parents who lack self-control themselves cannot communicate it to their children. Supervision and punishment in such families tends to be weak and inconsistent and there is a refusal to recognise the deviant acts that the children get involved in. As a result children of criminals are likely to become criminals themselves. Another factor is family size. Child-rearing is more effective in small families than in large ones. This is not necessarily because of any lack of affection on the part of the parents but because of the difficulties in finding the time and the energy to monitor and control large numbers of children. The lack of time and energy and the absence of adequate alternative supervision are also the reasons why children from single-parent families and from families with mothers who work outside the home have a higher risk of becoming deviant or criminal.

Control theory has had considerable attractions to many commentators and in particular to other conservative criminologists such as James Q. Wilson (see, for example, 1986) as it argues that the source of the upsurge in crime in countries like the United States since the 1960s has been the decline in discipline and child-monitoring. It also suggests that reducing crime and delinquency does not require a major redistribution of resources. What is needed is the restoration of adequate levels of social and individual control and discipline. As Gottfredson and Hirschi (1990: 272–3) put it, 'policies directed toward enhancement of the ability of familial institutions to socialize children are the only realistic long-term state policies with potential for substantial crime reduction.'

Labelling Theory

All of the above theories share a common feature. They see social control and the institutions – such as the policing and punishment ones – that society has designed to ensure social control as being *responses* to crime and deviance. By contrast, labelling theory sees these institutions as being active participants in its creation (see Becker, 1963). According to the theory a distinction must be made between rule-breaking and deviance. Rule-breaking behaviour is widespread in society. Many juveniles have, for example, committed offences for which they could have been arrested. Yet only some come to the notice of the police and only these have their acts labelled as acts of deviance and as criminal. Labelling theory argues that it is in what happens to those who are singled out in this way that the sources of deviant behaviour can be found. In other words, it is in the processes through which the police, the courts and the prisons select out and process some of those who break the rules in society that the motivation for crime and deviance can be located.

According to the labelling perspective, these processes represent an attack on the self-identity of the individuals involved. Those who are arrested and charged with crimes are no longer seen as normal and as 'just like everyone else'. Their distinctiveness is emphasised by the way in which they are treated. They find themselves in prison cells without their shoe-laces and belts. They find themselves in a courtroom where they are now called 'the accused'. They end up in prison stripped of their own clothing, dressed in a prison uniform and with their hair cut. From being individuals with a name they become transformed into prisoners with a number. These experiences make it difficult for them to maintain their sense of being like everybody else. They are also cut off from people like family and friends who might support their previous sense of self-identity. In such circumstances and under these pressures they may accept the new identity that is being forced on them. They may come to see themselves as criminal and, as behaviour is related to self-image, they may act accordingly.

The pressures created for people by being labelled a 'criminal' are far reaching and their influence should not be underestimated. It can, for example, change the way people in authority such as social workers and probation officers view their personal histories. Incidents in their past lives that were normal to them now become redefined as symptoms of a latent delinquency. The criminal label in society also carries with it a series of auxiliary traits that are assumed to be intrinsically linked to it. If one is a 'criminal' one is also assumed to be 'tough', 'aggressive' and 'dangerous'. We react to labelled individuals as if they had all of these traits. You can see this if you ask yourself how many criminals do you have as friends? Finally we exclude 'criminals' from situations that might help them lose the criminal label. They are, for example, cut off from certain kinds of employment, such as in the civil service, and are denied access to certain kinds of scarce resources, such as visas to the United States. Each pressure may in itself appear small but the combined effect of the accumulation of pressures to become what one is labelled as is intense.

The argument as outlined so far shows why people might become persistent offenders. It does not explain why most offenders are from working-class backgrounds. For that we need to return to the initial stage of the labelling argument. Labelling theory argues that rule-breaking is common in society so how is it that only some is selected out and reacted to? Other things being equal, the visibility of rule-breaking influences the attention it receives. Glue-sniffing in the street, for example, is more likely to be reacted to than dope-taking in a private residence. The power of rule-breakers and the social distance between them and the police is also important. Contrast the reaction to students' behaviour during rag-week with the reaction to the same behaviour from a group of skin-heads. This means that some groups in society – the less powerful and those who use the streets more as living and leisure space – are more vulnerable to official reaction and labelling than others.

Assessing the Theories and their Application to Ireland

We have presented here a set of theories that attempt to explain why it is that particular groups in a society might be motivated to commit crime. There are a number of difficulties in assessing these, both in the general sense of their utility as theories and in the particular sense of their suitability to the Irish context. As general theories, it has been claimed (see Bernard, 1990) that while aspects of each of the theories have been modified as a result of research findings, none of these have ever been successfully rejected. As a result major criminology textbooks expand to accommodate new perspectives rather than remain the same size by excluding old and redundant ones. In the more limited sense there have been no attempts to test the applicability of the theories to the Irish context. However it is possible to derive from these theories some indications of what they might look at and what they might conclude if they were applied to asking why the bulk of offenders in Ireland are from working-class backgrounds.

Three of the theories – Robert Merton, radical criminology and new realism – may differ in the way in which they characterise modern societies and in what they believe should be done about crime, but they are remarkably similar in the way in which they explain criminal motivations. For them these can be found in the gap between the expectations and aspirations that a culture creates and encourages and the way society distributes the means to realise them. A society that restricts access by certain groups to social success generates the frustration and resentment out of which criminal motivations emerge and against which they seem justified. In this sense the pattern of disadvantage experienced by working-class people provides the basis out of which deviant motivations emerge.

This is not of course consistent with the views of control theorists Gottfredson and Hirschi (1990). For them, as we have seen, social disadvantage is not a relevant factor in explaining the low levels of self-control that cause crime. However critics of the theory suggest that social disadvantage should be given more importance (see, for example, Currie, 1985). If quality-parenting is a factor in preventing criminal behaviour then social disadvantage is not the most promising base from which to attempt such parenting. Social influences such as the level of social and material resources available are important in the ability of parents to offer high quality child care. As Harriet Wilson argues, 'in the world of poverty the material preconditions necessary for child-centered parenting do not exist' (Wilson, 1974: 246). Moreover the kinds of factors that they identify as interfering with good quality parenting – large families, single parent families and working mothers without adequate levels of support services – are related to and coexistent with levels of social disadvantage.

A stress on the role of social disadvantage in generating criminal motivations is also not incompatible with a modified version of labelling theory. This theory has been criticised for its inability to deal with or to recognise the importance of the initial reasons why people became involved in criminal behaviour (see, for example, Taylor, Walton and Young, 1973). Because of this critics argue that its most useful quality is its ability to deal with the consequences of people's involvement with institutions of social control. This suggests that the importance of labelling is as a compounding rather than an initiating factor in the generation of deviant behaviour. So if it can be argued that social disadvantage is the source of motivations to become involved in crime then the experience offenders have of institutions and organisations such as the police, the courts and the prisons can become the source of, and the reinforcement for, motives to continue with criminal involvement.

The importance of social disadvantage has some support in the Irish context. Over the last twenty-five years, according to Breen, Hannan, Rottman and Whelan (1990), the class structure in Ireland has changed from one based on family property to one based on educational qualifications. The education system is now the major allocator of positions in the occupational world and so it is the major means through which success can be achieved in Irish society. Yet significant sections of the working class are excluded from full participation in this system particularly from its higher reaches. As a result they are also cut off from the competition for the better occupations in the country. They find themselves either in low-paying jobs or else excluded from the labour force through unemployment. The extent to which unemployment is concentrated among the working class is significant. In a society which respects high occupational achievement and high monetary rewards, success in conventional terms is not a realistic option for many belonging to that class. The strain and frustration this creates then becomes both a motive for crime and a legitimation of it. It is not surprising then to find the high representation of working-class individuals among 'property' criminals.

Linking this to labelling theory is more difficult. Direct evidence of the effects of encounters with control organisations like the police, the courts and the prisons on working-class people, and in particular on the younger ones, is not available for Ireland. We do not know if they create, reinforce or undermine deviant identities. A study of a youth project in a working-class area of a large Irish city, however, provides some indirect evidence. Interviews with young people involved in the project revealed a strong sense of grievance among them that they were being picked on by the gardaí because they were presumed to be 'trouble'. 'When anything happens', one of them said, 'the police come straight to . . . [their area] . . . and stop and ask us questions.' They spoke of the risks of 'being hit for nothing at all' and they felt that they were there 'just for the cops to come over and pick on the quieter ones' (quotations from Lorenz and Mc Cullagh, 1984/85: 42). Some of the older ones felt they had been wrongly accused of criminal activities on these occasions and that they were being provoked into the kinds of responses that would give the gardaí grounds to arrest them. Also, all had stories of people who they believed had been unfairly treated by the gardaí. As a result their response to policing was one of deeply felt grievance. It is possible that this sense of grievance could become the impetus to engage in or to intensify their level of involvement in deviant activities.

If there is little research on the consequences of involvement with the gardaí, there is none on what the consequences of involvement with the courts might be for deviant self-identity. However the rates of recidivism in the prison system (see chapter seven) would suggest that prison reinforces rather than undermines deviant identity. As much as two-thirds of the prison population in any one year can have served previous prison sentences. It has been argued (see Mc Cullagh, 1986a) that offenders leave prison with an enhancement of the criminal skills with which they entered it. It is also likely that this is accompanied by an augmentation of their self-identity as people who are capable of using these skills. The high rates of recidivism suggest, of course, that their assessments of their own abilities are wrong.

The argument being proposed here is that motivations for crime are rooted in the patterns of exclusion and disadvantage created by the operation of the class structure and in the experience of offenders with the institutions of social control in Ireland. If we combine these with the increases in the level of criminal opportunities and with increases in the size of the pool of potential offenders then we have an explanation that embraces many of the salient features of the crime problem that is revealed to us by garda statistics. One question remains unanswered – why is there not as much crime here as there is in other countries? This is addressed in the next section.

Comparative Criminology and Low Crime Rates

Ireland's low crime rate has been remarked on but its causes have never really been addressed by criminologists. It might be tempting to attribute this to the unwillingness of criminologists in Ireland to court the unpopularity of going against the grain of political rhetoric about crime. The reason is however somewhat more prosaic. It lies in the nature of the discipline that they work within. The study of crime has been dominated, in the twentieth century at least, by the work of scholars from the United States. As a result its major concerns have been with a society which has extraordinarily high levels of crime. The homicide rate in the United States between 1979 and 1983, for example, was fifteen times higher than that of Ireland. The result of this is that 'we remain greatly ignorant about the characteristics of countries with low crime rates' (Beirne and Messerschmidt, 1991: 612).

One of the few attempts to dispel this ignorance is that of Freda Adler (1983). She looked to see what countries with low crime rates might have in common. These were selected by dividing the world – fairly arbitrarily it must be said – into five regions – European capitalist, European socialist, Latin America, Islam and Africa. She then picked two countries from each region – Ireland and Switzerland were the European capitalist ones – giving her a total of ten countries to analyse. Their common characteristics were difficult to identify. Social, economic and political differences between the countries were extensive. In political terms, for example, some were democracies, some had military dictatorships and some were single-party states. In economic terms some had high levels of affluence and industrialisation such as Japan and Switzerland, and others, such as Nepal and Costa Rica, had little or no affluence or industrialisation. Some had high levels of unemployment while other had low levels. Half of the countries had capital punishment as the ultimate criminal sanction but, with the exception of Japan, their use of it was fairly restrained.

Two factors, Adler concluded finally, were important among the low-crime countries. The first was the high levels of participation, or at least confidence in, the criminal justice system. This certainly appears to be the case in Ireland. According to the recent European Value Survey (Hardiman and Whelan, 1994) the gardaí enjoy high levels of public support. The majority of people, 85 per cent of a national sample, said they had confidence in the police. While this is partly a product of the way the questions were asked (see chapter six for more on this), it still indicates a higher level of public support than is accorded to other Irish institutions such as parliament and the press.

The second factor Adler identified was the resilience of informal systems of social control, primarily the family and those institutions that emphasised the moral obligations of citizens to their community. In religious societies this was religious institutions; in the more secular ones it was political institutions and political parties. Again this applies to Ireland. A number of writers (see Beirne and Messerschmidt, 1991:

610) have remarked on the role of the Catholic Church and its contribution, through moral control, to low crime rates. Others have also stressed the importance of strong family ties (see Shelley, 1981: 70). Thus Ireland's low crime rate is, according to Adler, the product of the level of confidence in its police force and the strong sense of moral control exerted through religion and family.

There is both a certain sense of irony and a number of problems attached to this as an explanation for our low crime rate. The irony is that the source of crime in Ireland is seen by insiders as residing in the decline in those very institutions that are seen by outsiders as contributing to our low level of crime, namely the family and religion. The problems with Adler's analysis are primarily methodological. She has tried to identify those features that low-crime countries have in common. But in order to argue that these features are important it is necessary to show not just that low-crime countries share these characteristics but also that these characteristics distinguish them from, and are not present in, high-crime countries. It may indeed be possible to show this but Adler does not.

There are also problems associated with the depth of her analysis of the social structure of the different countries. For example, a superficial look at Irish society would attribute considerable power and influence to the Catholic Church. A more incisive analysis might point to a more nuanced version of this power. It is possible to acknowledge the power of the Catholic Church at a political and institutional level while remaining sceptical of its ability to influence the behaviour of its followers. Joseph Lee (1984), for example, has argued that while in most countries there is some gap between what people say and what people do, the size of this gap in Ireland is particularly large. This needs to be explained and the historical experience of colonisation and its psychological aftermath play an important part. The end product is a morality that has a 'relaxed attitude to lying' and that has conservative views on matters of sexual morality but 'relatively permissive ones on matters of public (or civic) morality' (Lee, 1984: 111). In England, Eamon de Valera is reputed to have said, 'one could say what one liked as long as one did the right thing, in Ireland, by contrast, one could do what one liked as long as one said the right thing' (Lee, 1984: 110). If this is true then the high levels of commitment to the family and the gardaí may be more verbal than behavioural, in which case their contribution to low crime rates may legitimately be doubted.

Conclusion

In this chapter we have considered the explanations that have been, and that can be, offered for the pattern of crime in Ireland as derived from official crime statistics. These show that crime has increased dramatically over the past thirty years, that it is mainly committed by young working-class males, that the major form of crime is property crime and that, despite recent increases, the crime rate remains low by international standards. Two explanations were considered for the increases. Both related them to wider changes in the society. The first – social disorganisation – related them to the way in which change undermined the traditional system of social control in the society. While this argument has some force and con-siderable public appeal it suffers from a somewhat misty-eyed view of the past and of the effectiveness of the traditional con-trol system. The second and more promising perspective locates the problem in the way in which social change has increased both the opportunities for criminal activity and also the size of the pool of potential offenders. The concurrence of these two sets of changes produced an increase in crime.

We went on to identify a number of shortcomings in this argument, most notably its inability to tell us why it is only people from working-class backgrounds who take advantage of increased opportunities to get involved in crime. This gap can be filled by considering the range of theories in sociology that try to identify the factors that generate criminal motivation. Despite their differences we argued that these theories can be seen as proposing that when the patterns of social exclusion and social disadvantage produced by the class structure of the society are combined with the responses of people to their involvement with the police, the courts and the prisons, the criminal motivations of working-class offenders become comprehensible. Finally the low crime rate can be explained in terms of the continued resilience of religion and family in the society.

These then are the kinds of explanations that can be offered for the Irish crime problem. Their utility and their persuasiveness depends, of course, on the validity of the base from which our knowledge of the crime problem is constructed. We have seen already how official crime statistics have a number of defects, most notably in their tendency to understate the level of crimes generally and particularly the level of crimes of violence. While this is true, it does not necessarily – as we argued in chapter one – undermine the belief that property crimes committed by working-class offenders constitute an important part of the crime problem. A more significant objection is that, for a variety of reasons, these statistics neglect the range of crimes that are committed by middle- and upper-class offenders. If these are significant then they have the potential to distort our picture of the nature of the crime problem in Ireland and to undermine the validity of the kinds of explanations for crime that have been considered here. Because of this it is necessary to examine the phenomenon of what has been variously described as white-collar crime, middle-class crime, crimes of the powerful and corporate crime. This is what we turn to in chapter three.

Notes

1. The Blueshirts were a private army that armed and marched in the country in the 1930s. They acquired their name from the colour of the shirts they wore as part of their uniform. They also adopted the straight-arm salute popular among fascist movements in Europe at the time. There is some dispute among historians as to whether they also acquired their politics from the same source. Their leader, Eoin O'Duffy, had been sacked as garda commissioner by the government of the day. They were banned by the government and merged with a number of other groups to form a political party which later became known as Fine Gael (see Lee, 1989: 179–84).

   The 'Emergency' was the name given in Ireland to the period known elsewhere as World War Two. Ireland remained neutral during this conflict.

3   THE CRIMES OF THE MIDDLE CLASS

Introduction

In the previous chapter we considered the explanations that have been offered for crime in Ireland. These stress the roles played by the factors of opportunities and of motivation. The increase in crime can be explained by the increased opportunities to commit crime and by the presence in Irish society of people who are willing to take advantage of these opportunities. However despite their individual differences in emphasis these theories share a factor in common. They assume that those who commit crime are mainly from working-class backgrounds and as such they accept that the picture of the typical offender contained in both police arrest statistics and in statistics on the prison populations is accurate.

This is also very much in line with the public's image of the typical criminal. Arguably this is of a young working-class man though depending on the politics of the individual or institution a different attitude may be adopted to the significance of social background. A liberal view might stress its deprived nature. The Council for Social Welfare (1983: 14–15), for example, has argued that criminals are mainly drawn from socially deprived backgrounds where poverty, poor education, alcoholism and unemployment are routine experiences. By contrast a less liberal version would stress the dangerousness of the people involved.

In this chapter we question the reality of this image by considering the crimes of the middle class. The chapter has two main sections. In the first we give a brief overview of white-collar crime and of the significance that it has for criminology. In the second section we examine the extent and seriousness of middle-class crime in Ireland and the degree to which it has become marginalised in the debate about crime.

I An Overview of White-Collar Crime

The term 'white-collar crime' is generally credited to Edwin Sutherland (1949, 1961). He used it to refer to 'a crime committed by a person of respectability in the course of his occupation' with the object of making a profit for his employer (Sutherland, 1949: 9). The offences he had in mind were breaches of anti-trust legislation and of industrial safety regulations, pollution offences, illegal payments to other companies, stock exchange manipulation, tax evasion, false advertising and price-fixing between companies. He concluded that these kinds of crime were frequent, widespread and routine features of American business. More recent research confirms that his conclusion remains valid today (see, for example, Braithwaite, 1984).

This research would also suggest that the term should now be seen to include two distinct kinds of crime. These are 'occupational crime' and 'corporate crime'. The first refers to crimes which involve the abuse of occupational position for personal gain. These are generally committed against employers through 'fiddling' or employee theft, for example, but the victim can also be the individual patient or customer as in the case of occupational fraud where individuals use the status of their occupations to defraud the public. One of the most common forms in the United States is fraud by physicians, primarily through unnecessary surgery, particularly coronary by-pass and hysterectomy (see Beirne and Messerschmidt, 1991: 180–3).

'Corporate crime' refers to crimes committed by people in the course of their occupations where the object is to gain benefit for the corporation or the company and to further corporate goals such as profit maximisation. As such it includes corporate violence where workers are exposed to danger through unsafe working conditions or where the public is endangered either through the deliberate sale of products that are known to be dangerous or through the flouting of pollution laws. It also includes corporate theft where the public are robbed through over-pricing of goods or deceptive advertising and where corporations rob the state through tax evasion. One of the most prominent forms this takes is where corporations bribe state officials and as such it involves the theft of the public trust placed in elected officials.

The Significance of White-Collar Crime

What the two kinds of white-collar crime have in common is that both are primarily crimes of the middle class. So while it can be argued that many forms of occupational crime are open to all employees, non-manual employees tend to have greater opportunities to commit more substantial thefts against their employers. They have, for example, greater access to locations such as computer facilities and large cash deposits from which significant embezzlement can take place. In an industrial world in which the fastest growing crime is computer-based theft, the contribution of the middle class to the problem of crime is not one that should be neglected.

Moreover white-collar crime has a particular significance for criminology. As we have seen in chapter two most conventional explanations stress the centrality of social class and social exclusion as motivating factors in acquisitive property crime.

The existence and extent of white-collar crime shows that these in themselves are not sufficient as explanations. Most of those involved in white-collar crime do not come from backgrounds where low levels of education and high levels of deprivation are present. If we are to continue to argue, as John Hagan (1994) has maintained, that inequalities of wealth and power are central to an understanding of both conventional and white-collar crime then we need to think about this relationship in a more sophisticated fashion than has been done so far. One way of doing this is suggested in chapter five.

II Studying White-Collar Crime in Ireland

White-collar crime is difficult to study in most countries but particularly so in Ireland. Some of these difficulties come from the crime itself which by its nature tends to be secretive and its success depends on it remaining at that level. This means that victimisation is often less apparent and because of the long time-lag between the event and its consequences, as for example, in the case of pollution and exposure to dangerous working conditions, it can often be difficult to establish. Similarly, occupational crimes like embezzlement have low rates of discovery and because of the potential embarrassment they are often not reported to the authorities by the victimised corporation or business. It does not do a lot for the reputation of a bank, for example, if it becomes public knowledge that it has been defrauded by an employee on a large scale and over a long period of time. It would also be damaging to their rationalisation plans if the extent of computer fraud and particularly that involving the manipulation of cash dispensers were ever to be made public (see Sieber, 1986).

Difficulties also arise from the perception that white-collar crime is not as serious as other kinds of crime. Thus James Q. Wilson (1975) has argued that conventional street crime is a threat to the ability of a society to sustain meaningful community life and white-collar crime is not. Similarly, Michael Clarke (1990: 20) claims that 'public order is not violated in business offences as it is in conventional crime' and such offences as a result have a 'much less threatening character'. Others, Steven Box (1983) among them, say that these kinds of arguments are inaccurate. It may be true that a business practice like tax evasion is not as threatening to us as physical assault. But crimes such as pollution, the mass marketing of defective drugs, or the neglect of safety standards pose very real dangers to a great number of people. Research on hazards at work, for example, shows that most workers are at greater risk in the work-place then they are in the street (Hagan, 1994: 104). At a purely financial level the cost of white-collar crime is also more substantial than that of most conventional crime. One well-organised fraud is likely to cost more and to create more victims than one 'ordinary' robbery.

The difficulty, which is specific to Ireland, is the absence of research. With one exception, noted below, there has been no research on white-collar crime in this country. This reflects the lack of research generally on crime but it also reflects the tendency for the available research to focus on the more conventional kinds of crime. This has particular consequences for our study as it means that the kinds of distinctions found in the international literature, between corporate and occupational crime, for example, cannot be utilised here. As a result our consideration of the topic must be tentative and to a considerable extent speculative.

The Extent and Seriousness of White-Collar Crime in Ireland

Nonetheless the sources that are available suggest white-collar crime is a serious problem. The Report of the Committee of Inquiry into the Penal System (1985: 55) put the combined cost of white-collar offences such as tax evasion, the evasion of the payment of debts, the non-payments of workers' tax liability and their social welfare entitlements, business sharp practices, company frauds, abuses of the social welfare system and a wide range of other such evasions at between £300 million and £1,000 million a year, that is between eight and twenty-eight times the amount taken in conventional crime in 1984. This is a very wide range but given the imprecision of the available data it is perhaps inevitable.

There are also some figures available on specific white-collar offences. The annual reports on crime for example, give figures for the amount of fraud that is reported to the gardaí. However as O'Mahony (1993: 55) points out, the information is not particularly useful as the classification system is not used with any consistency and no data is provided on the size of individual frauds. The figures show large increases in these offences but much of the increase is in minor offences such as receiving stolen goods and forgery. A more informative measure is available from the report of the Advisory Committee on Fraud (1992). This looked at the top fifty frauds under investigation by the Garda Fraud Squad in early 1992. The total amount potentially at risk was £26 million. Each of the top twenty cases averaged amounts in excess of £100,000.

It has been suggested that frauds such as these which comes to public attention are only the tip of the iceberg (see Magee, 1988). Up to 1988, for example, there had been only eight investigations of fraud in the meat industry and only one successful prosecution. Yet a businessman who was charged in Germany with defrauding the European Community said that Ireland was the easiest country in Europe to get away with such fraud (quoted in Magee, 1988). The problem is compounded by the unwillingness of many companies to involve the fraud squad. A security organisation which specialises in the detection of corporate fraud claims to deal with up to 500 cases a year and only 8 per cent of these end up in court (Magee, 1988). Many companies opt to avoid the publicity by simply sacking the individuals involved and 'one or two were actually given golden handshakes to terminate their contracts' (Magee, 1988: 15). The equivalent in conventional crime would be a free motoring holiday for every successful car-thief.

A study by accountants, Stokes, Kennedy, Crowley (reported in *The Irish Times*, 5 February, 1993), tried to get around the problem of non-reporting. It surveyed 301 companies but as just over half of them were available for interview, its results are also incomplete. One hundred and twenty eight of those said they had uncovered fraud in the past three years. Two-thirds of these involved amounts over £1,000. Just under 30 per cent involved sums greater than £10,000 and 2 per cent involved amounts over £1 million. Criminal proceedings were instigated in only 28 per cent of cases. This meant that just under three-quarters of the discovered frauds were never reported to the police and hence deprived of a mention in police statistics.

However, these kinds of data have serious shortcomings. They are limited in their coverage, both in terms of the level of detail they give on specific crimes and in the actual range of white-collar offences they cover. The Stokes, Kennedy, Crowley study, for example, was limited to fraud and did not cover other corporate offences such as unsafe working conditions, bribery of public officials or tax evasion. Moreover it only looked at fraud from the point of view of the companies who were being defrauded. It never asked whether they were themselves involved in offences such as tax evasion. Notwithstanding these limitations the conclusion from the data must be that there is, as O'Mahony (1993: 56) puts it, 'a real possibility that the illegal gains from "white-collar crime" far exceed the gains from the much more acknowledged and feared areas of robbery, burglary and larceny.'

Yet despite its extent and its seriousness white-collar crime does not form part of our consciousness of the crime problem. It does not, for example, figure as an issue in political party campaigns on crime and it seldom figures in public discussions of the topic. Moreover the people who are involved in it do not, as we have seen, figure as one of the elements out of which we construct our image of the typical criminal. In effect, white-collar crime in Ireland and the kinds of people who commit it have been marginalised in our understanding of crime. What we now need to look at is how this marginalisation has been achieved.

The Marginalisation of White-Collar Crime

There are three principal ways in which the marginalisation of white-collar crime is accomplished. The first and most important is through the laws that are enacted. The legal system in Ireland distributes the criminal label in an uneven manner. It sanctions some kinds of socially harmful behaviour and ignores others. The second way that white-collar crime is marginalised is by the law enforcement system devoting more energy and resources to the pursuit of some kinds of lawbreaking than to others. The final way is a court system that punishes some people and some offences more harshly than others. The end product is a criminal justice system which criminalises the offences of young working-class men and systematically ignores the crimes of the middle class.

(a) The Role of the Legal System

'Killing, injuring or molesting others, or stealing from them', the Committee of Inquiry into the Penal System tells us (1985: 28), 'are . . . unacceptable infringements of personal and property rights.' Yet all infringements of these rights are not treated as criminal and are not subject to the criminal sanction. In this sense the reach of the criminal law is uneven. Decisions as to what to treat as crime and as criminal are not a perfect measure of the objective dangers of particular kinds of behaviour. In Ireland the law has been formulated in such a way that the anti-social behaviour of those in business, corporate and commercial positions is either poorly regulated or if regulated it is not done through the criminal law. Consider these two examples.

(i) Bantry Bay   Just after 12.30 a.m. on the morning of 8 January, 1979, a small fire started on a tanker, the *Betelgeuse*, which was discharging fuel at the Gulf Oil terminal in Bantry Bay. Within a period of about fifteen minutes the fire became a major one and culminated in a huge explosion that killed fifty people. This is the largest number of people to be killed in a single incident in the history of the state. It was, for example, more than were killed in the loyalist bombing of Dublin in 1974. These deaths are not recorded in crime statistics for 1979 but they are recorded in Department of the Marine accident statistics as 'shipping casualties' (*Statistical Abstracts*, 1979/80: 309). The evidence presented at the tribunal of inquiry set up by the Irish government suggested however that the case may not have been that simple. Undoubtedly the elements of coincidence and of operator error were factors in the explosion. But the evidence also suggested that the attitudes and behaviour of the state and the companies involved were very important elements in what happened.

The state, it would seem from the evidence of the tribunal, may have failed to provide for the effective regulation of the activities of the companies working with oil in Bantry Bay. Gulf Oil, the corporation running the oil terminal, was, according to Chris Eipper (1989: 158), 'subjected to no coherent regulatory framework'. A Dangerous Substances Act had been passed by the Dáil in 1972, seven years before the incident. This gave the Minister for Labour extensive powers to control the storage of petroleum products and to regulate for safety standards. But the necessary regulations to bring the law into effect were not brought in until nine months after the disaster. The tribunal of inquiry concluded that the statutory obligations placed on Gulf Oil in relation to safety and fire-fighting 'were wholly inadequate' (Costello, 1980: 24).

A key element in turning the fire into an explosion was the fact that the ship split in two when its back broke. This was partly caused by a ballasting error. This error would not have happened if the ship had been fitted with a loadicator which calculates stress levels in the ship. The tribunal said that this 'is now virtually standard practice for large tankers'. Its installation would have cost a few thousand pounds. The tribunal records that it was given no adequate explanation for this omission, yet 'It had most serious consequences' (Costello, 1980: 212).

Furthermore, if the ship had been properly maintained the error would not have been as significant or as fatal. The ship had, what the tribunal described as, 'a seriously weakened hull' (Costello, 1980: 23), something which the crew could not have been aware of. A ship's inspector told the tribunal that on the day of the explosion, the *Betelgeuse* was 'a bloody awful-looking ship' (Costello, 1980: 210). It was in 'a seriously cor-roded and wasted condition' (Costello, 1980: 20). Repairs to the ship which in 1977 would have cost $311,000 were never carried out because the ship owners had been considering selling it. All of these decisions were taken by Total, the ship's owners, 'in the interests of economy' (Costello, 1980: 212). The tribunal concluded that 'the major share of the responsibility for the loss of the ship must, therefore, lie on the management of Total' (Costello,1980: 321).

Gulf Oil, the owners of the terminal, had also been less than responsible in the area of safety regulations. Their own procedures said that if a tanker was unloading oil there should be a tug in the vicinity on fire-watch duties. Instead the tug was almost three miles away and out of sight of the jetty where the oil was being discharged. Gulf Oil had also failed to provide 'suitable escape craft at the jetty' (Costello, 1980: 23). An automatically pressurised fire-main had been decommissioned in 1970. If it had been under pressure the fire could have been contained. There had been a decline in the quality of the training given to the jetty workers and 'there was no training or drill of any sort in the evacuation of the jetty' (Costello, 1980: 145). If many of these conditions had been met, the tribunal concluded that 'the lives of the jetty crew and those on board the vessel would have been saved' (Costello, 1980: 23).

This evidence suggests a significant level of corporate and state culpability. The companies involved eventually paid compensation to the victims' families. Their conduct resulted, in what Steven Box (1983: 25) has called, 'avoidable death'. Yet there were no criminal prosecutions directly concerned with the circumstances of these deaths.

(ii) The Gallagher Group   The second example concerns the activities of Patrick Gallagher and his group of companies (the Gallagher Group).[1] One of these, a bank called Merchant Bank, accepted deposits from the public. In turn it loaned money both to individuals and companies and in particular to other companies in the Gallagher Group. At the time of its collapse in 1982 80 per cent of the assets of the bank were in the Gallagher Group, something which was not known by the relevant regulatory authorities. Many of the loans were not loans within the usual meaning of that term. They were never repaid to the bank and there appears to have been little expectation that they would be. For example, monies paid for publicity for other companies in the Gallagher Group were reflected in the bank's books as loans outstanding. Gallagher also personally received a share in a race horse but the price of the share was reflected in the books as a loan outstanding. There appears to have been no security for these kinds of loans and little or no interest paid to the bank on them.

Part of Gallagher's business involved house-building. He used his bank and his depositors' money to finance this. As a normal part of major building projects, developers are required to deposit financial performance bonds with the relevant local authority as a guarantee that housing estates will be completed. Gallagher did this by giving the local authorities deposit receipts to suggest that he had lodged the relevant sums to accounts opened in their name in Merchant Bank. That this was in breach of Central Bank rules did not prove a major impediment as these transactions were simply never shown in his books. The receipts were also worthless as he never lodged the money in the bank to cover the alleged deposits. When the bank collapsed, £1 million was owed to the local authorities.

The dubious nature of Gallagher's banking operation can also be illustrated by the handling of the sale of the Donaghmede shopping centre in Dublin. In 1975 this was bought by the Merchant Bank from the Gallagher Group for £1.9 million. The bank held it for three years, during which time, according to independent estimates, its value increased to £2.5 million. But in 1978 the bank sold it back to the Gallagher Group for £1.9 million. This in effect was a loss to the bank of a potential £600,000. Despite having held an asset for three years the bank made no capital gain on the transaction. In 1981 the Gallagher Group sold the shopping centre for £4.5 million.

The sale of 'The Galleria', a shopping mall in St Stephen's Green in Dublin, also indicated an innovative approach to the use of property. In 1982 it was sold by Gallagher to Merchant Bank for the sum of £2.3 million. But the day before the sale, Gallagher gave the deeds of the property to the Bank of Ireland as security against loans of almost £6 million. So, in effect, there was nothing to sell. This did not prevent the sale appearing on the books of the bank but when the Merchant Bank collapsed there was no asset to claim on. In the end the bank's depositors lost £2.3 million through the bank's apparent purchase of an asset that the seller no longer had any effective control over. The Gallagher Group finally collapsed on 30 April, 1982. This empire also included a bank in Northern Ireland. Here depositors, because of legal protections in the jurisdiction, got back 70 per cent of their savings. In the South, by contrast, the 590 depositors, many of whom had invested life-savings, lost all the money – a total of £4.5 million – that they had lodged with the bank. Gallagher pleaded guilty to two offences in Northern Ireland – supplying false information to the regulatory authorities and theft – and served a prison sentence there. The latter offence involved the use of £110,000 of the bank's money to buy paintings for himself.

Yet, in the Republic, although the liquidator's report identified a number of possible offences under various acts, mainly those involving company law such as not holding AGM's, keeping false records and making false returns to the Central Bank but also possible offences such as obtaining an asset fraudulently and making fraudulent statements, no prosecution followed in the Republic. The liquidator's report was lodged with the high court in 1984. From here it was sent to the Director of Public Prosecutions on the grounds that there might be a case for criminal prosecution. The DPP referred the case to the garda fraud squad for investigation. When its report was sent back to the DPP no action followed. This was in marked contrast to what happened in the North.

It could be argued that, despite the example here, there is a range of legislation under which corporate offenders can be and are prosecuted. Relevant examples include environmental law, company law and the laws covering health and safety issues in the work-place. However it is important to recognise that these laws are not part of the criminal code. They cannot be found, for example, in the relevant texts on Irish criminal law. This means that those who are prosecuted under their terms are generally spared the criminal stigma, the imposition of which is an important feature of criminal proceedings. They are also spared the restrictions on subsequent life opportunities that, as we have suggested in chapter two, are experienced by those who acquire the criminal label.

(b) The Process of Law Enforcement

The second way in which white-collar crime is marginalised is through the manner in which the existing criminal law is enforced. We might anticipate that all serious law-breakers would be pursued with the same level of thoroughness and efficiency. Consider the following as suggestive of a selective enforcement of the law.

(i) Corporate fraud   The most common offence recorded in garda crime statistics is larceny. The range of crimes covered by the term includes larceny from the person, car-theft, and what is perhaps the most frequently recorded offence in garda statistics, larceny from unattended vehicles. In 1993, for example, just over 47,000 larcenies were recorded. About 45 per cent of these involved amounts of less than £100. Sixty-three per cent involved amounts of £200 or less. Only 8 per cent of larcenies involved amounts of £1,000 and over. The average amount taken in larcenies in which property was stolen was £446.

Let us look at a case involving £500,000, or over one thousand times the size of the average larceny. It first came to light in the Goodman Organisation in December 1986. The irregularities involved claims for European Community (EC) subsidies on meat which did not exist. The investigations section of the revenue commissioners, having investigated the matter, were concerned that serious criminal offences may have been committed. Their report was completed in September 1987. It recommended that the Goodman company, Anglo–Irish Beef Processors, be sanctioned and that the Garda Fraud Squad be called in. The report reached the Department of Agriculture on 5 October, 1987. Four months later, on 4 February, 1988, the fraud squad was called in though the Beef

Tribunal concluded that this delay was not inordinate 'having regard to the complexity of the matter' (*Report of the Beef Tribunal*, 1994: 402).

To begin their investigation the fraud squad had to get a copy of the report of the revenue officer involved. They went to the Department of Agriculture and were advised to contact the author of the report. A police officer contacted him on 2 May. He was told there was no problem in getting access to the report if the request was put in writing. This was done on 16 May but, according to the *Report of the Beef Tribunal* (1995: 402), 'the letter containing the written request does not appear to have reached the Revenue Commissioners'. On 18 October a copy of the letter was delivered by hand. The report was received by the gardaí seven weeks later on 2 December. While the beef tribunal report concluded that 'there was nothing sinister in the delay of the Customs & Excise authorities making the file available to the Garda Fraud Squad' (*Report of the Beef Tribunal*, 1994: 403), there appeared to be little evidence of a sense of urgency.

The result of the delay was that the garda investigation of the alleged fraud did not begin until two years after the fraud was discovered. The fraud squad spent a further two years investigating. The fraud was alleged to have taken place in two locations, Waterford and Ballymun, but the Waterford plant was never investigated. The Ballymun plant was. The reasons given were that the complexity of the matter and the resources available to them meant that one factory should be investigated in detail (*Report of the Beef Tribunal*, 1994: 403). Ballymun was chosen, according to the police officer involved, because of its proximity to the fraud squad offices in Dublin. The DPP decided in May 1991 not to prosecute. In the course of a letter written on 16 May, 1991 the senior legal assistant in the Office of the Director of Public Prosecutions said that '[W]hatever hope there might have been of bringing home criminal responsibility for such activities was effectively eliminated by the inordinate delays in completing the investigations and in particular in referring the matter to the Gardai' (*Report of the Beef Tribunal*, 1994: 398).

(ii) Tax evasion   Tax evasion is a criminal offence in Ireland. This has been the situation for over forty-five years since a supreme court ruling in the *State* v. *Fawsitt* in 1945 (*Irish Reports*, 1945: 183). According to the Collector General, it is not a victimless crime. 'The victims', he is quoted as saying (*Cork Examiner*, 25 September, 1990), 'are the complying public.' It also has what are, by Irish standards, severe penalties attached to it. Under the Finance Act 1983 the maximum sentence, if convicted on indictment, is five years in prison, a fine of £10,000 or both. As a crime it would seem to be fairly widespread. In May 1992, for example, it was alleged by the tax officers' union that the state was owed £2.5 billion in unpaid tax (*Cork Examiner*, 10 October, 1992). Despite this it is not always perceived as a crime. An accountant, quoted in Magee (1988: 16), said that as many as one in ten company liquidations in Ireland are the result of declining moral standards in the business community. But the quote from him shows some subtle differentiation in this area. 'Immoral management practices in business seem to be increasing. *Even if it is only* the non-payment of PAYE and PRSI' (emphasis added).

As a crime tax evasion has tended to be under-policed. According to the tax officials' union, a major cause of the high level of evasion is the virtual non-policing of the corporate tax sector (*The Irish Times*, 10 October, 1992). In 1990, for example, there were seven tax inspectors auditing the returns of the self-employed. At that speed, Greg Maxwell, general secretary of the then Union of Professional and Technical Civil Servants, said 'it will take 300 years to audit all of those making returns' (*Irish Independent*, 12 September, 1990: 3). Recent changes in staffing levels have increased the percentage of the self-employed who make tax returns but unfortunately the annual reports of the revenue commissioners do not say if this has been accompanied by a commensurate increase in the accuracy of these returns.

Thus while tax evaders may now have more fear of detection they are still fairly secure from the criminal sanctions available in the law. Criminal proceedings are seldom used against them. In the rare cases that end up in court a conviction has never 'led to a sentence of imprisonment' (Rottman and Tormey, 1986: 43). The situation can be summarised by saying that tax evasion is a fairly common activity where the chances of non-detection are still significant and the risks of being criminally adjudicated are relatively minor.

(iii) Insider-dealing Another form of corporate robbery is insider-dealing. This is where people in the financial world take advantage of privileged information that becomes available to them in the course of their work. It is generally information on the likely future movements of share prices of a company. It is also information that can be used to make substantial profits. If, for example, you have access to information that will, when it is made public, increase the share price of a company, you can use this information to buy company shares and then sell them when the price rises. The outcome is substantial profits with no risk. A judge in Singapore, quoted by Anthony Collins (1990: 32), said that essentially it was stealing information 'because, as in the case of theft of goods, the person using the information had no right to it'.

In the 1980s public concern about the practice of insider-dealing led to its being made a criminal offence in Britain and in the United States. It also produced a number of highly publicised cases where large amounts of money were made using insider information and where the individuals involved ended up being prosecuted for the offences and in some cases serving substantial prison sentences. The case of Dennis Levine and Ivan Boesky illustrates this. Levine worked for a number of stockbrokers in which he had access to information of business take-overs. He passed this on to Boesky who used it to turn an inheritance of $700,000 into a fortune of $200 million. He gave Levine 5 per cent of his profits for the use of the information (Box, 1983).

In Ireland, however, insider-dealing was up until recently a perfectly legal practice. Senator Shane Ross told the Senate 'it is happening all the time and it is just a historical fact on the Dublin Stock Exchange' (*Report on Debates in Seanad Éireann*, vol. 116, no. 9, 16 July, 1994: 2545). It is now an offence under the Companies Act 1990 but the manner in which it is made illegal is interesting. Under section 110 of the Act a person who is charged with insider-dealing will, on summary conviction, be liable to a maximum sentence of twelve months or a maximum fine of £1,000. If convicted on indictment, the maximum sentence is ten years in prison or a fine of up to £200,000. Initially the provision will be enforced by the stock exchange. 'Substantial duties are imposed on recognised stock exchanges who have an obligation to provide a report to the DPP if it appears to the relevant authority that any person has committed an offence under section 107' (Collins, 1990: 35). So in the end it can be enforced by the courts. The reality however is that these procedures are not particularly effective.

(c) The Process of Court Decision-Making

The final way in which white-collar crime is marginalised is through the manner in which it is dealt with in court. We can see this if we look at one of the few white-collar offences that is covered by Irish criminal law. This is embezzlement, the 'classic Irish white-collar crime' (Rottman and Tormey, 1986: 48). What happens when such offences lead to criminal prosecution? Research by David Rottman and Philip Tormey (1986) looked at all the indictments for six offences before the Dublin Circuit Court between 1980 and 1984. The offences were obtaining goods by false pretences, fraudulent conversion, embezzlement, customs violations, forgery, and receiving offences. This gave them 272 individuals who were involved in either professional crime – where criminal activity was their livelihood, or occupational crime – where the offences were carried out while involved in legitimate activities. Where occupational crime was concerned, they found that fifty-nine out of every hundred defendants are convicted by the courts. This is less than the rate of seventy out of every hundred for professional offences and, on the basis of 1,981 cases, the sixty-eight out of every hundred individuals found guilty of more 'conventional' crimes.

There is also a major difference when it comes to sanctioning. 'Imprisonment', they conclude (1986: 50), 'is used sparingly.' Only 20 per cent of such convictions resulted in a prison sentence compared to 50 per cent of 'conventional' crimes and 40 per cent of 'professional' crime. When a prison sentence is given it tends to be severe but typically the sentence is suspended if the offender pays a court-determined level of compensation. This was applied in almost half the cases. The researchers concluded that 'for those offences reaching the Circuit Criminal Court, the probability of conviction is low for occupational offences. Similarly, the prospect of imprisonment if convicted is low' (Rottman and Tormey, 1986: 52).

Other Considerations

In this chapter it has been suggested that in Ireland, as elsewhere, white-collar crime is a significant but under-appreciated problem. The main reason is that a range of processes marginalise the issue and save the behaviour from the stigma of criminality. White-collar crime is either not adequately covered by the law, treated as a matter for civil procedures even where it could be treated as criminal or not as rigorously policed as other forms of crime, or if it is brought to the attention of the criminal courts, convicted offenders seldom receive prison sentences.

However before we can conclude that the treatment of white-collar crime is in clear contrast to the treatment of the criminality of the working-class, a number of issues must be addressed. The first is the argument that, as Michael Clarke (1990: 20) has suggested, 'the criminal justice approach is largely inappropriate and ineffective' for business crime. It is inappropriate because criminal law is based on the notion of *mens rea* which means that to commit a crime those involved must have intended to cause harm or to have acted with recklessness. In the kinds of offences that we are dealing with here this form of intention is missing or with large and complex organisations particularly it can be extremely difficult and expensive to establish. It is ineffective in that the sanctions which it can mobilise are not the most effective and appropriate ones for such offenders. Hence it is argued that it is more appropriate to treat these as offences against regulations or as matters which can more appropriately be dealt with as breaches of contract or as torts which can be sorted out by litigation between the various parties involved.

This view is somewhat idealistic. It is based on the belief that as the law guarantees formal equality between the parties the process will always be fair but this divorces the law from its social context. Cases may proceed on the assumption that all parties are equal but they are not. At a very basic level the risks in litigation are not evenly distributed. The costs of litigation are high and they rise significantly the further up the legal pyramid that a case goes. The effect, as Curtin and Shields (1988: 123) put it, is that 'where the resources of wealth, information and possession belong to one group while the other group (although it may be in the right) has none of these advantages, there can be no real contest'.

The cases that are successfully concluded often require extraordinary commitment and exceptionally determined people to pursue them. The examples of John Hanrahan, the Tipperary farmer who pursued Merck, Sharpe and Dohme for a discharge of dangerous chemicals (*Hanrahan* v. *Merck, Sharpe and*

Dohme (Ireland) Ltd, 1988 *Irish Law Reports Monthly,* 1988, vol 8: 629–31) and Margaret Best who pursued a pharmaceutical company through a long and involved court process are cases in point. Hanrahan believed that the discharge from the plant had killed his cattle and damaged both his health and that of his family. He initiated a civil case against the company and ended up being involved in the longest civil action in Irish legal history. He lost the case in the high court. His family ended up with debts that were three times what they were worth and they were forced to put their land up for auction. They finally won a judgement in the Supreme Court and despite this it took two and a half years for the financial settlement to be paid over to them (O'Callaghan, 1992). Margaret Best took on a company with annual profits of £200 million from a situation of little money and no access to free legal aid. She lost a high court case and only won on appeal to the Supreme Court (*Best* v. *Wellcome Foundation Ltd, Irish Law Reports Monthly,* 1992, vol. 12: 609–50). In the end the case turned on a piece of evidence that was discovered by Ms Best among over 50,000 sheets of paper she had accumulated during the case. This was a memo between two of the company's scientists saying that a particular batch of a vaccine had failed routine tests and was particularly toxic but nevertheless had been released onto the market. Her lawyer described it as a 'stunning admission' but its discovery was accidental (see *Sunday Tribune,* 7 June 1992: A7).

It is true that the issue of intention can be difficult to establish and to resolve for corporate offences. But it is not impossible. As Braithwaite (1984) points out, to the outside world organisations present an image of diffused accountability for law observance yet they have very clear systems of accountability for internal purposes. They may present a public face of uncertain and imprecise systems of accountability but these do not operate when it comes to distributing the rewards for organisational success. James Gobert (1994) has developed this point. He argues that regulatory laws devalue the harm caused by corporate activities and they do not have a sufficient deterrent effect to prevent corporate misbehaviour. But while 'a "true" criminal backup is needed for serious offences and for deployment against serious offenders' (Gobert, 1994: 727), the present criminal law does not provide it. He maintains that the notion of *mens rea* is inappropriate and useless in the corporate context. In its place he proposes a model of corporate fault under which a company would be criminally liable 'where a crime is authorized, permitted or tolerated as a matter of company policy or *de facto* practice' (Gobert, 1994: 728). This would replace the concept of *mens rea* with one of *due diligence*. Under it a corporation would be required to show that it had taken the necessary steps to avoid the occurrence of harm, that is that it had acted with due diligence to prevent criminal activity.

This use of the criminal law against corporations raises questions about the appropriate sanctions and the level at which these sanctions should be imposed, particularly if individuals in organisations are not to be scapegoated for misbehaviour they were not solely responsible for. Some have suggested that it is the officers of the corporation who should be held responsible for corporate misbehaviour and it is to them that sanctions should be applied. Others such as Steven Box have argued by contrast that 'although individual offenders should be prosecuted in tandem . . . the level of intervention to regulate corporate crime has to be organizational rather than individual' (Box, 1983: 70). This means that, for example, a community service order imposed on an offending corporation could oblige it to build a nursury, a school or a library to make amends for its offence.

Those who argue for the inappropriateness of the criminal perspective also claim that the imposition of fines and the payment of compensation are more effective as sanctions than a prison sentence. Their arguments are part of the overall retreat from the justice model in dealing with corporate crime and their accuracy can be disputed. Francis Cullen and his associates (1983: 490), for example, have shown that 'instances exist in which the imposition of criminal penalties have had demonstrable deterrent effects on upper-world illegality' while Edwin Sutherland (1949, 1961), among others,[2] found that the use of administrative procedures against large corporations is not particularly efficient. Just over 97 per cent of the corporations he studied had two or more offences recorded against them.

It can also be argued that the penal sanction is not the most appropriate or effective sanction for more conventional criminal offences either. As we shall see in chapter seven, there are a number of difficulties in calculating the rate of recidivism in the Irish prison system but it is substantial. The *Annual Report on Prisons and Places of Detention* for 1991 shows that 51 per cent of the prison population in that year had served a previous prison sentence and 17 per cent had been in prison on six or more previous occasions. This suggests that prison is not particularly efficient for any kind of offenders but this does not detract from the fact that it is only the law-breaking of the working class that we choose to punish through imprisonment.

The failure to apply the criminal law means that the criminality of white-collar misbehaviour is seldom made public through court appearances and offenders tend to avoid the stigma which the imposition of the criminal label entails. Because of this we have difficulty in thinking of corporate misbehaviour as criminal and as on a par with other forms of robbery and killing. We also have difficulty in thinking of certain kinds of people as criminal. However what is perhaps the most significant effect of the marginalisation process is that it places enormous difficulties in the way of victims in establishing that such offences took place and that they have been victims. This again reinforces the blurring of the stigmatisation process and offenders, effectively, escape the slur of 'disrepute': 'the disparaged status that is associated with activities that . . . are called "criminal"' (Hagan, 1994: 1).

We need to consider also the argument that the weaknesses of the law and of the mechanisms for the regulation of corporate behaviour are simply problems created by the speed of development in the Irish economy. It could be argued that the industrial and financial structure has developed faster than the legal system thereby creating a problem of 'institutional lag'. Now, however, as the law is updated the gaps are being closed to match the complexity of the behaviour it is designed to regulate. The Companies Act 1990 is a case in point. Against this, it needs to be noted that while at a legal level gaps in the law are closing, the problem of enforcing this legislation remains a major one. There is no credible incentive to enforce corporate regulations and those charged with the relevant responsibility often do not have the resources to adequately discharge their role or function. An example of this is the way in which the task of enforcing many of the laws on pollution has been delegated to local authorities. As they are major polluters themselves they may lack the moral energy to enforce the law (see Leonard, 1988: 212). Also, because of a lack of personnel and resources, they may be unable to.

Similarly in relation to fraud it is evident that the garda fraud squad is considerably understaffed and under-resourced. In 1992 the fraud squad had a staff of forty-five and while it had little professional expertise itself, it had access to a panel of accountants. But as the Advisory Committee on Fraud (1992) discovered, this arrangement is of limited value. The committee proposed the setting up of a National Bureau of Fraud Investigation with an adequate level of staffing, a number of accountants and access to information technology. However while the Minister for Justice has agreed to set up such a bureau the key issue will be the level of staffing and other resources made available to it. No information is currently available on what these will be.

Finally, it should be noted that the political will to pursue corporate offenders has not always been a striking feature of Irish politics. It can be best illustrated by the hunt for the tax evader. There is, as we have seen, under-policing of the corporate tax sector. The Commission on Taxation (1985: 205) set up by the government made clear that 'it is emphatically not the case that the criminal law has no role to play in tax enforcement.' The level of staffing available to the revenue commissioners increased because of the reduction in the functions of the customs and excise service as a result of the open market within the European Union. The conditions were perfect for a major campaign against tax evasion using the full weight of criminal procedures.

The government's solution was to declare a tax amnesty on 26 May, 1993. Under its terms, tax evaders could confess their criminal offences in private to the revenue commissioners, agree to pay a tax of 15 per cent of their undeclared money and go in peace. This move proved somewhat unpopular among the general public and in response the Minister for Finance threatened that any tax evader who gave false information to the revenue commissioners would be at risk of prison. Indeed he was quoted as saying that he looked forward to seeing tax evaders serving prison sentences (*The Irish Times*, 7 July, 1994). However when the Tax Amnesty Bill became law the proposals for prison sentences had been replaced by a system of fines.

In these circumstances and in the light of the arguments outlined here, it is difficult to avoid the conclusion that the response to white-collar crime in Ireland is where possible to ignore it or if there is pressure to regulate it to do so through legislative structures that create the illusion of control but as they are inadequately resourced do not interfere unduly with the activities of anyone concerned. There is a fundamental reluctance to tackle the offences of the middle class and to respond to this behaviour with the resources of the criminal justice system. As a result, the stigma of criminality becomes yet another resource that is unequally distributed in Irish society, only in this case it is one to which the middle class are denied access.

Conclusion

In this chapter we have reviewed the issue of white-collar crime. We have stressed the extent and seriousness of this kind of crime and argued that despite its seriousness it has been marginalised in the public discussion of crime. The mechanisms through which this has been achieved are the system of law-making, the system of law enforcement and the system of punishment. Through the differential way in which these operate, the criminal activities of the middle class remain relatively unscratched and successfully escape the stigma of public shaming and censure that follows from this.

The existence of such crime has important implications for the explanations that we can offer for crime in Ireland. If white-collar crime is the problem we have suggested it to be then the kinds of explanations that we have offered in chapter two cannot be considered to be adequate. These are based on the notion that the bulk of crime is committed by working-class offenders. The argument of this chapter has been that this is not true. So if we wish to construct a comprehensive explanation for crime in Ireland then it must be one that can account for both kinds of crime. This is a task that we address in chapter five.

There is, however, one further issue about crime and about offenders in particular that needs to be discussed. In this chapter and in the previous one we have considered the consequences for crime of the stratification of society into social classes. But society is also stratified in other ways. Gender is the most significant of these. The ramifications of this form of stratification for crime are discussed in the next chapter.

Notes

1. This account is based on a *Today Tonight* documentary called 'The Collapse of the Gallagher Empire', screened on RTE on 21 February, 1990. The programme was based on a copy of the liquidator's report which came into the possession of the programme-makers. The liquidator was quoted in *The Irish Times* (23 February, 1990: 9) as saying that he had 'no argument to make' with the content of the programme.

2. For example, Lincenberg (1992).

4 WOMEN AND CRIME

Introduction

In this chapter we examine three aspects of the issue of women
and crime. The first is the low crime rate among women and
the explanations that have been offered for it. The second is the
experiences of female offenders in the criminal justice system.
Are they treated differently in court and in prison because they
are women? The third is women as crime victims. The focus
here is on rape, its extent, its causes and some of the myths that
surround it. It could be argued that devoting a separate section
of a book on crime to women reproduces and reinforces their
ghettoisation by suggesting that there is something different
about their relationship to crime. The justification is that there
is. The issues addressed here are unique to women and are not
part of the experiences men have with crime or with the criminal justice system.

I Crime Rates Among Women

The Low Involvement of Women?

As we have seen in preceding chapters the social background
of offenders is important to the study of crime. Most of those

arrested by the gardaí and imprisoned by the courts are from working-class backgrounds. The issue is complicated by police discretion in the prosecution of offenders and by the neglect of middle-class crime by the state. But whatever about the complexities of the relationship between crime and social class, the relationship between gender and crime appears to be simple and straightforward. Crime is predominantly a male activity. We can see this from garda statistics. In 1993, for example, the number of 'persons convicted or against whom the charge was held proved and order made without conviction' was 6,800. Of these, 6,044, or 89 per cent were male and 736, or 11 per cent, were female. The majority of the women were convicted for one of four offences but primarily for what the gardaí classify as 'other larcenies', a category which mainly involves shoplifting. This accounted for 404 women or 55 per cent of the total. 'Forgery and uttering' is the rather archaic way garda statistics refer to the passing of forged or stolen cheques. This offence accounted for 108 women or 15 per cent of female offenders. Fifty-six (8 per cent) women were convicted of burglary and fifty (7 per cent) were convicted for 'receiving stolen goods'. Together these four offences accounted for 84 per cent of the convicted female offenders. It is noteworthy that there was no indictable offence for which the number of women convicted was greater than the number of men.

The obvious exception to this should be what many would regard as the archetypal female offence – prostitution. It is not however that straightforward. In Ireland it is not illegal to be a prostitute but it is illegal to solicit, to importune or to have a brothel. In effect, it is not illegal to exchange sex for money but it is illegal to advertise that fact on the street. Loitering is the form of advertising that the law forbids. However since 1981 it has been difficult to prosecute offenders after the Supreme Court found the notion of 'loitering with intent' to be unconstitutional. Steps have been taken in the Criminal Justice (Sexual Offences) Act 1993 to sort out the legal intricacies and to introduce some level of equality into the law, though a number of Dáil deputies argued (see *Dáil Debates*, vol. 432, no. 7, 24 June, 1993) that the opportunity should have been used to decriminalise prostitution.

Section 7 of the 1993 Act criminalises both those who offer and those who ask for prostitution services. It applies equally to male or female prostitutes and to their clients. Section 8 makes it an offence to refuse to move on if asked to do so by a garda who suspects that a person is loitering for the purposes of prostitution. Soliciting from a motor-car is also an offence, thus criminalising the activities of kerb-crawlers. The effects of the Act have yet to be seen in crime statistics. However they are unlikely to give us many insights into the nature and extent of prostitution in Ireland as police use of these legal powers is not consistent. In effect if prostitutes confine their activities to certain parts of cities and if they do not provoke the hostility of residents they are allowed to operate with some immunity from police attention. Indeed as long as they behave in this way the attitude of the police is often one of paternal oversight rather than of draconian legalism.

If the involvement of women in crime is low they tend also to be involved in the less serious types of crime. We can establish this in two ways. One is by looking at the principal offence, 'other larcenies', that women are involved in. In general larceny in Ireland involves relatively small amounts of money. In 1993, for example, 45 per cent of larcenies were of less than £100, 63 per cent were of less than £200 and just over 1 per cent were of £5,000 and over. The other is to look at the participation of women in more serious offences. The only person recorded in garda statistics as convicted of murder in 1992 was male. Three were recorded as convicted of 'robbery with arms': all were men. Forty-four people were recorded as convicted of aggravated burglary, all but one of whom were male. Fifty people were recorded as convicted of the larceny of motor vehicles and all were male. Overall, then, the picture of the female offender that emerges from Irish crime statistics is very much in line with those of other countries (see Harvey,

Burnham, Kendall and Pease, 1992). Fewer women are convicted of indictable offences than men and they are convicted of less serious offences.

A number of writers respond to these kinds of figures by suggesting that they understate the level of crime committed by women (see, for example, Adler, 1975). They argue that a gender bias operates at two crucial decision-making stages in the criminal justice system and its effect is to divert women offenders out of the system and out of crime statistics. The first stage is the reporting of offences to the police. Crime victims can be reluctant to do this when the offender is female. Department stores, for example, despite stated policy to the contrary, may be disinclined to proceed against certain kinds of female shoplifters. Their reasons can range from the bad publicity that may follow from seemingly tragic cases to the perception that the punishments given by the courts are derisory and insufficient either as retribution or as deterrence.

The second stage is with the police. As we shall see in chapter six the police have considerable discretion in their use of the law to resolve troublesome situations. It has been argued that decisions to arrest or to charge can often be based on the demeanour or the gender of a suspect. If the police, for example, believe that informal ways are more effective with female offenders they may let them off with a warning for an offence that they would have charged a male offender with. If this happens, male offenders are more likely to show up in police statistics, consequently overstating the male contribution to crime and understating the female one. These arguments have received some support from research studies in other countries (see Heidensohn, 1985). Victims and, in particular, the police, respond to male and female offenders in different ways. However the important question is whether the gender differential would disappear if male and female offenders were treated equally. It probably would be reduced for minor offences but it is unlikely to disappear where serious crimes, like homicide or armed robbery, are involved. Female murderers do not get off with a friendly warning. Thus with the exception of the under-reporting of their involvement in the less serious forms of property crime like shoplifting, police statistics appear to be a fairly accurate reflection of women's low level of involvement in crime.

Theories of Women and Crime

What we need to explain now is the low participation rates of women in crime. This is an issue that, until recently, has largely been ignored in criminology. There are however some theories which examine gender and crime. We can divide these into two broad types, those that stress issues of biology and physiology and those that deal with sociological factors.

(a) Biological Theories

Explanations in terms of biology and physiology have a history going back to the late nineteenth century. They come in two forms. Ceasare Lombroso (1913) argued that women who were involved in crime were unfeminine and were biological abnormalities. Pollak (1961), by contrast, argued that women in general were more criminal and deceitful than men but the chivalry of men kept them out of crime statistics. For both theorists, however, the criminal behaviour of women was determined by their biological make-up. Such theories have been refuted and their claims to scientific status shown to be specious. But the attitudes that underlie them are often just below the surface of public debate about women criminals. Women criminals are presented in the media as anomalies, as monstrous or as lacking in feminine feelings.

These kinds of arguments surfaced in a particularly public way in Ireland during the Kerry Babies Tribunal in 1985. This enquired into the circumstances surrounding the prosecution of Joanne Hayes for the murder of a new-born baby. It transpired that although she had given birth to a baby who died she could not have been the mother of the baby whose death she was charged with. In the course of the tribunal an attempt was made by the counsel for the state during the cross-examination of a number of psychiatrists to suggest that she was a sociopath. She had not responded as they anticipated a woman should – she did not seem to feel sufficient guilt over the death of her child – so she must lack normal feelings (see McCafferty, 1985: 160–3). By contrast no attempt was made to suggest that the man, who fathered a baby by Joanne at the same time as he fathered a child by his wife, was deviant in a similar fashion.

(b) Sociological Theories

A second set of explanations for women's criminality has emerged in the last twenty years from mainly women criminologists and sociologists. These explanations have been provoked by the women's movement and by the way in which women academics have begun to look at their subject areas and to ask if women have been excluded and if so, what needs to be done about it. In the sociology of deviance this has manifested itself in the attempt to explain the low crime rates of women in social terms (see, for example, Heidensohn, 1985). The explanations proposed emphasise two particular social factors – socialisation and opportunities.

Socialisation is the process through which society instils in us the attributes it wants us to have. Through child-rearing practices, educational processes and media content it encourages us to develop characteristics, perspectives and values which we will share with others in society. It also encourages us to develop the attitudes and personalities that are considered appropriate for males and females in our society. As a result the self-perceptions, self-consciousness and self-identities developed by males and females differ. Women are socialised to be patient, understanding, passive, dependent and female roles tend to reflect these qualities. They are encouraged to find their identities in the home – the 'real' woman's role – or in the labour market in gender-specific jobs that reflect their 'female' qualities such as clerical work and nursing. Men by contrast are socialised to be self-confident, independent, active, competitive and aggressive. They are expected to use these qualities in the workplace rather than in the home.

Socialisation has implications for criminal involvement. The qualities that men are encouraged to develop are important in the world of work but they are also prerequisites for careers in crime. Ann Oakley (1972: 72) has argued that 'the facets of the ideal male personality . . . physical strength, a certain kind of aggressiveness . . . are very close to those of criminal behaviour'. 'The dividing line', she continues, 'between what is masculine and what is criminal may at times be a thin one.' By contrast, the qualities that women are encouraged to acquire disable them from successful involvement in crime. There are few opening for the caring, maternal bank-robber. So as a result of socialisation there are more male criminals than female ones.

The pattern of female socialisation is also used to explain the limited range of crimes that women get involved in. There are, for example, important parallels between the attributes of the female role and prostitution. Women are socialised to see sex, and to use their sex, as a means of acquiring social status. They exchange participation in sex for the social status of marriage. 'To become a prostitute', according to Oakley, 'simply requires an exaggeration of [this] one aspect of the role type of the non-deviant woman.'

However there are a number of problems with the socialisation argument. The main one is that it over-simplifies the socialisation process and as a result its predictions on levels of criminal involvement are exaggerated. If it is true that males are encouraged to develop qualities that are essential for an involvement in crime then there should be significantly more men involved in crime than there are. But despite the amount of crime in society and despite the fact that it is mainly men who are involved it is still only a small minority of men who commit crime. This suggests that the extent of male socialisation is not exhausted by the development of particular masculine attitudes.

Men are also socialised into positive attitudes to authority and respect for the values and normative standards of a society. So if men get involved in crime there must be other factors motivating them to break with socially acquired patterns of behaviour. The same is true for women. They are also socialised into particular patterns of the acceptance of authority and social morality so they too must be motivated in some way to break with them. Consequently a key question in any theory of criminality must be the identification of the sources of motivation for criminal involvement. The socialisation process is not a sufficient explanation of this.

What is called 'restricted opportunities theory' tries to fill the gap (see Heidensohn, 1985). The restricted opportunity theory argues that the opportunity structure in society is such that there are few opportunities for women to be other than what society expects them to be. This social structure has two elements – the legitimate and the illegitimate. The legitimate opportunity structure gives access to legitimate means of earning a regular income in a regular job. As such this is more restricted for women than it is for men. Because of this the opportunities to engage in occupational crime and corporate crime are limited. Access to the illegitimate opportunity structure or to the means and opportunities to commit ordinary crime is also limited. Most criminal enterprises are controlled by men who are for the most part reluctant to engage in job-sharing. They prefer to work with other men. As Steven Box (1983: 183) puts it, 'crime is not "an equal opportunity employer"'.

This means that the low participation of women in crime can be explained in terms of the opportunity structures in society. Women are cut off from access to the opportunities to commit crime so their crime rates are low. As an explanation this has the same problem that all theories which stress opportunity share. It fails to take sufficient account of the willingness or unwillingness of people to take advantage of opportunity structures, in other words the motivational factor. The solution to this has been to put the two factors – socialisation and opportunities – together to produce a complete theory. The low rates of crime of women are to be explained in terms of their socialisation and the lack of opportunities. Socialisation does not give them the personal qualities necessary for criminal activity and the opportunity structure only allows them access to a very limited range of criminal opportunities.

As an explanation this has considerable appeal but it also has significant limitations. These can be seen if we examine the kinds of predictions it makes about the future involvement of women in crime. It has been suggested that as women are progressively freed from the constraints of family life such as child-rearing and as they take advantage of new educational and occupational opportunities, they will begin to commit more crime (Adler, 1975; Simon, 1975). Put in more sociological terms, the claim is that if restricted socialisation and restricted opportunities explain low rates of female crime, then when women are socialised to be less passive and more independent and when, along with this, the opportunity structures available to them widen to increase the availability of work outside the home then crime by women will increase.

It is difficult to know if this prediction of increased crime by women has come true. While the proportion of total crime committed by women in Ireland has remained fairly stable over the past thirty years, the number of women convicted of crime has increased, from 845 in 1961 to 1,258 in 1991. However we are unable to say if this is due to an increase in the amount of crime committed by women or to changes in the willingness to report and process women offenders. It has been argued in the United States, for example, that social change does not lead to increases in criminality among women, but it does change perceptions of women's criminality (see Beirne and Messerschmidt, 1991). The police have been influenced by the images of women as liberated and, as such, potentially dangerous. So the chivalrous basis on which they used to operate has dissolved and they are now more willing to prosecute and charge women than was the case twenty years ago.

However if there has been a real increase in women's criminal involvement then has 'liberation' led to increased crime? There are two reasons to doubt it. The first objection is a theoretical one. As we have suggested already the socialisation argument has serious flaws hence any argument that relies on it as part of an explanation is also flawed. Simply because one element of the socialisation process changes to encourage women to develop what previously were male qualities does not mean that those aspects of the process that stress conformity to the existing social order are abandoned. Moreover we have argued that if the fact that men are encouraged to develop qualities of aggression and independence is not sufficient to explain their involvement in crime then the fact that women may now be encouraged to develop these qualities is also insufficient to explain their increased criminal involvement. In both cases there must be some other factor or influence encouraging them to abandon their commitment to central social values.

The second objection to the 'liberation' notion is an empirical one. The theory suggests that recent changes have increased the range of opportunities available to women. However this is to ignore an important aspect of these changes. Where material changes have occurred their benefits have been mainly confined to middle- and upper-class women. As a result these changes have not improved the situation of many women, particularly those in the working-class, all that dramatically. Gains in the area of employment and taxation, for example, have brought more benefits to women with professional qualifications than to women who work as cleaners. They have also brought more benefits to women who work in the formal rather than the informal economy and as many working-class women have traditionally worked in the black economy (beyond the reach of the tax system but also of employment protection legislation) many of the changes have been of little direct benefit to them (see Daly, 1989).

For these reasons then the 'liberation' argument is unconvincing as an explanation for the increased involvement of women in crime in Ireland. The search for reasons for the involvement of women in crime must be pursued in a different direction. We need to attend to the process that has accompanied the improvement in the social situation of some women, namely the increased marginalisation of others. While some women have made inroads into male occupations and while poverty among women has declined, the risk of poverty is still high among female-headed households where the woman is under thirty-five (see Callan, 1994).

A number of factors are responsible for this. One is the rising rate of marital breakdown (in other countries this is called divorce) and the way this has increased the number of households headed by a woman and by a woman who is often unemployed. Another is that many women are in insecure, low-paid, unskilled, part-time work, with limited job prospects and a recurrent pattern of unemployment. Both groups find themselves increasingly dependent on the welfare state and on its benefits. As these have either been static in real terms or actually declining due to cuts in government expenditure, living and rearing a family becomes increasingly more difficult. Crime becomes attractive as an element in the repertoire of survival strategies used by marginalised women (see Carlen, 1988). In this situation, resisting the temptations and the pressures to commit crime becomes more difficult.

Two items of evidence support the marginalisation argument, one of which is stronger than the other but both of which depend on official statistics. The first is that if the liberation thesis is true we would expect that the increases in women's crime would be in those offences that women had not previously been involved in. Yet the evidence from garda statistics is that the increases in crimes committed by women have not been in new or 'male' areas such as armed robbery but in the 'traditional' female areas of larcenies such as shoplifting and forging cheques. The second is that we would also expect that a wider range of women would now be involved in crime than was previously the case. Yet, to the extent that we can judge, there has been no significant change over the recent period in the social backgrounds of women who are convicted of criminal offences. Female prisoners in Mountjoy prison in 1989 were overwhelmingly from the lower social groups (see O'Mahony, 1993: 198–200), a pattern that is broadly in line with the results from the studies of the female prison population in the 1970s.

A final point about women and theories of crime. We have argued here that the roles of socialisation and restricted opportunities are overstated in the understanding of women and crime. Instead we have suggested that the process of marginalisation is of central significance. We will be arguing in chapter five that marginalisation is also important to the understanding of the involvement of many men in crime. So in a sense we are left with the original problem that we began this section with, namely why, if both women and men experience marginalisation, women's involvement in crime is so much lower than that of men. The difference is in opportunities. For cultural and social reasons the criminal opportunities available to men to solve issues arising from marginalisation are simply greater than those for women. This point is dealt with in more detail in chapter five.

II Women and the Criminal Justice System

Research on women and crime has not confined itself to theories about crime. It has also focused on how the formal processes of the courts and the penal system treat female offenders. Where courts are concerned, the main focus has been on whether there is a gender bias in sentencing. Are male and female offenders treated differently by the courts? The focus of interest in the penal system has been on the conditions under which women are imprisoned.

The Courts

The expectation that there might be a gender bias in court derives from the existence of an ideology of patriarchy in society, an ideology which is used to justify male domination and control. This can lead to different treatment of women criminals through the attitudes to women and their crimes that it produces and through the way in which these attitudes influence judges who in Ireland, as elsewhere, tend mainly to be men. Patriarchal attitudes can be characterised in three ways but each has a different effect on the sentencing of offenders.

The first is what Pollak (1961) calls 'the chivalry factor'. According to this judges and other court personnel are reluctant to proceed against women with the full rigour of the law. This is because as women they are not really 'criminal' in the same way that men are. So where chivalry operates it will result in lower sentences for women and less use of prison. The second set of patriarchal attitudes can be characterised as 'paternalism'. This is a variant of chivalry in that it sees the criminal justice system as having an obligation to protect the weak in society such as women and children. As a result it has a duty to be a 'father-figure' to female criminals. Like all displays of parental authority this attitude has unpredictable effects on sentencing, producing either harsh ('a spell in prison will do you good') or lenient treatment. The underlying justification in both cases is the same: it is for the good of the person involved. The final way in which patriarchy can manifest itself is in the 'evil woman' thesis. This is the view that as women who commit crime are no ladies they must expect to be punished with the full rigour of the law. In committing crime they have exceeded the bounds of acceptable female behaviour and so need to be dealt with severely to bring them back into line.

The only research on the sentencing of women in Irish courts, that by Ann Lyons and Paul Hunt (1988), concludes that there is a gender bias in Irish courts. Lyons and Hunt took one offence – larceny – and looked at how male and female offenders were dealt with. They examined court records for the Dublin metropolitan area for the first half of 1979. As this is the area in which almost 60 per cent of all crime in the country occurs its courts should deal with a representative cross-section of male and female criminals. They found that the factors which influence the severity of sentencing were the seriousness of the crime, the previous criminal record of the offender and whether the offender was male or female. Thus they concluded that there was a gender bias in that when women are charged with the same offence as men they receive shorter sentences than the men do.

The study relied on court statistics and did not have access to the reasons judges used to justify particular sentences. As a result it was unable to make clear why the gender bias occurred. Was it the operation of paternalism? Did the courts gave a different weight to family background and family responsibilities where women were concerned? Did the fact that a woman offender might have children weigh more heavily with the courts than would the same information about a man? If it did then it can be argued that this is control in the guise of chivalry as it reinforces the notion that the true place for women, and the true role for them, is in the home (Eaton, 1986).

The Prisons

It is probably just as well that a gender bias prevails in the criminal justice system because the picture of life in women's prisons in Ireland has, until recently, been a dismal one. But let's begin with some basic information about women and prison. There are two prisons for women in Ireland. One is the Mountjoy female prison in Dublin with forty single cells and one multiple one. The other is Limerick prison with nine single cells. The number of women committed to prison each year varies considerably. It was over two hundred per year in the 1960s. This figure declined in the 1970s, due mainly to a change in the interpretation of the laws on prostitution that we discussed above. It rose again in the 1980s and in 1989 reached its highest since 1951 with 290 women imprisoned. These increases were due mainly to a growth in the number imprisoned for larceny or theft and, to a much lesser extent, for the possession of drugs. The numbers have fallen somewhat since then and 233 women were committed to prison under sentence in 1992. In general women tend to receive shorter prison sentences than men do. In 1992, for example, 47 per cent of women prisoners were serving sentences of less than three months whereas 39 per cent of the male prisoners were.[1]

Despite the small numbers of women going to prison and the short sentences that are imposed, there are a number of features of women's imprisonment that are worthy of note. The first is overcrowding. Though this has declined somewhat in the recent past it can still be a problem. According to the *Annual Report on Prisons and Places of Dentention* for 1992 the daily average number of offenders in the female prison in Mountjoy was thirty-four but it was sometimes as high as forty-four. Yet the report also indicates that the prison has a capacity for only forty offenders so in effect there is a shortfall in accommodation at peak times. When overcrowding occurs, the extra people are put on mattresses between the beds. This is a considerable improvement on what the situation was in the mid to late 1980s when overcrowding was close to crisis proportions. The change is partly due to the refurbishment of the prison and partly to a decline in the numbers being sent to prison.

The refurbished prison in Mountjoy was opened in 1991. An important improvement was the provision of single-cell accommodation. Apart from the extra comfort that this represents for prisoners it has also, according to the Department of Justice, lead to a reduction in lesbianism. It is clear from the department's comments that this is something to be welcomed. The report of the Visiting Committee for 1991 was less sanguine about the changes in the prison. It stated that many of the prisoners 'cannot read or write and find a single cell unbearably lonely' (*Annual Report on Prisons and Places of Detention*, 1991: 54). This is particularly the case given the long period at night – from 7.30 p.m. until 8.15 a.m. the next morning – in which prisoners are confined to their cells. As a newspaper report (*Sunday Tribune*, 7 March, 1994) described it, 'night time is nightmare time'.

The second feature of women's imprisonment is the lack of segregation between prisoners of different ages and for different offences in Mountjoy (*Annual Report on Prisons and Places of Detention*, 1988: 47) – a long-standing feature in the women's prison. This involves, according to the Visiting Committee (1988: 47) 'drug-pushers and users, long and short-term prisoners, young teenagers and experienced convicts and emotionally disturbed people all confined together'. As a result someone in for a short sentence for fine default or shoplifting could be mixing with the few long-term serious women criminals. This is hardly the best situation for the encouragement of rehabilitation.

The failure to provide more than one type of prison facility for women prisoners has been described by one Visiting Committee as discriminatory (*Annual Report on Prisons and Places of Detention*, 1989: 50). The absence of open prisons or low-security centres for women offenders is of particular concern. If a male prisoner is sentenced to Mountjoy prison, he can, if he is deemed suitable, be transferred to Shanganagh open prison to finish his sentence. At present there is no such facility for female offenders. For them, there are no half-way houses on the road out of prison.

The final issue goes beyond the immediate problems of the female prison and relates to the degree to which prison can be considered to be a suitable location in which to deal with the women involved. It is not clear from the profile of women prisoners whether prison is doing anything to reduce their level of offending or if indeed it is the appropriate place in which to deal with a group of women who have the range and depth of problems that they have.

Rates of recidivism are high among women prisoners. A survey (reported in O'Mahony, 1993: 198–203) of women in prison in 1989 found that 82 per cent of them had been in prison before. Just under a half had been there on six previous occasions and a quarter on ten or more occasions. It indicates, as O'Mahony (1993: 200) says, that for women 'prison is aptly described as a revolving door experience'. It may keep them off the streets for a limited period of time but it does not keep them away from crime.

Prison life also does nothing for the range of problems that women prisoners have. They share many of these with male prisoners but the problems are present to a greater extent among women. Thus, for example, 85 per cent of female prisoners were on psychiatric medication. This is three times greater than the proportion among male prisoners. The extent of suicidal behaviour was a serious problem. Over two-thirds had self-injured or overdosed at some point in their lives, including a number who managed this while in prison. Addiction to illegal drugs is also a serious problem. Over half the women in prison are drug addicts (see *Sunday Tribune*, 7 March, 1993). In addition it is difficult to describe them as a serious danger to the public or to social and political order. Few are convicted of violent offences; most are in for repeated petty theft. In effect most of the female prisoners are a greater danger to themselves than to society.

These features provide the context in which to consider the building of a new women's prison, as announced by the Minister for Justice in December 1993. This is intended to be a state-of-the-art prison and to solve many of the problems associated with the current prisons. It will provide places for sixty prisoners and as long as judges do not react to its availability by increasing the numbers they send to prison it should solve the overcrowding problem. It will solve the segregation problem by providing separate units within the prison for dealing with the different categories of offenders. The intention is also to provide special services aimed at the personal and emotional problems of the prisoners. If the prison becomes a reality – the women's prison previously planned for Wheatfield, Clondalkin in 1979 was never built and the present plans were put on hold in the summer of 1995 – then it will be a considerable improvement on present facilities. But the fundamental issue will remain unresolved. Prison does little to break the cycle of repeated and persistent offending and it is not a suitable location in which to deal with the range of social and psychological problems that many women prisoners suffer from.

III Women as Victims: The Crime of Rape

The fear of crime is a significant factor in the lives of people in modern societies. But this fear is more pronounced and more focused for women. According to the 1992 British Crime Survey, for example, women were more worried about crime than men. Forty-nine per cent of women said they felt unsafe out at night compared to only 14 per cent of men. The crime women are most concerned about is rape. Almost half of the women (42 per cent) aged between sixteen and twenty-nine described themselves as 'feeling very worried' about rape as against 23 per cent in the same age-group who were worried about theft from their cars (Mirrlees-Black and Maung, 1994). We do not have comparable information about the fear of crime and in particular about the fear of rape in Ireland but there is little to suggest that the situation here is significantly different from that in Britain.[2] In this section we examine the range of issues that must be addressed in any consideration of the crime of rape in Ireland.

Rape as a Crime: Data and Definitions

In 1993, 590 sexual offences were recorded in garda statistics. These are made up primarily of sexual assault (368 cases or 62 per cent of the offences) and rape (143 cases or 25 per cent of the total). The Rape Act 1990 created the offence, 'sexual assault', which is neutral with respect to gender, but it is clear from the statistics that all of the victims were women. As such sexual offences constitute under 1 per cent (.6 per cent) of all recorded indictable crime. Their detection rate is considerably higher than that for many other forms of crime. In 1993 it was 75 per cent for rape and 83 per cent for sexual assault.

It has been argued that figures such as these understate the true level of sexual violence against women. The main reason is that the majority of rapes are not reported to the police. The Dublin Rape Crisis Centre, for example, claims that less than 20 per cent of the offences reported to them are subsequently 'made known' to the police (Braiden, 1992: 21). This is accepted by the gardaí who, in their recent corporate strategy document, described violence against women and children as 'probably our most under-reported crime' (*Garda Síochána*, 1994: 10).

There are a number of reasons for this high level of non-reporting. Many victims are reluctant to get involved with the criminal justice system. They feel that they have to fight to establish themselves as victims and that the process through which this is achieved is degrading and humiliating. Rape victims can become 'double victims', victimised first by rapists and then by the criminal justice system. Madigan and Gamble (1991: 7) have argued that the second rape, that by the criminal justice system is 'more devastating and despoiling than the first'. Indeed the unique feature of rape as a crime is that the victim's 'credibility is more often doubted by prosecutors than the credibility of victims of other violent crime' (Deming and Eppy, 1981: 361).

In Ireland we may need to distinguish between the experience of victims with the gardaí and their experiences in the courts. A number of recent changes, including the provision of specific training for the gardaí in dealing with rape victims and the assignment of female officers to deal with complaints of rape, has lessened the ordeal for victims who approach the police. Their experiences in the courts, however, have been and continue to be very different. Olive Braiden (1992: 22), former director of the Dublin Rape Crisis Centre, argues that women who have been through a rape trial say that the experience 'felt like being raped publicly again and most would not, given the chance to go back in time, report the rape at all'.

The Criminal Law (Rape) Amendment Act 1990 allows for judges to hear rape cases in camera but it does not solve the problem of male dominance among court officials. The previous character of the victim can be brought up at the discretion of the judge and, according to those who work in the system, if such a request is made it is generally allowed (Shanahan, 1992: 91). The experiences of other countries with 'rape shield' legislation such as this is that it has not constrained the nature of the cross-examination of the rape victim or changed the outcomes of rape trials (see Matoesin, 1993: 17–18).

The relationship between the victim and the offender is another important factor in the decision not to report rape. The classic image of rape is of an attack by a stranger in a dark street. The reality is that a woman is more likely to be raped by someone she knows than by a stranger and she is more likely to be raped in her home than in a public place (Smith, 1989). However victims are more likely to report 'stranger-rape' than rape by friends or family members. Moreover the police are more likely to record reports of stranger-rape as criminal offences than they are reports of the more typical kinds of rape. As a result police statistics seriously understate the amount of rape in society and overstate the proportion of stranger-rape.

The problem of non-reporting creates a particular difficulty for the assessment of rising rape figures. In 1961 the gardaí recorded seven rapes. In 1981 the figure had risen to fifty-one and in 1993, as we have seen, reached 143. These are, by any standards, substantial increases. Yet we do not know if they reflect a real increase in the number of offences, a change in the willingness of victims to report the offence to the gardaí or a combination of both. The answer to this would require data from a series of victim surveys and this is not available in Ireland. Research from other countries suggests that changes in the attitudes to rape are reflected in changes in the willingness of victims to report the offence and that this is a major factor in explaining changes in rape statistics. In the United States, for example, crime statistics from 1973 to 1985 showed substantial increases in the number of rapes. But the results from victim surveys conducted over the same period suggested that the actual number of offences had remained stable (Beirne and Messerschmidt, 1991: 76). The amount of rape had not changed significantly but the willingness of victims to report it had.

Some criminologists argue that there is a further reason why official crime figures understate the extent of rape. This is because figures for rape are based on a definition of the offence that emphasises the threat or the use of physical violence on the victim. As a result many incidents in which a woman's consent to sexual intercourse is absent are not covered. Examples include what Steven Box (1983: 128–9) calls 'exploitation rape' where male employers use their power of hiring and firing to 'encourage' female employees to have sexual intercourse with them, 'conjugal rape' where husbands use the notion of conjugal 'rights' rather than physical violence to coerce their wives into having sexual relations and 'date rape' where males expect that sex will be the return for dinner and drinks. Box argues that rape needs to be re-defined to take account of these kinds of situations. His proposal is that it should be seen as 'sexual access gained by any means where the female's overt genuine consent is absent' (Box, 1983: 125).

Others disagree. David Finkelhor and Kersti Yiio, for example (quoted in Beirne and Messerschmidt, 1991: 71) argue that widening the definition risks diluting its meaning. They accept that many forms of coercion can be used to force women to have sexual intercourse. But it can be very difficult, if not impossible, to determine when non-physical forms of coercion such as the economic and the psychological have been used. By contrast the use of, or the threat to use, physical violence is generally easier to establish if only because it produces visible injuries and so the term rape should be retained for situations in which it is a factor.

Both positions are in agreement on the centrality of the absence of consent to the crime of rape. They differ over the extent and significance of the forms of coercion that are used on women. It is unclear which position the law on rape in Ireland is closest to. Under the terms of the Criminal Law (Rape) Act, 1981 as amended by the Criminal Law (Rape) Amendment Act 1990, rape is unlawful sexual intercourse with a woman against her consent if the man knows she does not consent or does not take adequate steps to make sure that such consent is present. The key question is the meaning of consent and of what should be considered to be evidence of its absence. There is no strict legal definition of the term. It is, as Charleton argues (1992: 273), 'not completely settled as to what type or character of threat will vitiate consent'.

It is clear that consent is not an issue in cases of sexual intercourse with a girl under fifteen. With a girl aged between fifteen and seventeen, sexual intercourse is a crime but it requires the absence of consent to be considered as rape. With adults the fact that the relationship between the man and the woman is one of marriage does not do away with the need to establish consent. Neither can failure to resist be taken as an indication of consent. Apart from these circumstances it is, according to Charleton (1992: 274), up to a jury to decide if the circumstances in a particular case constitute consent and here they should bring their 'collective common sense' to bear on the issue. The problem is that their collective common sense may reflect and embody the range of sexual stereotypes of rape that exist in Irish society. Thus while the law may not require evidence of resistance or signs of physical injury as indicators of the absence of consent they may be the very factors that are important to jurors.

The final limitation on the discussion of rape is that it is treated as a sexual crime. This is misleading. If the objective of rape is sexual then it is difficult to explain the level of violence that accompanies it. Amir (1971), for example, found that 85 per cent of the rapes in his study involved the use of violence and of forms of sexual humiliation such as repeated intercourse and forced fellatio. This suggests that there is more to the crime of rape than the satisfaction of sexual urges. It is about domination and humiliation of the women involved. This means that it should not be treated in isolation from the wider problem of violence against women generally.

The Myth of Victim Precipitation

The issue of definition is also at the heart of another controversy in criminology. This is over what Menachem Amir (1971) has called 'victim-precipitated rape'. He defined this as occurring in 'those rape situations in which the victim actually, or so it was deemed, agreed to sexual relations but retracted before the actual act or did not react strongly enough when the suggestion was made by the offender(s)' (Amir, 1971: 266). Victims indicate their agreement either verbally or through gesture or body language and then at a crucial stage in the process they change their minds. Amir has suggested that hitchhikers who have been raped fall into this category. The rape is 'victim precipitated' because getting into a stranger's car could be construed as 'inviting' a sexual relationship (Nelson and Amir, 1975). This notion has also been extended to the idea that being present in certain parts of cities at certain times is an indication of availability for sexual relations.

The proportion of rapes that can be described as 'victim precipitated' is a matter of dispute among theorists who are committed to the idea. However the concept itself has been criticised on the grounds that it embodies and reinforces a number of potent and dangerous myths about male sexuality and female rights. Thus it has been criticised for failing to acknowledge or respect the victim's right to change her mind. It also involves taking the justifications offered by the rapist at face value – 'she was asking for it'. Finally it encourages inappropriate responses to rape by suggesting that prevention is entirely a matter for women. If they did not provoke men through the way they dress, through their behaviour in public places and through their use of public space they would not be raped. What this kind of belief represents is a critical curtailment of women's freedom to dress, behave and use public space in the manner in which they choose. It also and most crucially shifts the focus of blame and of responsibility from the offender to the victim.

Explaining Rape

In considering the explanations that have been offered for rape, two particular views need to be disposed of at the outset. The first is the argument that because of the violent nature of the offence rapists must be mentally disturbed. This may be true of some but it is not true of most convicted rapists. According to Diane Scully (1990: 41), for example, less than 5 per cent of rapists have been diagnosed as being clinically psychotic at the time they commit the offence. In effect the vast majority of rapists are not psychologically or emotionally disturbed in the normal sense of these terms.

At the other extreme is the explanation that proposes that men rape because it is possible for them to do so. Writers like Susan Brownmiller and Andrea Dworkin argue that men rape because they are natural predators and as such they are also potential killers of women (see Box, 1983). This is not a particularly helpful formulation. The reality is that more men commit rape than is recorded in police statistics and if the definition of rape was widened the number of men who could be regarded as rapists would be far greater. But even with these changes it is still a minority of men who rape. Also to the extent to which this explanation stresses the inevitability of male urges it reduces rape to an unchangeable feature of male biology. As a consequence the social factors that make it possible for some men to utilise their capacity to rape women and for others to control it are ignored.

Many contemporary studies of rape stress the importance of four social factors in explaining the level of rape in a society (see, for example, Smith, 1989 and Matoesin, 1993: 10–18). The first is the presence of a sexist culture and the extent of its impact on male and female socialisation. Steven Box (1983), for example, argues that there are particular stereotypes of the ideal or the 'real' man in our culture and the acceptance of these stereotypes facilitates rape. The way to be a 'real' man is to be strong, powerful, independent and dominant. Superiority over women can be achieved by charm and cunning or, if these fail, by the use of physical strength. The socialisation of women complements this. It encourages women to 'need' men, to be emotionally dependent on them and to look to them for protection. They are also taught that male sexual urges are very powerful forces and that women need to be careful about setting them off. If things get out of hand it will be the woman's fault: she has given off the wrong signals. The pervasiveness of such attitudes, according to Schwendinger and Schwendinger (1983), explains the enormous sense of guilt experienced by many rape victims.

While socialisation is undoubtedly important this kind of explanation, as we have seen, runs the risk of over-simplifying cultural stereotypes and of over-emphasising the degree to which they are internalised by men and women. The processes are more complex than this. There is not one single definition of appropriate male or female behaviour in a culture but a range of them. The key question is which is most dominant and most rewarded in a society. Steven Box (1983) argues that all that is required for violence against women is that a significant proportion of individuals regard cultural prescriptions about masculinity and femininity as applicable and as appropriate. And he contends that research indicates that they do.

The second factor is the level of gender inequality. Sanday (1981), for example, has argued that rape is more prevalent in societies with male domination and high levels of gender segregation. Rape-free societies are mainly tribal ones in which there is a significant level of gender equality. In these the productive and reproductive roles of women are valued and rape is comparatively rare. Rape-prone societies are ones in which men dominate politically, economically and ideologically. Women are seen as objects to be dominated and they lack resources and power. As a result they are particularly vulnerable to male violence. Thus gender inequality encourages and affirms negative cultural attitudes towards women and creates conditions in which rape can happen whereas gender equality in a society produces attitudes which prevent rape.

The third factor in explaining rape is the presence in a culture of what sociologists call 'techniques of neutralisation'. These are verbalisations that enable people to engage in culturally prescribed behaviour without feeling guilty for having done so. Where rape is concerned these verbalisations allow men to condemn rape but also 'free' them to engage in it by providing socially accepted 'legitimate' excuses for it. In effect these verbalisations are sets of rape-supportive attitudes. The most common are the loss of control due to drink, the contributory negligence of the victim in leading the man on and the conviction that the raped woman was not, because of her style of dress or her demeanour, a 'real' victim. These attitudes are, according to researchers, deeply embedded in the lived culture of Western societies and are shared by many men and women.

The criminal justice system is the fourth factor. It contributes to the level of rape, or to what Box (1983) terms the

'rape culture', in two ways. One is through the weak enforcement of rape laws. The police are unwilling to believe rape
victims and to proceed against rapists. For the small minority
who are found guilty in court, sentencing is unreliable and
inconsistent, and its deterrent effect is limited. The other is the
criminal justice system's willingness to accept social stereotypes
of male motivations and of raped women as mitigating factors
in cases of rape. In effect, Box argues, the criminal justice system
is saying to men that it is okay to rape certain kinds of women.

Overall this argument is that rape is not due to some inherent feature of men's nature but an inevitable feature of a sexist
culture, high levels of gender inequality, the availability of
techniques of neutralisation and the operation of the legal
system. The first two factors are best considered as background features or necessary conditions for the existence of
rape. When the other two are added the occurrence of rape is
facilitated and socially enabled. It follows from this that while
short-term solutions such as more active enforcement of the
law are important and necessary longer-term solutions involve
the elimination of the sexist culture and of gender inequality.
They require the creation of, what Klein (1981: 76) calls,
'conditions supporting egalitarian intimacy'.

The advantage of this argument is that it takes our attention
away from a limited consideration of the characteristics of particular offenders and places it very much on the nature of the
society in which these offenders act. It is the society which provides much of the social space in which offenders can operate.
There are, however, two difficulties in assessing its relevance as
an explanation for rape generally and specifically in applying it
in the Irish context. The specific problem is the absence of the
necessary research on the extent to which these factors are part
of the cultural inheritance of the Irish male and female.

The more general problem is that the theory fails to give due
weight to other factors that inhibit rape. Thus, for example,
techniques of neutralisation facilitate rape by providing rapists
with a range of justifications for their behaviour; but there are

also factors present in a culture which prevent men from either considering the possibility of rape or violence against women or from actually engaging in it. The degree of importance to be attached to this shortcoming depends on what one believes is the actual level of violence against women in society. If one believes it to be part of the experience of most women and thus by implication part of the behaviour of most men then such broad factors as the sexist nature of the culture will be sufficient to explain rape and other forms of violence (see, for example, Russell, 1984). If, however, one argues that a minority of men are rapists and users of violence against women then it is important to consider either what factors inhibit other men from behaving in this way or alternatively what factors allow a minority of men to attack women. In this sense our attempts to explain rape are hampered by a lack of knowledge about its true extent.

Punishment

The final aspect of the issue of rape and violence against women has been the way in which it has put the role of punishment very firmly back onto the political agenda. The respectability of the notion of punishing people had been suppressed by the traditional and predominant liberal attitude that the society that punishes best is the society that punishes least. Imprisonment is cruel and ineffective so it should be used sparingly.

Feminist writings on rape and sexual assault have challenged this. They have resurrected the idea of severe punishments for crimes. They accept that prison does not either rehabilitate or deter. But long prison sentences, they claim, have a symbolic effect. They are a statement by a society of the social serious-ness of rape and an unequivocal indication of a society's attitude to violence against women (see, for example, Box-Grainger, 1986). Much of the debate on rape in Ireland has concentrated on its punishment with calls for more consistency in sentencing and for mandatory sentences for rape victims. In 1988 the Supreme Court declined to set guidelines for sentencing in rape cases though one of the judges argued that it was only in exceptional circumstances that a custodial sentence should not be given. It is, however, generally accepted that a guilty plea by the defendant should be taken into account in sentencing. Since then the use of suspended sentences in a number of highly publicised cases led to the provision in the Criminal Justice Act 1992 for the state to appeal against what it perceives to be excessively lenient sentences and for the courts to take the long-term effects of the offence on the victim into account. What effects these will have is as yet unclear. They may satisfy the desire for symbolic demonstrativeness but in the absence of appropriate modes of rehabilitation in the prisons they are unlikely to cure rapists.

The Key Issues

Much of the debate about punishment remains at a rhetorical level. The reality that must first be dealt with is that most rapes are never reported and most rapists are never caught. A number of key issues follow from this. One is the need to increase the amount reported to the police. As we have seen, the gardaí are trying to encourage this by adopting an attitude to the investigation of rape that 'is one of sympathy and understanding but one in which either consideration does not give way to misdirection' (Nolan, 1992: 45). The second is that we need to increase the number of offences that come to trial. At present well over half the offences reported to the gardaí never reach the courts. Why this is so is not clear but presumably it relates to the judgement of prosecutors on the quality of the evidence against the accused and their assessment of the ability of the victim to sustain detailed and potentially devastating cross-examination. It may also be due to the unwillingness of victims to allow themselves to be 'raped' again in court proceedings.

How this issue can be resolved is even less clear. Recent legislation, as we have seen, has attempted to improve the conditions under which rape trials are held and to reduce the trauma for victims. However the private nature of the offence, the lack of other witnesses, the absence of other kinds of evidence and the need to respect the rights of suspects mean that a central part of the trial process will almost inevitably focus on the reliability of the major witness to the offence, namely the victim herself. There have been few proposals to get around this problem other than retrospectively 'compensating' the victim by the imposition of long sentences.[3]

The final problem is the punishment process and, in particular, the nature of the pleas for mitigation that are used in and accepted by the courts. Judges are required to take pleas for mitigation into account in sentencing convicted offenders. But we know little about the kinds of factors that are considered as 'mitigating' either in the sense of those offered by defending counsels or those that judges indicate they accept. It is an area that would repay detailed research because it is here that particular attitudes to women and to responsibility for rape can have their most impact. If, for example, the courts accept that the failure of control due to drink or to the victim's demeanour or style of dress is a mitigating factor in rape then they are playing a part in perpetuating myths about rape in society and so indirectly contributing to its continued existence.

Conclusion

In this chapter we have reviewed what is known about women and the criminal justice system in Ireland. As we have seen, this is surprisingly little. Yet it is potentially one of the most important areas for research on crime. If we can understand the reasons for the low participation of women in crime then it may provide us with insights that would be useful in reducing crime among men. If there are, for example, features of the socialisation of women that influence their low involvement in crime then they may provide a vantage point from which the appropriateness of male socialisation can be assessed. Moreover if we wish to reduce the level of violence in our society and in particular the level of violence against women then we need to explore the nature of masculinity and what its implications are for the ways in which men and women relate to each other. This is a topic that is beginning to be explored in the growing literature on masculinity and crime (see, for example, Walklate, 1995).

Notes

1. These figures have been calculated by including those imprisoned in St Patrick's Institution in the total number of male prisoners.
2. There are occasional surveys in the media (see for example, *Irish Independent*, 9 October, 1994) but their results tend not to be broken down by gender, by age or by social class.
3. The final chapter of Kate Shanahan's (1992) book on violence against women reviews suggested changes in the way rape is dealt with but it has no proposals on how the central role of cross-examination in rape trials can be modified or reformed.

5   BACK TO EXPLANATIONS

Introduction

We are now in a position to outline the salient features of crime in Ireland and to acknowledge the shortcomings of existing attempts to explain them. From what we have seen in the previous chapters the five key features of crime in Ireland are the rising amounts of crime since the mid-1960s, the coexistence of property crime committed by young working-class males and the occupational and corporate crime committed by middle-class men, the low participation rates of women, the degree to which crimes of violence have, despite their recent increases, remained relatively low, and finally the extent to which crime is urban and particularly Dublin-based. The kinds of explanations that we discussed in chapter two are limited by their inability to account for crime committed by people other than working-class men.

It is the contention of this chapter that an explanation to cover many, though not all of these phenomena, can be sought in the social changes that began in the late 1950s and early 1960s.[1] If it was around this period that crime, and particularly acquisitive property crime, began to increase then the sources of crime must lie in other changes that were co-temporaneous with it. In other words these kinds of crime must be closely linked to the process of development that took root in Irish society at this time. As Rottman (1980: 147) puts it, 'the increase in crime was one offshoot of the adjustments being made to deep-seated structural change'.

To characterise and comprehend this process of change we need to turn to the sociology of development and to the theoretical perspectives that it has to offer on the relationship between crime and social change and development. There is a problem here in that while one of the striking features of many developing countries is their high rates of crime, the study of the relationship between crime and development has not been a central part of the research agenda in either the sociology of development or the sociology of deviance. Furthermore, those studies that do exist are almost all done from a particular, and as shall be seen below, a limited perspective (see for example, Clinard and Abbott, 1973). This means that in the later parts of this chapter we shall be situating crime in a framework that has seldom been applied and so has at least the virtue of novelty.

The two major perspectives on development in the sociological literature are those of modernisation theory and of dependent development. In this chapter we outline both of these and discuss which is most relevant to account for the key features of crime set out above. As it may appear that at times in what follows the issue of crime seems to disappear it is well to be aware that the argument is that crime in Ireland can be best understood within the perspective provided by arguments about dependent development. In order to substantiate this argument it is necessary to give some detail on the perspectives through which sociologists understand the development process.

I Modernisation Theory and Crime

The basic tenet of modernisation theory is that because developing countries experience in one or two generations the kinds of changes that have taken several centuries in the currently developed countries of the world, severe social disruption and high crime rates are inevitable. The orderly series of stages by which it is assumed First World countries moved from being agricultural to being industrial societies is not possible for developing countries and as a result social changes are telescoped into a short time-frame.

This can be seen most clearly in the way in which the process of industrialisation is accompanied by a particular form of urbanisation. This is one which concentrates the process into a few major cities in the developing countries. As these cities grow, they act as a magnet attracting rural dwellers in search of the good life. They come with high expectations of a good education and of lucrative employment. But their numbers overwhelm the capacities of cities to deal with them and they are forced into marginal existences in marginal slum areas.

This process is captured by the notion of 'over-urbanisation', the view that the level of urbanisation is not synchronised with the level of development. A number of problems follow from this disparity between the rate of urbanisation and the ability of cities to absorb new residents. One is the inability to incorporate the new urban dwellers into productive employment. There are insufficient employment opportunities in the new manufacturing industries to meet the level of demand. As a result the new migrants are forced into the tertiary sector in search of work. This becomes the most rapidly expanding sector of the economy but the work here, operating food stalls, selling postcards, driving taxis, is characterised by poor pay, poor conditions, under-employment and a pattern of irregular employment.

Cities are also unable to provide the basic physical infrastructure for the new migrants. This results in the proliferation of shanty towns with few facilities such as adequate housing and water and generally poor living conditions. These become populated by young, unskilled males from rural areas who have few relatives and friends to help them adjust to city life. When this is combined with the lack of employment and the poor living conditions such people become marginal to city life.

At the same time as this process is unfolding, traditional systems of social control are breaking down. Increased secularisation through the opening of societies to the mass media, the disruption of the extended family and the undermining of traditional communities through migration, the replacement of value systems that promote fatalism and resigned acceptance with those that promote the values of materialism and achievement: all conspire to break the hold of traditional forms of social control.

As a result developing countries are dominated by a small number of cities and these in turn are dominated by their shanty towns. These are populated by people with no significant employment prospects, with few of their ties to home and village still intact, who are freed from the constraints of traditional forms of social control and who have no productive role in the society. When this is combined with the general pattern of social disorganisation produced by change many of them experience a sense of personal disorganisation, the indicators of which include involvement in drugs and in crime. Thus the high rates of crime in developing countries are a product of the disjunction between the speed of economic and social development.

Criticising Modernisation Theory

There are a number of ways to respond to the kind of analysis proposed by modernisation theory. One is to consider the level of support that it has at an empirical level. Another, related, way is to examine its adequacy as an explanation for crime in Ireland. At both levels, as we shall see, it fails to provide a satisfactory account of the relationship between crime and development.

At an empirical level a number of studies have found some support for a relationship between economic development and crime, though the low crime rates and the high levels of development of Japan and Switzerland remain important complicating exceptions. Other studies, however, suggest that it is not possible to come to any conclusion on the relationship between crime and development. As Arthur (1991: 503) puts it, studies on the relationship have 'consistently yielded both negative and positive correlations'.

There is also the problem that beyond fairly general statements about a relationship between crime and growth it is not clear what precisely modernisation theory is suggesting. There is, for example, some confusion as to what the precise relationship it is proposing between property crime and violent crime is. Some theorists claim that modernisation reduces homicide rates and that this view has empirical support (see, for example, Bennett, 1991). Others suggest that both kinds of crime increase with modernisation but that the rate of increase in violent crime is slower than that for property crime. This, too, they claim has empirical support (see, for example, Arthur, 1992 and Abbott and Clinard, 1973). To complicate the matter further Arthur (1991), in a study of crime in eleven African countries, found that both property crime and homicide decreased with increased economic development.

What is perhaps the major difficulty with these empirical studies is the way in which their reliance on official crime statistics leads them to ignore major forms of crime in developing societies. These statistics, like those in developing countries, either ignore or understate the level of white-collar crime and corruption generally. Thus, for example, Clinard and Abbott (1973) mention the importance of white-collar and state crime in their study in Uganda. Yet when they go on to investigate the causes of crime their attention becomes narrowed and focuses on working-class crime and on the urban, marginal and detached youth. Explanations which confine themselves in this way remain seriously incomplete.

Finally there is the issue of the applicability of the modernisation perspective to the Irish situation. While David

Rottman (1980) addresses this issue his approach is limited by the inability to include or to allow for white-collar crime in any comprehensive way. Moreover he argues that as research stands in Ireland there is insufficient evidence to accept or reject this perspective. Yet there are a number of pointers that indicate that it may not be particularly useful. The major one is that while it can be shown that there was considerable dislocation in urban, but particularly rural, Ireland in the 1950s, this did not produce the kind of urban growth and consequent social and psychological marginalisation that is central to the modernisation argument. As we shall see, an underclass or marginalised class did emerge in Dublin but this was not, as predicted by modernisation theory, a product of rural/urban migration.

From the 1950s onwards there was considerable urban and rural dislocation in Ireland. Just over half a million people, for example, emigrated from the state in the twenty-year period from 1951 to 1971 and the population of Dublin grew from just over half a million in 1951 to over 800,000 in 1971. But there was little relationship between the two: urban growth cannot be accounted for by movement from rural areas. The emigration from rural Ireland over this period was not to Irish cities but to those in England and the United States. Between 1946 and 1961 eight out of every hundred migrants in Ireland moved to Dublin. In the period 1961 to 1971 this had increased to twenty-one per hundred.[2] This means that, as Rottman (1980: 29) puts it, 'Dublin and other Irish cities did not share with other European cities the catchment role of sheltering and socialising successive waves of rural migrants'. The primary factor in the growth of Dublin was the high rates of natural increase in the existing population. This means that the kind of urban dislocation that modernisation theory sees as important to crime did not occur in Ireland.

The other factor that makes the Irish situation different is that the typical migrants to Dublin were not unskilled, uneducated males but mainly from well-off middle-class families and with the level of skills and job prospects associated with such class positions. Thus they did not become part of a marginalised and alienated mass but were integrated into the growing middle-class sector of urban and suburban Dublin.

These considerations lead us to conclude that modernisation theory does not provide us with a useful framework for understanding crime in Ireland. It is inadequate at both a conceptual and an empirical level. This conclusion does not require us to abandon the attempt to understand Irish crime but it does require us to set it in a different framework. The framework that I propose here is that supplied by the concept of dependent development. This remains true to the need to link crime and social change but it proposes a different means of conceptualising change and its consequences for Irish society generally and for crime in Ireland in particular.

II Dependent Development – The Model Outlined

According to theorists of dependent development it is necessary to transcend the frame of reference of the nation state if we wish to understand the process of social change in peripheral countries like Ireland. For them, the essential starting point is at the level of the world system or the international economy. They argue that this system is to be understood as composed of a 'core' or centre group of countries that are capable of independent development and of development which is responsive to their own needs and of a 'periphery' which is only capable of reflex development. This means that periphery countries do not change by responding to their own needs but by adapting to the requirements of the developed centre. Thus the links which have been established between periphery countries and the developed core create dependent societies in which the possibilities for autonomous growth are restricted. It is the nature of their integration into the world system that creates their dependence and so shapes the form which change and development takes in them (see the account in Hoogvelt, 1983).

These links between the core and the periphery, however, are not invariant and unchangeable. As the needs of the core countries change and as the balance of power between them shifts, the nature of the links alter. Peripheral countries have moved from their eighteenth and nineteenth-century position as suppliers of raw material to the core economies to their present position as suppliers of cheap labour to multinational enterprises. This move parallels to a considerable extent the shift in power in the centre from Britain to the United States and, to a lesser extent, to Germany and Japan.

Some versions of this argument, such as that of André Gundar Frank (1967), see the internal dynamics of dependent societies as totally determined by their external dependency, so that the process of change in dependent societies is totally conditioned by their external dependency. Once incorporated into the world economy, certain development consequences inevitably and unquestionably follow. However, more sophisticated versions, like that of Fernando Cardoso (1973), do not see the process in such deterministic terms. He argues that incorporation into the world economy does not produce identical effects and does not initiate identical processes in every dependent country. Economic dependency sets the manoeuvering limits of dependent societies but the manner in which these limits are accommodated is a product of the interaction between external forces and the internal political and class forces in the dependent society.

These factors mean that when there are major economic changes in the core economies, the response of peripheral countries is not automatic or predetermined. It is the outcome of an organised negotiation or struggle between different groups in the dependent societies and the outcome of this struggle will vary from society to society. For Cardoso, the effects of dependency on any particular country depend on the particular interaction of the forces of the core economies with the forces of the national power and class system. Because of this, the mere fact of dependency does not allow us to predict the effect it will have on the form that change and development takes in a dependent society.

If a situation of dependency is not a totally determined one then it is important to analyse the processes through which internal and external forces reach an accommodation and in which the effects of development are decided on. Arguably this process can be best observed when one model of development becomes exhausted and the alliances on which it is based collapse and there is a transition to a new one. Ian Roxborough (1979) has argued that the three important stages in the development of the relationship between core and periphery are:

(i) the period from the 1850s to the 1930s when Great Britain was the world power and peripheral countries were integrated into the world system as export economies producing raw materials and food for the core countries;

(ii) the period of crisis from the 1930s to the 1950s when relationships between core countries disintegrated into economic protectionism and war and so weakened the links between them and peripheral countries. In these circumstances peripheral countries responded with policies of import substitution and the encouragement of the development of native industry behind tariff walls;

(iii) the third period is the one that began in the late 1950s and early 1960s and in which the United States and multinational companies are the major power brokers. In this period foreign investment is being directed at peripheral countries, changing their internal structure and providing a form of what Cardoso (1973) has called 'associated dependent development' in which a certain level of prosperity becomes possible in peripheral countries.

If this periodisation is accepted then the key points in the study of development are the transitions between the phases or more specifically for our purposes here the transition between the second and the third phases of the world economy. It is here that the key mediation between foreign and domestic interests take place, the results of which shape the form that development takes in the new period.

However while Cardoso is prepared to acknowledge that both development and dependency can go together and that foreign investment is not a zero-sum game where all the benefits go to one side, it is also not a costless experience for a society (Cardoso, 1973). This form of development has a price. It has a regressive effect on income distribution, it generates increasing levels of foreign indebtedness and it creates unemployment and social marginality. The existing income distribution is made more skewed by two factors. One is that much of the increased affluence accrues to élites and to the middle class. Their patterns of consumption favour the purchase of imported goods and so the benefits of their affluence go outside the country. The other is that the higher wages paid by the multinational companies only accrue to a small group of workers, thereby creating what is in effect a labour élite which is slightly, though significantly, better off than the mass of workers and thus has a vested interest in the form that development takes.

The effect of dependency on the level of foreign indebtedness is produced by the demonstration effect of new affluence. It raises the level of material expectations but it is accompanied by insufficient levels of foreign investment to create the amount of employment that would enable most people in the society to satisfy their new expectations. The state has to step in either to meet these expectations through increased welfare-spending or to suppress them through coercion. Both cost money and as the tax base does not necessarily grow with the increase in foreign investment – it comes in search of low or non-existent tax rates – the extra costs of this kind of development must be met by borrowing.

The increase in unemployment arises because this new economic regime is generally accompanied by free trade which undermines domestic industry. Furthermore, the concentration of the new foreign investment in capital-intensive sectors means that its presence does not necessarily compensate for the lost jobs. The degree to which each or all of these is a factor in dependency is a matter for empirical investigation of particular cases but their existence reminds us of the price that some pay for the development of others. Those included in the development process gain both in income and in power terms while those who are excluded lose. As we shall see this has an obvious connection to crime in that the willingness of the losers to pay this price cannot be taken for granted.

Applying this Perspective to Ireland[3]

Ireland has been and undoubtedly still is a dependent country. Its growth and development have been conditioned by the growth and development of the world economy and its phases of change fit comfortably into the model proposed by Ian Roxborough to account for the experiences of Latin American countries. From the middle of the nineteenth century, if not earlier, the Irish economy, then predominantly an agricultural one, became essentially a mono-crop economy producing meat for the market in Britain. This was a factor in the attempts to consolidate land holdings over the period (large farms are more efficient for producing cattle), in the decline of the farm labourer, in the rising power of large farmers and in the periodic famines to which the peasantry of the time fell victim. From the 1930s to the 1950s, when the world economic crisis and the subsequent world war weakened the links between core and peripheral countries, space was created for peripheral countries to attempt to build up an industrial base from which to launch a process of independent development. The encouragement of import substitution and industrial protectionism was central to this policy and at the level of job-creation at least the policy could claim to have had some success in Ireland.

However, with the end of the World War Two and the reassertion of economic power by the United States, which emerged from the period confirmed as the new core of the world economy, the developmental context changed. Peripheral countries such as Ireland came under internal and external pressure to 'open' their economies to the outside and a new phase of development began – 'industrialisation by invitation' or the attempt to get a share of the massive investment funds of multinational companies that were seeking to expand their dominance beyond that of the economy of the United States. Arguably this phase of development is now coming to an end as changes in the nature of the world economy are forcing realignment within the developed core and in the nature of its relationships with less-developed peripheral countries, particularly as the collapse of the Soviet empire has widened the number of peripheral countries available for foreign investment.

However, even though the changes in the world economy have conditioned and do condition change and development in the Irish economy, they did not and do not *determine* it. The final form that development took and takes in each case is the outcome of the balance of power between the external and internal social forces. Thus in the 1930s the influence of external forces was weakened by the war but the model of development through import-substitution industrialisation was one which did not bring the state into conflict with major power groups in the country. Neither was there much opposition from what was perhaps the most powerful groups in the country at the time, the large cattle farmers. They used few industrial inputs in their type of agriculture so their imports were limited. There was also little opposition from native capitalists as controls on the extent of possible foreign ownership in Irish industry ensured that the new industry would remain under native control. The tariff walls also protected against foreign competition in the home market thus guaranteeing Irish capitalists high levels of profit. So while the developmental context was conditioned by the state of the international economy and by the nature of the links between core and peripheral countries, the precise form that development took in a peripheral country like Ireland was the outcome of the accommodation reached with the powerful interest groups in the country.

In this way, the key to the form which development and change take in a dependent society lies in the nature and balance of power between the key social actors in the development and those whose interests are reflected in the context against which development is being attempted. 'It is', as Denis O'Hearn (1990: 33) remarks, 'the interaction of domestic and transnational forces – their conflicts and alliances – that determines the direction and forces of change in "developing societies"'. We can use this perspective to argue that the shape that change and development took in the period from the late 1950s onwards was the product of an alliance between native capital, foreign capital and a national state in a context which was structured by the interests of the United States and those of multinational companies.

The social crisis of the 1950s was the background against which the new development strategy was negotiated. Balance of payments problems in 1951 and 1955 provoked deflationary measures by the government which in turn produced major recessions in 1952 and 1955 respectively. Industrial employment ceased to grow. Output stagnated. Emigration reached record proportions yet still left unemployment at 10 per cent and Gross National Product fell. For all effective purposes the import substitution process was exhausted. It is difficult in retrospect to appreciate or indeed to convey the sense of disaster that permeated Irish society in this period. John Healy (1968: 70), a journalist, described the emigration from the West of Ireland as 'our own Auschwitz-like trains of dumb emigrants going'. Corporation houses in Dublin were boarded up as there were insufficient tenants. The bitter joke began to circulate that the last person out of Ireland should remember to turn out the light.

In theory two developmental options faced the state. The first option was to acknowledge the failure of local capitalists to develop the economy and for the state to take a more direct role in planning and investing in the economy itself. In other words, to institute a much higher level of state control of the economy. This would have involved an extension of the kind of model that had been the basis of successful semi-state companies such as the Irish electricity company, ESB. The second option was to remove the restrictions of foreign involvement in the economy and to open the Irish economy to foreign investment.

The first option was rejected because domestic capital was unhappy with it. It seemed to this group to be essentially 'sovietisation on the sly' and was viewed as a threat to its members' rights to use their capital in whatever manner they chose. This class was, however, split over major policy issues and its moral authority had been eroded by its failure to deliver on the promises of tariff protection. It had made considerable profits from this but these had been invested outside the country. It had also failed to produce industries that could survive in the harsh world of international competition. Given this, its ability to influence policy was correspondingly circumscribed.

Increased state control of the economy was also rejected because the United States was against it. Since the late 1940s the US had been utilising its position as the major world power to place pressure on regimes all over the world to liberalise trade. More specifically it was utilising the structures created to distribute Marshall Aid in Europe to bring pressure on governments, including the Irish government, to establish free trade in Europe and to ensure its maintenance after the ending of the aid (see the account in O'Hearn, 1990: 18–24). Thus the US was involved in creating situations within the international economy in which direct multinational investment could take place in peripheral economies (see, for example, Cardoso and Faletto, 1979: 149–71) and it was prepared to use its considerable political and economic power to achieve it.

The final reason this option was rejected was that it was proposed by a weak state that lacked sufficient autonomy from the powerful interests in the society to enforce or enact such a policy. The state's continued legitimacy depended on its ability to produce some level of economic performance yet it was circumscribed by the fact that, since independence, the Irish state had never become a developmentalist one, that is one which is capable of acting independently of powerful interest groups in the society. It never became an 'entrepreneurial state' in the sense of going beyond what Freeman (1982: 91) called 'entrepreneurial assistance', where the state gives assistance to the private sector, to 'entrepreneurial substitution' where the state either takes entrepreneurial initiative or takes a controlling interest in productive enterprises. Unlike countries such as Brazil where local capital was positive in regard to an entrepreneurial role for the state, this was never the case in Ireland. The state never had the capacity to formulate and implement policies which were independent of the interests of powerful groups, such as native capital and large farmers. This contrasts, for example, with the case of South Korea where the disarray among the major social classes in the 1960s and 1970s allowed the emergence of a strong state which pursued independent development policies (see Lie, 1992). Thus the Irish state was never in a position to dictate the direction of development but merely to assist in the direction that others wanted it to go in.

With no sufficiently powerful group to pursue the option of state ownership and state direction of the economy, it never became a realistic prospect. The process of dismantling tariff walls was begun and with it the opening of the economy to external investment. It was a policy that had benefits for all the groups involved, although the level of benefit tended to reflect their respective power in the policy-making process. Despite their overall weakness domestic capital won a major concession. This was that the kind of multinational industry that qualified for state aid and for inclusion in its regime of low corporate taxation must produce for export and not for the domestic market. In this way, its products would not be in direct competition with those of domestic industry. It is also alleged that in some cases at least domestic capital negotiated with foreign investors to ensure that wage rates they paid were not sufficiently out of line with local ones to become a source of discontent for their own workers. The state was provided with a means to ensure its legitimacy through directing policies to entice a large share of multinational investment to locate in Ireland and thus generate prosperity here. Finally, multinational investment was guaranteed entry to an economy with an educated labour force, easy access to the European market, low taxation and little danger of onerous government regulation.

III Bringing Crime Back In

The significance of this account to the study of development is obvious. But what, it might reasonably be asked at this point, has all of this got to do with crime in Ireland? Its importance comes about in the following way. We have been arguing that crime is linked to the process of social change and social development in Ireland over the past thirty years. However the nature of the explanations offered for the link between social change and crime depends crucially on how we characterise the process of change. To the extent that there is a traditional view in the sociology of crime it would understand this link in the terms of modernisation theory. However we have argued that modernisation theory is not adequate for this purpose. It makes erroneous assumptions about the nature of development, it is not supported by empirical evidence on the patterns of crime in developing countries and the pattern of migration and urban growth in Ireland does not follow that anticipated by the theory. We have suggested that the pattern of change and development in Ireland is best considered through the model of dependent development. What this section will do is show the link between dependent development and crime.

Development and Opportunities for Crime

Dependent development has influenced crime in four ways. What these have in common is that they are made possible by the form that dependent development took and by the relative power of the groups that formed the development alliance. The first influence is that this form of development strategy was successful in the, very relevant, sense of generating new levels of affluence in the society. This in turn led, as we have seen in chapter two, to new opportunities for crime. This can be seen in the obvious sense that the new level of ownership of material goods such as cars and televisions produced new levels of opportunities for theft. However the change was not confined to the opportunities for 'conventional' crime. It also extended through the increased generation of business activity to opportunities to engage in 'conventional' white-collar crime. Opportunities to commit fraud and to engage in dubious business practices were extended by the increased level of activity in the economy, especially when these were combined with the presence of a weak state with a conditioned unwillingness to respond to it (see O'Toole, 1995, on the inability of the state to regulate the activities of cattle ranchers and of the meat industry in particular). The increase in the opportunities for, and the profitability of, corporate and middle-class crime, coupled with a weak or non-existent system of regulation, inevitably meant significant increases in the behaviour.

Development and Corporate Crime

The second influence is the weakness of the state. This is relevant to the way in which this model of development allowed for the phenomenon of crisis-transfer to take place. The background is this (the argument is more fully developed in Keohane, 1987): the opening of the Irish economy to foreign investment from core countries took place at the same time as many of these core countries were facing a crisis. The exploitation of labour, of nature and of natural resources has created major problems in the core industrial societies of the world. These are manifested in class conflict and environmental depletion. The state in these societies has been forced to place limits on the economic system, thereby creating the potential for further crisis pressures. The form of development initiated in the late 1950s and early 1960s in many peripheral countries like Ireland offered a potential solution to these problems. It allowed developed countries to transfer the problems they were experiencing to peripheral societies. An example here is the pressures that polluting industries came under in core countries, such as the United States, which led them to search for peripheral societies that would allow them 'the right to pollute' (Leonard, 1988). The administrative systems of peripheral countries had to take on the problems that this kind of crisis displacement created. But these systems were, as we have seen in the Irish context, already weak and inadequate to the task.

Two studies in particular illustrate the extent to which the state was resistant to calls to regulate these industries and the degree to which, when it was forced to, it resorted to a policy of 'token deterrence' (Eipper, 1989: 158). Chris Eipper's study of the operation of Gulf Oil, a major multinational, in Bantry Bay, found that state officials adopted a placatory attitude to the company. They enacted, what he termed, draconian legislation on oil spillages but this legislation was not enforced and 'the costs of contravention were virtually non-existent' (Eipper, 1989: 158). Kieran Keohane (1987) has shown the way in which state regulation took an administrative rather than a criminal form. The ADR agreement, for example, which regulates the transportation of dangerous substances by road is administered by the Department of Labour. In other countries it is enforced by the police.

In effect, the state became the broker for multinational capital and operated with a deferential stance towards multinational companies. This, however, does not imply or more importantly require corruption by state officials. Leonard (1988: 227), for example, argues that in the course of his research he found some examples of 'efforts by local officials or government inspectors to elicit bribes from big US companies in lieu of enforcement of certain environmental regulations'. He also claims that in the late 1960s and early 1970s the Industrial Development Authority told local government officials that some of the dirtier industrial facilities should be allowed into Ireland on less stringent pollution terms than operated in Europe or the United States (Leonard, 1988: 127). However his main conclusion is that 'in Ireland, bribery is probably not very common' (Leonard, 1988: 227).

These pressures to adopt a more relaxed attitude to the regulation of multinational companies were in fact inherent in the choice of development policy adopted by the state in the late 1950s. The promotion of an industrial policy that would produce some level of prosperity and that would guarantee the continued legitimacy of the state was incompatible with the strict regulation of multinational companies. It was the absence of such controls that attracted many companies to Ireland in the first place. As we have seen, they were trying to escape from the increasingly restrictive regulation in their home countries, particularly the United States where there was considerable use of the criminal sanction against corporate offenders in general and against environmental ones in particular. So, in effect, the state was caught in a number of the classic double-binds that characterise situations of dependency. It wanted industry so it had, to a large extent, to take it on the terms on which it was prepared to come. If the state tried to regulate, then the companies called on their ultimate sanction, the threat to pull out. In this the companies often had the support of those particular sections of the local business class who benefited from their presence (see Eipper, 1989: 147). At the same time the state was under increasing pressure from other local groups to regulate the industry (see Allen and Jones, 1990). The solution was pragmatic but cosmetic: a series of restrictions and controls were set up that are, in some areas at least, as stringent as those that operate in other European countries, but they are simply not stringently enforced (see Leonard, 1988: 211).

In this sense then the solution has been to ignore the misbehaviour of these corporations or, if placed under pressure to regulate it, to do so through legislative structures that create the illusion of control but which are inadequately enforced, resourced and policed. As a result they do not interfere unduly with the activities concerned. When this structure is superimposed on a society that has already had problems of regulating the behaviour of native capital, the way is open for the kinds of middle-class misbehaviour outlined in chapter three.

Development and 'Conventional' Crime

The third influence that the form of development had was its effects on conventional crime. Development in Ireland has generated a range of social benefits and this, as we have seen, has also generated new opportunities for crime. In addition the manner in which these benefits have been distributed has been such as to create a group in society who are prepared to take advantage of the new criminal opportunities. As development has proceeded, increasing numbers of young working-class people have been marginalised to positions of almost permanent unemployment and disadvantage. In such situations crime becomes a mode of economic and social survival.

Part of the crisis that foreign investors were in retreat from was one of state regulation. The other was organised trade unions. So when they selected Ireland as a location for investment they were looking for non-unionised labour or labour that would be reluctant to flex its industrial muscle. This led multinationals to locate outside major urban areas and in particular outside Dublin which has a reputation for organised trade union activity. They were encouraged in this by state support for job creation in rural areas. This kind of policy had deep roots in the rural fundamentalism of the Fianna Fáil party but it also had a pragmatic aspect in the sense of creating alternatives to agricultural employment for small farmers with limited economic viability (see Whelan, Breen and Whelan, 1992). Foreign investors also had a preference for the employment of female workers who are traditionally considered to have ambivalent relationships to union activity. Much of this was disguised through talk that the kinds of skills they were seeking were less likely to be found among the male population (see Murray and Wickham, 1985). However as these levels of skill were generally fairly low there was little evidence that they were gender specific. This in effect meant that much of the new employment that was created was rural and female. It also meant that the cost of this policy was paid by the urban working class, particularly the less skilled and younger sections of it. Effectively speaking they were marginalised by the kinds of development policies that the state pursued.

The new policies encouraged these new kinds of employment but they did nothing to halt the decline of many of the traditional Irish industries most of which were urban-based and male dominated. As a result large numbers of low and unskilled jobs that were previously available disappeared (Drudy and Lynch, 1993: 147). The consequences were to produce forms of unemployment which were intensified by other features of the society and transformed into new forms of social exclusion with male urban workers being forced into a situation of permanent marginality from the labour force.

An important contribution was made by the education system. It now plays a major role in 'allocating' positions in the world of work. But despite the opening of new educational opportunities in the 1960s and the 1970s through, for example, free primary and secondary education, participation in second- and third-level education has remained restricted along class lines. Research indicates that among lower working-class families, 45 per cent of the boys and 28 per cent of the girls left school without, what was then, the intermediate certificate (Rottman, 1984: 177). This contrasts with the experiences among upper middle-class families where only 4 per cent of the boys and none of the girls left school without their intermediate certificate.

This level of disadvantage has clear implications for employment. It has enabled the middle class to get the kinds of educational qualifications that have allowed it to secure the new white-collar and skilled industrial employment created by economic development. We can see this if we look at the relationship between education and unemployment. The unemployment rate among those without a post-primary certificate, according to Richard Breen (1984), was 29 per cent whereas for those with a completed leaving certificate it was 8 per cent. The middle class has also been prepared, in a time of economic recession, to use its superior educational qualifications to move into traditional working-class careers, like apprenticeships for skilled work, in the search for permanent employment, thus pushing young working class males further out of the labour market (Breen, 1984). In effect then, development created new jobs that the urban working-class did not have the education and skill levels to compete for at the same time as it eliminated the kinds of jobs they could compete for. In this way a growing prosperity for some was accompanied by a marginalisation for others.

This marginalisation was primarily along class lines but within the working class it was particularly concentrated in certain urban areas, especially inner-city ones where the dependence on traditional forms of male employment had been intense. When social disadvantage is concentrated in this way it tends to form a syndrome which persists over generations and provides the conditions in which a criminal culture can be created and perpetuated. Michael Bannon has argued that this kind of geographic concentration of disadvantage is more pronounced in the Dublin area than in other major European cities and in particular more so than in parts of inner-city London. He argues that for most inner-city residents in Dublin there is no realistic hope of getting a stable job, no matter how badly paid (Bannon, Eustace and O'Neill, 1981: 262–3). The notion of continued attachment to the labour force becomes irrelevant when the prospects of getting into it are non-existent. Faced with what many see as a hopeless situation, crime becomes an acceptable response to this level of social exclusion.

John Hagan (1994) has described this process as one of capital disinvestment in urban areas. Crime represents a means of adaptation to it and to dealing with its attendant consequences such as restrictions of access to socially desirable goods and services. Crime becomes the means through which individuals recapitalise their lives. It involves them using whatever resources and avenues are available to them, whether legitimate or not, to achieve the kinds of social goals that others are also striving for. William Wilson (1991: 10) has developed this point in his discussion of how the accumulation of disadvantages attendant on a decline in labour force attachment mutually reinforce and reproduce themselves, producing a downwards spiral which increases marginality to conventional society and increases the possibilities for, and the attraction of, a criminal lifestyle. He argues that

> a social context that includes poor schools, inadequate job information networks, and a lack of legitimate employment opportunities not only gives rise to weak labour force attachment, but increases the probability that individuals will be constrained to seek income derived from illegal or deviant activities. This weakens their attachment to the legitimate labour market even further.

It is this process of attempting to recapitalise their lives that allows the development of what Hagan (1994: 77) calls 'deviance service industries' such as prostitution and drug-dealing, while at the same time explaining their apparent tenacity and intractability. They represent an attempt by the individual entrepreneurs in inner-city and deprived areas to recapitalise their lives through the income and the profit generated by such activities. It is instructive in this respect that the search for the assets of major Dublin drug-dealers was not particularly difficult. They did the same with their income as most conventional middle-class families do with theirs. They bought their own houses.

This marginalisation is now a well-established feature of life in many working-class areas in that the pattern of poor education and unemployment experienced by parents has become the experience of their children also. In effect the marginalised class is being reproduced by and through the same social processes that created it. The process of capital disinvestment which Hagan (1994) speaks of, has, despite the efforts of many community groups, continued across generations. This has intensified the conditions that support a criminal culture and that support the use of crime as a means of recapitalisation. We can see this in the studies of the social backgrounds of criminals that we discussed in chapter one, a striking feature of which was the extent to which criminals who were unemployed at the time of their arrest came from families where the father had also a significant history of unemployment.

Development and Gender

The final issue here is that of gender. If, as we have been arguing here, the process of development marginalised a significant sector of the working class from participation in the new affluence then presumably this marginalisation was equally a problem for men and women. Yet, as we have seen in chapter four, the participation rates of men and women in crime are significantly different. So if marginalisation affected entire communities or urban areas why was the response of men and women different? There are two possible answers here.

One is that the experience of marginalisation was *not* a communal one but one whose effects can be differentiated along gender lines. There is some evidence that this might be the case. A lot of the new employment that was created by the new form of development was work for women: the amount of unskilled assembly work that emerged in the electronics industry, for example. This process is referred to as the 'feminisation of the labour force'. Its effects may have been that working-class women have been less marginalised than working-class men and so have less incentive to engage in crime. Unfortunately the nature of employment statistics in Ireland is such that we cannot establish if this 'feminisation' actually took place and so this argument is difficult to substantiate.

The other possibility is that the experience of marginalisation may have been the same for both men and women but the manner in which women adapted to it may have been different. There may be accepted social roles into which young working-class women who are unable to get work can fit. One of these may be that of mother. If the prevailing attitude is that, for women, work is an interlude before marriage or parenthood then there may not be a significant stigma attached to missing out on the work part. By contrast, where men are concerned, the dominant role model may be that of provider. For men, notions of identity and masculinity may be tied up with earning an income and in the prevailing circumstances earning this through crime may not be unacceptable. In this way then social definitions of appropriate gender roles may intervene between the experience of marginalisation and the responses to it.

This account of crime has stressed the central role of marginalisation in the production of crime. It is important to recognise however that while crime is one of the major forms of response to the marginalisation of sectors of the working class, it is not the only one. Two others are important. One response is the internal migration represented by drug addiction. Through this, addicts withdraw from the demands of reality and replace them with the demands of the drug. It can relieve the pain of marginalisation but the manner in which it does so is destructive both to the addict and to the community in which drugs circulate freely. Addicts expose themselves to the risk of contracting the HIV virus, a major source of which is the use of contaminated needles, and the costs of feeding their drug habit lead to the kinds of crimes such as assault that further undermine already marginalised communities.

The other response to marginalisation is what we might term external emigration. For the marginalised working class the exit has always been to England where employment in a wide range of unskilled work, particularly in the building trade, could be found. However it is increasingly the case that this escape route from marginalisation is becoming less viable as England too experiences a decline in unskilled and low skilled work for men. This means that in effect working-class men have 'escaped' from marginalisation to marginalisation, the only difference being that until recently the British welfare state paid them more.

Conclusion

In this chapter we have proposed an explanation for crime in Ireland that is intended to account for many of its salient characteristics. These include the central role of young males from a working-class background in conventional property crime, the neglect of and the inability to control the crimes committed by the middle class, the low participation rates of female offenders in conventional crime and the concentration of crime in urban areas. We have argued that this pattern of crime must be understood in the context of the social changes that have occurred in Ireland over the past thirty years. But we have also argued that such changes are inadequately conceptualised through the conventional approach to the study of social change and crime, namely that of modernisation theory. These changes need to be placed within the model of dependent development because it is this form of development that created the 'double marginalisation' that is at the heart of crime in Ireland.

Development marginalised corporate élites and the middle class from effective processes of state control and so intensified the extent to which their anti-social behaviour has been free from the stigma of criminality and from any effective regulation by the processes of criminal law. It also marginalised significant sectors of the working class from the benefits of the material progress that development produced. It did this through undermining the traditional sources of employment that the working class had been dependent on and replacing them with new kinds of employment which were rural rather than urban-based and for which they had neither the education nor the requisite skill levels. For young working-class men this situation represents a form of marginality that has to be accommodated and this accommodation was made more difficult by the fact that emigration is no longer an option for those without skills or qualifications. In this context crime becomes a form of adaptation to this kind of marginality and an attempt to overcome it. For young working-class women the experience of marginality is similar but perhaps not as intense and the range of social roles through which they can deal with marginality is somewhat wider, including as we have argued, premature parenthood. Finally we argued that this kind of marginality is being reproduced by the failure of the state to deal with the development strategies that are creating it and by the fact that this marginality is now becoming part of the experience of a second generation of the urban working class.

However it is appropriate to conclude by emphasising the point that what is being advanced here is an argument which draws on and utilises available empirical data but which has not itself been the subject of empirical investigation. The detailed substantiation of it would require a number of levels of empirical research. The first is at the comparative level to see if other countries that have undergone dependent development have experienced similar forms of marginality and similar patterns of increasing crime. The second is the kinds of ethnographic community-based research that are beginning to form an important part of the 'new criminology' (Hagan, 1994: 59–99). These are being used to study the manner in which marginalised sections of the urban working class are adapting to the social exclusion that they are being subjected to by the process of social and economic change. The third is the area of the misbehaviour of the middle and corporate classes in Ireland to see if the picture drawn here of their marginalisation from the legal processes is accurate. This would be the most difficult area to research because of the well-recognised capacity of the powerful to conceal their behaviour from public scrutiny. The kind of research suggested here would be a large undertaking and as it would challenge official definitions of the nature of the problem of crime it is difficult to see it emerging in the near future. However it is essential if we are to establish a theory that accounts for crime in Ireland in any comprehensive and sociological fashion.

Notes

1. In particular the explanation being proposed here cannot explain why crime in Ireland is relatively speaking fairly low.
2. Figures in Rottman (1980: 29).
3. This section draws on the account in Mc Cullagh (1993).

6   POLICING IRISH SOCIETY

Introduction

In the remaining chapters we shift the focus of our attention from the causes of crime to the responses to it. The main responses are policing, through which criminals are identified and apprehended, and punishment, the process through which they are sanctioned. Policing is the subject of this chapter and punishment that of the next. The policing role is one that we think of as the exclusive prerogative of the state and of its professional police force. But as we shall see there is more to it than that. There are forms of policing that complement the activities of the state and there are others that compete with it.

We can identify four types of policing in Irish society. These are:

(i) policing by a professional police force;

(ii) policing by an alliance of police and people as in community policing and neighbourhood watch;

(iii) direct policing by people and communities as in vigilante groups and in the Concerned Parents Against Drugs in Dublin and;

(iv) policing by private security firms who are becoming an increasingly prominent feature of urban life in particular.

In this chapter we look at the range of issues that have been raised in sociological research and in public debate about each of these kinds of policing. We begin with the gardaí.

I Professional Policing –
The Role of the Gardaí

In this section we look at a number of features of Ireland's
professional police force, the Garda Síochána or 'guardians
of the peace'. They have become such an accepted part of the
society that any discussion of policing in Ireland tends to be
concentrated on them. We begin with a brief account of the
historical origins of the gardaí.

Origins

Prior to the late eighteenth century, policing in Irish society
was primarily the responsibility of unpaid justices of the peace,
watchmen and unpaid constables. This system was replaced in
Dublin in 1786 by a force centralised under three commissioners. In this way the city achieved the distinction of having
the first statutorily created police force in the British Isles (as it
was then called). The force was conceived primarily as being a
bulwark against Irish nationalism and peasant agitation. This
was reflected in its recruitment policies. Members were to be
young, in good health and Protestant (see the account in
Palmer, 1975).

The Dublin model was extended in 1787 to rural Ireland. As
a concession to its political opponents the new force was
initially confined to Munster where there were high levels of
peasant agitation. However by 1836 a national centralised
constabulary, the Royal Irish Constabulary (RIC), had been
established under the control of Dublin Castle. The urban and
the rural forces were amalgamated by the new state in 1925 to
become the Garda Síochána. What unfolded over the following
period was the gradual establishment by the state of a monopoly over the role of policing. This monopoly had not been
challenged until the 1980s when other forms of policing such as

community self-policing and policing by private security companies began to make themselves visible in the society.

Significant legacies remain from this formative period. The first is that the police force is a national one under centralised control. This has produced, what Salmon (1985: 92) termed, 'a great, top-heavy, over-centralised bureaucracy in its Phoenix Park headquarters'. Moreover, unlike the police forces in England, accountability is not to a formal police authority but directly to a government department. This has meant that a high level of control has been exercised over the gardaí by the Department of Justice and by successive ministers. This has left the force open to forms of political interference such as, until recently, the highly politicised nature of appointment of garda commissioners (see Mc Cullagh, 1988b).

The second legacy is also a matter of organisational structure. The divisional structure of the gardaí, particularly outside the Dublin metropolitan area, is the one that was inherited from the RIC. As a result the bulk of the police force is located in rural Ireland. In 1965 31 per cent of the force was located in Dublin (Rottman, 1984: 127–8). When the size of the force began to increase after 1972 it grew within this organisational structure so that the rural bias persisted. By 1991, 37 per cent of the force (excluding those in garda headquarters) was located in the Dublin metropolitan area. This may make sense in terms of the relative size of the population of Dublin but as almost 60 per cent of all crimes took place in the capital city it does not make sense from a crime prevention and detection perspective.

The final legacy is that the force started out and continues to be, at a formal level at least, an unarmed one. However with the security demands of the Northern situation and the increase in the number of criminals using guns, this policy has come under strain. While it is generally accepted that an increasing proportion of the force is now armed or has access to arms and while there have been controversies over their skill in using them (see for example, *Garda Review*,

:, 1990: 24–5), it is not possible to obtain precise
ition on the number of police officers that routinely
irearms. Estimates suggest that as many as 1,500
carry guns, that is about 15 per cent of the force (see
Garda Review, March, 1991: 17).

The Role of the Gardaí

When the gardaí were set up as an organisation their goals had
a clear law enforcement bias. Their aims were 'the prevention
and detection of crime, the security of life and property, and
the preservation of the public peace and good order' (Garda
Síochána Code, 1922: 5). Later accounts emphasise the service
dimension of their work. The Commission of the Garda
Síochána, more popularly known as the Conroy Commission
(1970: 4), for example, stressed the role of 'befriending any
person who needs help, and by assisting in any emergency that
might arise'. Research suggests that while the service role is the
better characterisation of public expectations of the police,
there is in fact considerable tension in the organisation between
its service and law-enforcement roles.

The research has approached this issue from the perspective
of the policed rather than from the formal statements of the
police themselves. It asks what kind of assistance people are
looking for when they contact the police? A study of tele-
phone calls and personal callers to police stations in Dublin,
Waterford and Thurles found that the majority of the calls (64
per cent) were of a service nature, though this fell to 46 per
cent in the station in central Dublin. Almost a third of the
service calls was for advice, information and direction.[1] These
included a caller wanting to know the result of a match in
Croke Park (Harris, 1988).

These findings, which are very much in line with those of
international research (see the review in Harris, 1988),
suggest that people view the police force not merely as

crime-fighting but as a more broadly based service organisation. This has a number of implications for policing. One is
that it points to an underlying tension in police work,
between the police view of their work as being primarily
about crime detection and the more mundane reality that the
bulk of work they do is routine service work. Harris (1988)
found that uniformed gardaí spent most of their time on
service-related work. Gardaí on foot-patrol, for example,
spent more time sorting out traffic congestion than dealing
with crime. Yet the tasks that they rated as most important
to them were mainly related to crime. Eight of what they
considered to be their ten most important tasks were law-
enforcement ones whereas eight of the ten 'least liked'
aspects were forms of service work. Fourteen of the eighteen
tasks that gardaí said should be performed by some other
agency were service-related.

This suggests that there may be a lack of appreciation of
the importance of service work. Yet surveys show that the
way in which the police deal with the public in service-
related situations is a more important element in building
high levels of public satisfaction with them as a force than
their level of success in crime-fighting. Public satisfaction is
unrelated to their ability or inability to control the level of
crime but is based more on the kinds of non-adversarial
interaction that the public have with them (Taylor, 1986).

The other implication is for the way in which the police are
trained. Until recently garda training was narrowly focused on
crime-related activities, learning the law and achieving high
levels of physical fitness. Many garda cadets felt the skills
which were least developed were communication ones yet
these are central to the successful accomplishment of service
work. A new system of garda training introduced in 1987 was
intended to remedy this and to provide a better reflection of
the reality of police work. Its success in preparing recruits
more adequately for the kinds of situations they are likely to
encounter has yet to be assessed.

Police Culture

The new training scheme includes a large element of what might be termed 'work experience'. Recruits spend about one year of the two-year programme in selected garda stations where they work under the guidance of training sergeants. This gives them their first encounter between the ideals of police work learned in training and the reality of the attitudes of working police officers as contained in and expressed by the occupational sub-culture. If the experiences of other police forces is anything to go by youthful idealism may be the first casualty of this process.[2]

According to sociologists every occupation develops a particular way of relating to the social environment it deals with and operates in. This perspective includes the attitudes adopted by the holders of the occupation to the people for whom and with whom they work. A number of studies have identified a distinctive set of attitudes or what might be called a sub-culture among police officers (see Reiner, 1992, for a summary). It is made up of a combination of the following elements:

(i) A sense of mission: this is the notion that police work is not just a job. It is a way of life or a vocation. Police officers are the 'thin blue line' protecting decent, respectable people from the 'scruff'.

(ii) Suspiciousness: the culture encourages police to be wary, watchful and suspicious of people they come into contact with, and to be always on the look-out for trouble and for indications of danger. This, according to Reiner (1992: 114–15), is partly a response to the conditions of the work but it is also a characteristic that is encouraged by police training.

(iii) Aggressiveness: a number of studies have identified a tendency for the police to be aggressive in their dealings with the public. Many police officers believe that the public, or those parts of it that they come into contact with, is either dangerous or else hate them (see the classic study by Westley, 1970). This, they feel, can best be dealt with by being aggressive first, thus setting the tone of, and controlling the manner in which, encounters with the public will proceed. It has been argued that the aggressiveness of the police in dealing with the public and particularly with the young has increased in the past decade (see Benyon, 1986).

(iv) Related to aggressiveness, and to the sense of danger that is alleged to go with the work, is the quality, which Reiner (1992: 124) refers to, as 'old-fashioned machismo'. Many police officers see their work as exciting, tough and dangerous and so as 'men's' work. The travelling companion of this attitude is an equally old-fashioned sexism. Women officers are considered to be good at those activities that require 'maternal' qualities such as dealing with rape victims and keeping the filing up to date.

(v) A final element of the culture is political and social conservatism. Police officers tend to be very much part of a lower middle-class culture, have a pronounced tendency to vote for conservative candidates in elections and tend to see social problems in terms of individual rather than social failings. As Fielding and Fielding (1991: 39) put it, they 'subscribe to a harsh, narrow, and unforgiving view of human nature'. This is guaranteed to make them somewhat unsympathetic to the kinds of solutions to the crime problem that are proposed in chapter eight.

An important factor in producing and reinforcing these attitudes is the social isolation of police officers. Numerous studies have indicated that they tend to socialise primarily with other police officers (see Reiner, 1992: 115–16). This is partly because shift work makes it difficult to maintain friendships with people who do not have similar schedules. It is also partly because of attitudes in the community to them. Many people tend to be reserved in their company, particularly in pubs. Police training also plays a role. It discourages them from getting too actively involved with members of the community as the nature of their work may involve taking action at some stage against the people they have befriended.

In the absence of the relevant research we do not know the extent to which such a sub-culture can be found among gardaí. Some of the conditions that foster and propagate it are present such as a certain isolation from the communities they police. This is a product of the pattern of recruitment to the force and of organisational practices in relation to the posting of gardaí. In 1966 when 38 per cent of the population were living in urban areas (that is, centres having more than 10,000 residents) only 12 per cent of new garda recruits came from such areas. By 1986 the proportion of the population living in urban areas had increased to 43 per cent while the percentage of urban recruits had increased to 36 per cent (Harris, 1988). This means that there has been some decline in the extent to which urban areas are policed by people who may have little experience of the nature of urban life. At the same time however they are prevented from policing the areas they are familiar with by the practice of not posting gardaí to their native areas.

The degree to which these produce a full set of the cultural attributes of a sub-culture is open to question. Liam Harris (1988) did not look at the nature of the sub-culture in the gardaí since such an analysis would have required a different type of research approach to the social survey one that he used. Yet it is important to know if such a sub-culture exists among the gardaí as studies in other countries have shown that such a culture has a number of consequences for police work. One is the degree to which the contradiction between the image of the work contained in the culture and the reality of the work creates a problem of boredom. Despite the centrality of the crime-fighting image in the culture, much routine police work such as beat patrolling is often aimless and boring (see, for example, Smith and Gray, 1983). Just over 10 per cent of the gardaí interviewed by Harris did not speak to anyone when on foot-patrol.

It is this boredom that may explain the rapid decline in idealism that Harris documents. The main reasons officers gave for joining the gardaí were non-instrumental in character, involving in particular the desire to render community service.

However the high levels of dissatisfaction and disappointment with the job that he found suggest that this idealism does not survive the experience of police work. These were slightly higher among those with under five years' service than among those with longer periods in the force (Harris, 1988) though much of this dissatisfaction may be due to the kind of work younger gardaí ended up doing – protection post duty, for instance – rather than dissatisfaction with police work *per se*. In much the same way many studies have found that there is, among the lower ranks in particular, considerable antipathy to the more service elements of their work. These duties are perceived to be boring and to prevent them doing 'real' police work (see, for example, Manning, 1977).

The other important consequence of a police sub-culture is the way it produces a strong sense of solidarity between officers. This has positive benefits in that it creates a willingness to go immediately to the assistance of an officer in danger. Police officers, according to Bittner (1981: 63), say that one of the most important aspects of their job is the 'spirit of "one for all and all for one"'. The negative aspect is that unquestioning loyalty can create an unwillingness to take complaints against fellow officers seriously or to testify as witnesses in cases where the malpractices of other officers are involved. This makes it particularly difficult to successfully prosecute complaints against the police.

Police Discretion

Research suggests that police officers exercise considerable discretion in their work, particularly where decisions to use the law are concerned. A number of aspects of their work facilitates this. One is that they seldom witness directly many of the events they are called on to respond to. They have to rely on witnesses who in circumstances either of shock or self-interest may not be perceived to be reliable. There is also what

ciologists refer to as 'a hierarchy of credibility' in society,
eaning that some people's accounts, those of middle-class,
older men perhaps, are believed to be more reliable than those
of others such as working-class people, travellers and women.
In these circumstances police use their discretion to decide
whether an incident would benefit from police intervention
and what form such intervention should take.

The other aspect of police work that facilitates discretion
is the difficulties in the direct supervision of their work.
Much of what the police do is 'invisible' to their supervising
or superior officers. They can make 'on-the-spot' decisions
about the use of the law which are not subject to oversight
by their superiors and may reflect their self-interest or their
social prejudices as much as the needs and demands of good
policing. In addition the Irish police have a range of discre-
tionary powers that do not have an equivalent in the police
forces of the United States (on whom much of the research
on police discretion is based). As Rottman (1984: 64) points
out, this level of discretion is 'inherent in deciding whether
to seek a court prosecution in the first instance and the
ability to determine the manner of prosecution in the lower
court'. Its effect is that around 50 per cent of people arrested
by the gardaí end up not being prosecuted (for a dissenting
account, see *Garda Review*, March, 1985: p5).

It has been argued that such discretion is a necessary part
of police work. Literal enforcement of the law would lead to
massive work-loads in the courts, considerable public hostility, as, for example, with the intense enforcement of parking
regulations and, in many cases, inappropriate responses to
incidents. The intelligent use of discretion can diffuse and
disarm situations that could be threatening. The problem is
that while discretion may be necessary, it can lead to abuses.

Corruption is one such abuse. Though there have been a
number of cases in Ireland in which individual police officers
have abused their powers for personal profit, there are no
examples of the systematic and often deep-rooted and highly

organised levels of corruption that have been documented, for example, in the West Midlands police force in England, in the Metropolitan Police in London, and the New York police, whose members were major drug suppliers in the city (Punch, 1985).

Differential policing is another abuse. Groups that may be particularly vulnerable include social minorities such as travellers and young working-class people where the reactions taken by the police may be as much a reflection of the officers' attitudes to the different groups as it is of the objective danger that they pose. This is an area of policing in Ireland that would benefit from research as it may be an important factor in explaining what the Association of Garda Sergeants and Inspectors (AGSI) (1982: 7) have referred to as, 'a tendency for sections of the public to become alienated from the police'. This trend, they claim, is evident in larger urban areas and particularly in some working- and lower middle-class areas of Dublin in which the gardaí feel they are less than welcome.

The Level of Confidence in the Gardaí: What the Research Shows

Arguments about the level of confidence in the gardaí and whether it is in decline or not are difficult to evaluate. The results of the Irish part of the 1990 European Values Survey suggest that it is very high. Eighty-five per cent of a national sample said that they had confidence in the gardaí (Hardiman and Whelan, 1994: 103). This is higher than the proportions who had confidence in the civil service, the Dáil or the press. However the levels of confidence vary by age and occupation. They are higher the older the person and the higher the occupational status. Unemployed people are 'substantially less likely to have confidence in the police' (Hardiman and Whelan, 1994: 129).

Confirmation of these results and a more nuanced view of attitudes to the police can be found in Bohan and Yorke's

1987) study of the perceptions of the police held by a sample of the population of the Dublin city borough. They found high levels of satisfaction with the gardaí but when they asked more specific questions the levels of confidence were not so impressive. Almost 57 per cent of respondents agreed with the statement that 'the Garda Síochána sometimes exceed their powers by abusing suspects physically or mentally'. Forty per cent felt that 'in court, some gardaí would rather cover up the facts than lose face', 44 per cent felt the police had enough power and 50 per cent agreed that 'the gardaí are never around when you need them'.

But what comes across strongly is the less favourable attitudes of what Bohan and Yorke (1987) call 'the lower social categories' and young people. 'The lowest social categories expressed the greatest reluctance', they tell us (Bohan and Yorke, 1987: 81) to contact the police 'if they knew someone was selling stolen property'. They are also less satisfied with the police and were more likely to perceive them as 'unfair and inefficient'. Where young people are concerned those who had a high level of contact with the police tended to be least satisfied.

In general terms, these findings are fairly typical of the responses in many countries to the police force. The first British Crime Survey (Hough and Mayhew, 1983: 29), for example, found that attitudes of the young and unemployed people to the police were significantly different from those of the population as a whole. What is significant about the Irish results is that they support the perceptions of the AGSI of a change in the relationship between people and police. They suggest that the legitimacy of policing in Ireland can no longer be assumed. It is something that has to be worked for.

Responding to Rising Crime: The Effectiveness of the Gardaí

In the early 1980s the legitimacy and recognition that the gardaí had established in a gradual fashion since independence began to come under pressure. Criticisms centered on a number of issues including allegations of the extraction of false confessions in a number of celebrated cases, including the Kerry Babies and the Christy Lynch cases, from 1970 to 1983 (Kerrigan, 1984a, 1984b). Both involved people 'confessing' to crimes they could not have committed. However the main focus of criticism has been on the failure of the gardaí to deal with rising crime.

The police have responded in two ways to rising crime rates. The first has been the appeal to what Baldwin and Kinsey (1982: 52) called 'the holy trinity of policy, more men, more powers, better equipment'. The second has been to suggest that new forms of policing based on a different relationship with the public are needed. We will deal with the first part of their response here and ask if implemented will it be successful? The second response will be dealt with in the next section.

The call for more personnel has been the most popular proposal for reducing crime in Ireland. Successive governments have responded to it. For a start they have recruited more gardaí. The size of the force increased from 6,612 in 1971 to a peak size of 11,396 in 1985. Its 1994 level (at 1 January) was 10,900. Governments have also sought a more effective deployment of existing numbers. Moves to achieve this include the closing of rural police stations and it has been suggested that this be extended to urban areas where the closure of police stations that are under-utilised at night would release extra numbers to patrol the streets during the day (Culligan, 1994). The move to 'civilianise' a range of administrative tasks, particularly clerical duties, is another way to increase efficiency. This process began in the gardaí in 1970 and the number of civilian staff in 1993 was 680 with the intention to increase that to 730 in 1994 (*Annual Report of An Garda Síochána*, 1993: 6). With commendable honesty the garda commissioner says that while the effect of civilianisation is to free more gardaí for operational duties, the 'reasons for this development are largely economic'.

Despite these increases, the level of policing in Ireland remains a matter of some controversy. International comparisons of police strength are difficult to make, particularly as the precise size of police forces in other countries can be hard to establish. Many have substantial reserve forces that they can call on at times of peak demand whereas the gardaí do not have such a facility. The comparisons that have been made suggest that the level of policing in Ireland is high. There is one police officer for every 640 people in New Zealand, a country with a similarly sized population (Mc Cullagh, 1986c). Denmark has one for every 500 people; England and Wales one for every 390 and Scotland has one for every 360 people (O'Mahony, 1993: 69). All of these have higher crime rates than Ireland yet we have one police officer for every 325 people (for a dissenting view, see Kenny, *The Irish Times*, 23 August, 1994).

The effects of the size of the police force, and of the increases in it, on the level of crime is also a matter of considerable controversy. Effectiveness in preventing and detecting crime may not be the only terms in which the importance of police numbers should be assessed but there is no compelling evidence that increasing the size of the police force has any dramatic influence on crime levels (Rottman, 1984). The Irish figures support this. In 1961 there were the 6,612 gardaí, just under 15,000 indictable offences and a detection rate of 60 per cent. By 1994 the size of the police force had risen to 10,900, the numbers of indictable crimes had risen to 99,000 and the detection rate was 36 per cent.

Numerous studies in the United States and elsewhere have shown that increasing the size of the police force does not necessarily have the anticipated pay-off in terms of reduced crime, more arrests or more convictions (see Mc Cullagh, 1983 for a review). This is partly because some of the extra numbers are absorbed into the 'public service' or 'support' role of the police which, as we have seen, consumes considerable portions of police time. This is partly because changes in the demands made on the police through, for example, concern about terrorism, also absorb extra personnel. However the main reason seems to be that while, initially, increases in the visible police presence on the streets lead to reductions in 'street' crimes such as car-theft and robbery, over the longer term criminals adapt to the new situation and their old pattern of activities resumes.

This has led to the argument that police efficiency may not be a question of numbers, but of how the police are deployed on the streets and what they do there. It has been suggested that as the traditional forms of policing such as preventative patrolling are not particularly productive, in terms of crime detection, they should be dispensed with and replaced with more innovative patrolling strategies. These include 'focused' or 'targeted policing' which involves the police selecting particular kinds of crime and the targeting of policing resources at their control and detection. Here again however the evaluations of these alternatives suggest that while they may have some impact on the levels of certain crimes they do not alter overall crime levels (see Mc Cullagh, 1983).

In Ireland, focused police work has taken the form of specialist units aimed at particular criminals or at particular crimes such as drug-related ones, armed crime or shoplifting. The history of specialist units within the gardaí has been an uneasy and unclear one with squads being set up and disbanded in what often appears to be an *ad hoc* fashion. Their level of success has never been assessed. We do not know if these kinds of activities suppress the types of crime they are aimed at or if they simply lead to temporary reductions in the crime or else to the displacement of criminal activity on to other less heavily policed crime. As armed criminals are less bureaucratic in their forms of organisation, they may be able to move their areas of criminal specialisation with greater ease than the gardaí can.

Overall the research suggests that increasing the number of police officers or changing the ways they are deployed does not have a significant effect on the level of crime. As Reiner (1992: 155) puts it 'neither more of the same (nor marginally different) tactics are likely to improve their capacity for detection or prevention to any substantial degree'. Moreover the financial costs of this very limited success may be extensive. It has been estimated that a 10 per cent increase in personnel in the British police force would only raise the detection rate by less than 1 per cent and there is no guarantee that these increases will be in the more serious crimes.

However there is one important qualification to this general pessimism. Increasing the size of a police force and the level of resources available to it may have only a negligible effect on levels of crime but it may improve the skill and the proficiency with which it provides other services, such as helping victims and resolving disputes. Moreover while many kinds of patrolling activities have limited effects on crime, they do have other effects. A number of studies have found that increasing the number of police officers on the street can reduce the fear of crime (Reiner, 1992: 149). This is of course an important benefit in that it can improve the quality of the life of those who experience it. It can also be important for the way in which it allows the police to retain the confidence of the public. The problem is that the increase in manpower required to increase the level of foot patrols in most urban areas may be significant.

The demand for increased levels of technology is also one that has been, and continues to be, responded to. Two areas are of particular importance. One is the installation of a modern communication system, the Command and Control System, in the Dublin metropolitan area at a cost of £2 million. The other is the increased level of spending on information technology. Both have their uses as management tools as they can be used to assess individual and organisational performance and they are part of a wider scheme of professionalising the gardaí (see Carty, 1991). They are also intended to contribute to increasing the efficiency with which the gardaí deal with crime. At that level their impact is a matter of some dispute.

The Command and Control System, through which all calls are automatically logged onto a central computer and sent from there to the relevant officers, is intended to reduce their response times. When the technology works (see the debate about this in *Garda Review*, vol. 20, no.5, 1992) it is undoubtedly successful in doing this. What is more open to question is whether this has any effect on the detection rate. Research such as the 'Kansas City Response Time Analysis' (see Morris and Heal, 1981) suggests not. This found that while technology increased the speed at which the police could respond to crimes – their response time was on average three and a half minutes – this was effectively neutralised by the delay of victims and of witnesses in reporting crimes. By the time the victim reported the offence the chances of apprehending the offender at the scene had gone. This is not to suggest that rapid response is not to be valued. It obviously makes a difference to some crimes. It may also be taken by the public as an indication of the level of police concern for them and through that it may have an effect on their level of fear and anxiety about crime. It is just that it does not do a lot for the detection rate.

The benefits of information technology are similarly open to debate. There are a number of crime-related areas where information technology has been shown to be important in police work but it also raises certain concerns about civil liberties. Harper (1991) found that the installation of a computerised crime-reporting system, as has been proposed in Ireland, was useful to English detectives in their investigations of crime. It gave them quick access to a wide range of information on particular crimes such as the use of similar *modus operandi*. This meant the police could quickly narrow the field of suspects for particular crimes, be more extensively briefed before they interviewed any of them and be better able to negotiate with them as they had particular advantages in the 'bluffing about information', which is a central feature of police interrogation.

The negative aspect of information technology is the kinds of civil liberties issues that are raised by the existence of national information systems that record more than just information about crimes. It was estimated in 1980 that police computers in Britain had low-level intelligence information on 10 per cent to 15 per cent of the population (Baldwin and Kinsey, 1982). When this is combined with police information on vehicle owners it gives them access to information on over half the population. The difficulty is that the relevant data protection legislation in Britain allows a citizen to check the accuracy of computer records but information collected for crime prevention purposes is specifically excluded. This means that people who have no criminal records are unable to find out if there is information about them on police records.

In Ireland the Dublin Criminal Record kept by the gardaí is a computerised record of all the convictions of anyone who has been found guilty by the courts here (O'Mahony, 1993: 119). The *Gardaí's Corporate Strategy Plan* (1993: 15) says that information technology will be the means by which 'information which is essential for the prevention and detection of crime can be collected and correlated'. However it is not clear if this will include information on people suspected of criminal activities and on people who are found not guilty by the courts. It may also be difficult to find out what this information is. The Data Protection Act 1988 allows citizens to establish if personal information is kept on them by state agencies but it does not confer an automatic right of access to the information. This is because there is an exemption for information that is kept either for law-enforcement purposes or which is necessary to safeguard the security of the state. There also does not appear to be any statutory control over how long the gardaí can keep information on their files. This may be reasonable or at least arguable in the case of convicted criminals, but it is less so in the case of people who have at one point come under police suspicion. As a society we may be willing to subscribe to the notion that 'once a criminal always a criminal' but do we feel the same way about 'once a suspect always a suspect'?

The demand for increased police powers has been a constant feature of the garda response to criticisms of their level of effectiveness. Like other police forces, the gardaí perceive many aspects of the legal system to be obstacles to their ability to catch criminals. These demands focus currently on two specific rights: the right to silence and the right to bail. Bail cannot be refused to defendants in the Irish courts on the grounds that they will commit further offences while awaiting trial. Yet it has been argued that offences committed on bail make an important contribution to annual crime figures (see Mc Cullagh, 1990, for a review of this debate). Similarly, the right to remain silent under police questioning is seen as a significant obstacle to the ability to deal with major criminals.

These issues were addressed in the Criminal Justice Act 1984. Sentences for offences committed while on bail are now consecutive to the sentence passed for a previous offence or offences. People are also required to provide particular kinds of information to the gardaí and the courts are allowed to draw inferences from the failure to provide this information. However these changes have not dampened the enthusiasm for changing bail law or for the total abolition of the right to silence (see, for example, Culligan, 1994).

It is possible to question what the effects of such legal changes would be. Research in other countries suggests, for example, that few suspects use their right to silence (see Mc Cullagh, 1984). Removing the right may encourage them to talk but if they have the will-power to remain silent in the first place then the only talk it might generate is denial and what kind of inferences could the courts draw from that? In the absence of other evidence against them this would have to be accepted. In the presence of other convincing evidence their silence would be irrelevant. There are similar problems with bail law. Since the Bail Act of 1976 in England and Wales, bail can be refused if there is a risk that a suspect will commit offences while awaiting trial. Yet recent research suggests that offences committed on bail remain a significant problem with around 10 per cent of those given bail committing further offences before trial (Henderson and Nichols, 1992).

Thus, the first response of the gardaí to the rising crime rate has been the traditional one of more personnel, more legal power and more technological power. The research we have considered above suggests that these kinds of changes are limited in their capacity to produce radical alterations in the level of crime or in its detection.

II An Alliance of People and Police

The second response to the rising crime rate was potentially more fundamental. It came from the Association of Garda Sergeants and Inspectors who acknowledged in 1982 that there was something radically wrong with the traditional model of policing (AGSI, 1982). The AGSI argued that gardaí faced two major problems: rising crime and the strained relationships they had with sections of the population, mostly notably with those in a number of working-class and lower middle-class areas. The solution to both was the involvement of the community in crime prevention, an involvement that could be achieved through a system of community policing.

The system the AGSI suggested had three levels to it. The first was a return to beat patrolling. It was argued that police officers should be assigned to specific beats in local communities. This would enable them to get involved in that community through visits to schools, shops and houses while at the same time doing the 'normal' police work of issuing summons and making arrests. The second level was organising crime prevention committees in local communities. These committees would include people who worked in the local area such as local government officials, social workers, doctors, priests as well as residents. They would identify community needs and the kinds of problem-areas that breed crime and do something about them. The gardaí would play a central role in co-ordinating their activities. The third level was organisational. The community relations office in the garda headquarters needed to be extended to provide the back-up services that the community-based crime prevention committees would need.

These proposals represented the most explicit and liberal statement made by members of the gardaí on how to deal with the crime problem. Their analysis did not appear to be shared by senior police officers. What we got instead was a system that involved neighbourhood policing, Community Alert and, most importantly of all, Neighbourhood Watch. These differ in a number of significant ways from community policing, most notably in how the community and the neighbourhood are to be involved. In community policing these are groups that are to be consulted with. In Neighbourhood Watch they are involved mainly in receiving and acting on police advice, putting stickers on doors and locks on windows, and reporting suspicious activities to the police. Thus, while the gardaí may be prepared to allow the public to be their eyes and ears, they are not prepared to allow them to be the brain.

If growth is the only measure of success then Neighbourhood Watch has been successful. In 1986 there were 322 schemes involving just under 93,000 households, most of which were in Dublin. By 1993 this had risen to 1,709 schemes involving over 300,000 households in the country, most of which again were in the greater Dublin area. The number of Community Alert schemes in rural Ireland has also grown from 175 schemes in 1985 to 528 in 1993. However their impact on crime is a matter of controversy. The gardaí believe that these have been very successful and are an important factor in reducing crime but this view is not based on any systematic research or published evaluation.[3]

There are legitimate doubts about these schemes. The degree of involvement of the public in many cases may be little more than putting a sticker on a house or on a car. We know nothing about how long the schemes last. If fear of crime is a factor in getting them going, then the decline in such fear may reduce the commitment to them. There are also questions about the degree of involvement of the gardaí. They may be little more than sticker distributors. The association between the schemes and falling crime is also in need of systematic evaluation. In 1986 when there were 322 Neighbourhood Watch schemes, the number of recorded burglaries from dwellings stood at 29,000. By 1994 the number of schemes had grown to 1,709 but the number of burglaries had not declined. Just over 32,000 were recorded in 1994.[4] The number of burglaries that may have been prevented remains, of course, unknown.

Where such schemes have been evaluated, the results are depressing. There have been four large-scale and carefully designed studies of Neighbourhood Watch, three in the American cities of Seattle, Minneapolis and Chicago where four schemes were evaluated and one in London where two schemes were evaluated. Two of the schemes recorded small decreases in crime but the remainder recorded either no change or marginal increases in the amount of crime. Similar results were found with regard to the fear of crime. With one exception the level of fear was either unchanged or else increased in the areas with the schemes in place. The researchers were also unable to find many changes in the reporting of crime, in the levels of home protection or in the level of surveillance engaged in by residents in the schemes. 'One of the basic conclusions', Rosenbaum (1988: 363) argues, is that Neighbourhood Watch-style schemes have 'been oversold as a stand-alone strategy in the war against crime'.

In this section we have considered the attempts made to change the basis of policing in Ireland to include a greater role for the public. As the new schemes have evolved they have been very firmly under the control and direction of the gardaí. No new systems of control by or accountability to local communities have developed. Many claims have been made for the success of these schemes but they are not based on any kind of systematic evaluation. However, as will be argued, the significance of these schemes may not be in their ability to reduce or to prevent crime. They are also important in the way in which they make it possible for the police to share the responsibility for rising crime with the public without conceding to them their monopoly over crime control in society.

III Self-Policing

The third way in which the policing function can be performed is by local groups and communities acting alone. This kind of self-policing takes two forms. The first is vigilantes or forms of citizen patrol. This tends to be a localised and short-lived response to particular situations. It often springs up, for example, in housing estates in response to increases in vandalism or car theft. Residents – usually the men – take on the patrolling and surveillance of the estates, especially at night. But as the immediate situation dissolves the groups break up as the need which brought them together is gone. They are also difficult to sustain because much of the surveillance involves people watching their property in the early hours of the morning. This is not always the ideal preparation for the next day's work. Efforts to capitalise on the motivation that underpins such groups have not been successful. In 1984 an organisation calling itself 'People Against Crime' claimed it could mobilise 200,000 people to patrol local areas as an auxiliary to the police (McAleese, 1987). However it never materialised.

The more organised form of community self-policing is represented by the Concerned Parents Against Drugs (CPAD). The group emerged as a response to the drug problem and to the perceived failure of the gardaí and statutory authorities to respond adequately to it. Prior to the late 1970s the problem had primarily been one of marijuana use and it had been mainly confined to middle-class students who thought of themselves as part of a counter-culture. However when the amount of heroin increased in Europe, Ireland and in particular the city of Dublin was no more resistant than elsewhere to its enticements (see Flynn and Yeates, 1985). But this time the population of abusers was different.

The communities in which drug-dealing and drug-taking were concentrated were mainly the poorer, working-class ones in which there was already a high concentration of social problems such as unemployment. According to local residents, the official response was slow and many of them argued that as long as the problem was confined to these areas the response continued to be lethargic. The gardaí, for their part, reject such suggestions. They point, for example, to the restrictive and dated legislation with which they were operating. When this was changed through the Misuse of Drugs Act 1977, and the Criminal Justice Act 1985, the pursuit of drug-dealers became a police priority. By then however the gardaí were almost irrelevant. The CPAD had become the main weapon used by communities to combat their drug problem.

By that time, the CPAD had developed an organisational life of its own (this account is drawn from Bennett, 1988). The basic structure was simple. Groups organised in areas in response to local perceptions of the problem and in imitation of other groups. They were mainly made up of parents who met regularly, monitored the use of drugs in their areas, identified addicts, and more importantly drug-pushers, and took action against them. They also sent delegates to a central committee which co-ordinated information and support for the city as a whole.

The methods used to identify drug-users and drug-pushers were the classic policing ones of surveillance and a strong flow of information from the public. The CPAD kept watch on particular spots where syringes had been found, observed groups of addicts gathering in particular locations at regular and predictable times, a sure indication that drugs sales were about to the made, and followed suspected pushers and couriers across the city to find out who they came in contact with and who they were buying from. They also relied on information from parents, who were worried that their children were behaving in ways which indicated drug-use, and from taxi-drivers, who were concerned that some of the passengers they were carrying were involved in drug-dealing.

The holding of a particular style of public meetings was one of the most striking features of the work of the CPAD. The residents of the community were invited to them and, in the initial stages in particular, attendances were high. The accumulated evidence of the organisation's surveillance and information-gathering was presented. Drug-pushers in the area were publicly named and given an opportunity to defend themselves. The evidence against them had to be of a high standard and they were offered the opportunity to stop their activities or to leave the area. If this did not work, sanctions were imposed on them. Local groups carried out a number of evictions of people whom they believed to be drug-dealers.

The level of success of the CPAD in combating the drugs problem is difficult to assess. Bennett (1988) claims it has been significant. In the early stages of the movement it appeared to have achieved some restraint on the supply and sale of heroin. It is, for example, no longer sold openly in O'Connell Street in Dublin. This may simply have meant it had been displaced to areas where the CPAD did not operate. The decrease in supply may also have been related to the AIDS problem which in Ireland is mainly located in the population of illegal drug-abusers where the use of dirty needles has facilitated the spread of the HIV virus. It could also be argued that the most significant effect of the CPAD is the way in which their activities and the attendant publicity spurred the gardaí into taking action themselves which resulted in the successful prosecution of many of the major drug-dealers in Dublin. They are now serving long prison sentences.

Either way the success of the CPAD was short-lived. The amount of heroin available on the street is rising again and the level of abuse in Dublin is again becoming a source of concern. This time around, however, the CPAD does not appear to be capable of functioning as an effective form of policing against it. It has, according to Barry Cullen (1989: 271), 'lost credibility and relevance as a community action movement'. Its membership base has eroded, its democratic ethos appears to have dissipated considerably in that many of its actions were seen as having 'questionable intent' and it is now 'perceived by many who are most vulnerable as an organisation to be feared.'

Cullen argues that two kinds of forces undermined the CPAD. The external forces included the level of institutional opposition to it, a reflection of the inability of many state institutions to deal with local working-class organisations. Some of this opposition was justified by the belief, expressed by the then Minister for Health, Barry Desmond, that they were a front for Sinn Féin; others alleged there was Provisional IRA involvement. Whatever about the truth or falsity of these allegations the effect was to damage the public image of the CPAD and it discouraged many community groups from being publicly associated with them. This was not helped by a central committee decision to adopt a policy of non-co-operation with the gardaí, a policy which, according to Cullen (1989: 287), did not reflect the practices of local groups. The internal force that undermined the CPAD, it is claimed, was the actions of some of its membership. Also, the new centralised structure led to a certain loss of independence for local groups and created a situation in which actions were taken in the name of the organisation that did not appear to have the full support of local groups. These ranged from alleged kidnapping to attempts to evict drug-users from local communities.

As a result, the CPAD, at least in its centralised form, appears to be largely a spent force yet its fate encapsulates many of the problems of self-policing. Their origins are in the perceived failure of the police to adequately maintain order in communities. Yet self-policing groups have a better chance of surviving when they have the support of the police, a support which tends to be conditional on a significant element of police control (see Einstadter, 1984). Their survival depends on their willingness to become an ancillary to the police rather than an independent force. They also depend on levels of local support that are difficult to maintain. Once the problems they were designed to deal with either recede or move elsewhere the level of local involvement tends to decline. This leaves them open to being taken over by small sections of the community and used in ways that do not reflect the wishes of the wider community. If they lose their representative base in the community then they also forfeit the basis of their legitimacy, which is that they are under the control of and accountable to the communities they police.

IV Private Policing

The increasing resort to self-policing has been the most publicised development in the policing of Irish society. It has not, however, been the most significant one. The growth in private policing and in policing by private security firms has been more notable and more extensive. It is a form of policing about which there appears to be less concern. There is certainly less research available on it and yet its growth raises important issues about equality and access in Irish society.

This growth is linked to a series of changes in the organisation of space in modern urban areas, characterised by Shearing and Stenning (1983: 496), as the growth of 'mass private property'. This refers to the way in which public life increasingly takes place on property, such as large shopping complexes and stadiums, which is privately owned. As these places are not normally policed by the 'public police', private security firms have been delegated the function of maintaining order in them. This process has been characterised by Shearing and Stenning (1983: 503) as 'a "new feudalism": huge tracts of property and associated public spaces are controlled – and policed – by private corporations'.

Though this argument is difficult to transfer to the Irish context, there is sufficient impressionistic evidence to suggest that it may have a certain validity. Private security is pervasive in the work-place, in shops and supermarkets, at sporting events and at pubs, discos and dance halls. There is general agreement that the number of private security firms has increased but precise figures are difficult to come by. There were over six hundred security firms in Ireland in 1991 (*The Irish Times*, 4 May, 1991). However as there is no system of obligatory regulation for such firms and as the industry's representative body – the Irish Security Industry Association – has a membership of only fifty-three firms, more precise information about the size of the industry is not available. We do know, however, that the number of security workers – defined as caretakers and watchmen – has exceeded the number of gardaí since 1981 and now stands at almost three thousand more than the national garda strength (Corcoran, Sexton and O'Donoghue, 1992).

The current prominence of private policing has come about largely without much public awareness and without much public debate. This is partly because the powers used by the industry have seldom become a matter of controversy. In the case of shopping centres, for example, these powers derive from the rights of the owners to restrict access to their property. The sanctions available to them are mainly the right to deny access to the property and to the resources which such access provides. How and against whom they use these sanctions is therefore a matter which clearly requires study. If, as Spitzer and Scull argue (1977: 26), private police have 'the privilege but not the obligation' to use their power, it is important to know how they exercise this privilege. Does it, for example, vary with the social class or the age of the people they come into contact with?

Again, the evidence is impressionistic but there may not be equality of access to locations like shopping centres which increasingly have replaced the street and the street corner as places of congregation and of socialising for young people. It often seems from the numbers congregating outside them and from the routine harassment inside them that being a teenager is a legitimate reason to be denied access to the facilities. Travellers may not be any more successful in gaining access either. As a result much of what was formerly public space may increasingly become the domain of the middle aged and the middle class.

In this way the growth of private security poses particular problems for certain sections of the population. Its growth also poses issues for sociology of the police. Traditional explanations of the growth of policing have emphasised the centralisation of the public protection function in the hands of the state. This, it was argued, has been a part of the development of the modern state. However, the growth of private security firms raises a series of questions about the degree of state control over private interests. It suggests that we need to investigate the degree to which the state is conceding control over the policing function, not to local communities and local areas, but to unaccountable private interest groups. It also raises the question of why the delegation of policing to such interests is not a matter of controversy and contention while the desire of local people to police their own areas is.

Conclusion

In this chapter we have considered the various forms that policing takes in Irish society. The conclusion is that we are likely to see a continuation of the dominance of policing by the gardaí and by private security firms. Policing by citizen groups will come and go in response to particular local needs but it is unlikely to become a significant challenge to the others forms of policing. This is partly due to the difficulties in organising and sustaining the level of community commitment and involvement that is necessary for organised policing. It is also due to the hostility of the gardaí and of state institutions generally to organisations that they do not have effective influence or control over.

The continued dominance of traditional forms of policing will not necessarily be accompanied by reduced levels of crime or increased levels of detection. The range of policing proposals discussed here may have an impact on particular criminals but they will not have a major impact on overall crime or detection levels. What we can expect as crime rates rise and detection rates stabilise or fall is an increase in the calls to remove legal constraints on the gardaí and changes in the way in which the gardaí publicly present the issue of crime and particularly the allocation of responsibility for its control and reduction. The garda commissioner (*The Irish Times*, 19 September, 1994) has asked yet again for increased legal powers and has suggested that the maintenance of law and order is not just a police function but a community responsibility.

However while the gardaí will continue to be the dominant form of policing in Irish society, an issue that may become more prominent in time is the degree to which, given the cost of policing, they can remain structurally and organisationally unchanged. As with other police forces, such as those in England and Wales, they may come under political pressure to streamline their own structures. The model of two-tier policing being proposed there (see, for example, Brogden, 1994) may become a feature of the Irish debate.

This model takes its point of departure from the observation that there are in effect two different crime problems, a large one of relatively minor crime and a small one of serious professional crime, and from the observation that the bulk of police work is of a service rather than a crime-fighting nature. Two-tier policing structures build on these. The first structure is one of a well-paid but relatively small élite of police officers trained in the detection and prosecution of complex serious crimes such as murder, drug importation and those of a white-collar or corporate nature. The second tier is one of a constellation of local police services organised and accountable through local government structures. These would perform the service type functions that occupy so much police time and would also deal with the large volume of petty, opportunistic crime where local knowledge can be the key to detection and local support can be the means through which offenders can be dealt with in a non-stigmatising manner.

These forces would require different forms of training and, given the differences in the complexity of the work they would be doing, different levels of remuneration. Those of the local forces would be lower and this would enable the provision, for example, of more police on the beat without significant and unsustainable increases in the costs of such policing. The difficulties involved in moving to such structures in Ireland are obviously enormous given the strong power and likely resistance of garda representative bodies and the weak structure of local government. But they are not insurmountable given that many aspects of two-tier policing may already be present in embryonic form in the current structures of the gardaí. However what this kind of discussion points more clearly to is the need to move the debate about the future of policing beyond its current limited focus on the issue of police powers.

Notes

1. Harris (1988) classifies calls for help with family disputes as service calls. This procedure has been criticised by Kinsey, Lea and Young (1986). They argue that such calls may be treated by the police as service calls but they generally involve the crime of assault and so should be classified as law-enforcement matters. However as the number of such calls in this study was small their classification does not have a significant bearing on the overall results.
2. See the account of the fate of idealism in the New York police (*New York Times*, 21 November, 1988)
3. Neighbourhood Watch was evaluated by researchers in the Department of Sociology in St Patrick's College, Maynooth but the results have not been published.
4. These figures are taken from the annual reports on crime for the relevant years.

7 PUNISHING CRIMINALS – IRISH STYLE

Introduction

If the policing system is the first line of defence against criminals then the second is the means through which criminals are punished. In this chapter we discuss the operations of the courts and the system of punishment with particular emphasis on the use of prison. We begin with a consideration of the path to punishment. This starts with an arrest so we first discuss what happens to those who are arrested by the gardaí. We then look at what happens to them in court and at the extent to which court cases for criminal offences end in conviction. Finally we look at the range of sanctions that the courts impose on those whom they find guilty. Having considered all of these we move on in section two to look at prison. As in all the areas we have considered in this book, our understanding will be limited by significant shortcomings in the quality of the published data.

I The Path to Punishment

Stage One – Being Arrested

The first step on the road to punishment is arrest. In general the legal requirements for arrest are that the gardaí either

witness a person committing the offence or they have reasonable suspicion that the person committed the offence, though
the Offences Against the State Act 1939, provides somewhat
more relaxed conditions for an arrest for specific named
offences. More recently the Criminal Justice Act 1984,
extended the power of arrest to include the right to arrest
and detain for questioning for serious offences, including
those not covered by the 1939 Act. On this basis one might
assume that in most circumstances a high proportion of
individuals who are arrested by the gardaí would later be
charged with a criminal offence. This however does not
appear to be the case.

David Rottman (1984) analysed the fate of those who were
arrested by the gardaí in the Dublin metropolitan area in 1981.
Only half of those arrested went on to be prosecuted in court.
This suggests that there is significant diversion out of the
system prior to court. One possibility is that they were diverted into the Juvenile Liaison Officer Scheme (JLOS). Under the
terms of this scheme juveniles can be dealt with informally by
the gardaí. They are cautioned by a superintendent and required to remain in regular contact with the Juvenile Liaison
Service (JLS). The relevant conditions for inclusion in the
scheme include admission to the offence, the agreement to co-
operate with the relevant juvenile liaison officer, and the agreement and consent of both parents and the victim. The scheme
was originally confined to first-time offenders but it was
extended in 1991 to include second- and third-time offenders.
However diversion to the JLOS does not account for the full
fall-out from arrest to prosecution. In 1981 around 10,000
people were arrested and not subsequently prosecuted, whereas only 1,488 juveniles were admitted to the JLOS.

Rottman's research was completed before the passing of the
Criminal Justice Act 1985, so it means that legally the people
his research was based on could not have been detained for
questioning. If they were not detained for questioning or to be
charged then what were they arrested for? Is the power to

arrest being used, for example, as a power to harass? Are people being arrested for whom there is insufficient evidence to charge? These concerns must remain at the level of speculation. We know little about the process of moving from arrest to charge and about the reasons why such large numbers of people are diverted out of the prosecution stage. In particular, as the National Economic and Social Council (1984) pointed out, 'very little is known about the criteria used in deciding whether to prosecute or not'.

Stage Two – Being Convicted: Slow but Sure?

Table 7.1 shows the proceedings against people for indictable offences in both the district and the jury courts for a number of years from 1961 to 1991. It excludes the bulk of the work of the courts, which is concerned with non-indictable offences and in particular road traffic offences. The district courts deal, for example, with about fourteen non-indictable offences for every indictable one. Almost 70 per cent of their work is dealing with traffic offences and two-thirds of these are parking offences (Rottman, 1984). However it is not particularly useful to deal with the information on non-indictable offences because, as we have seen in chapter one, the category is a very broad one. It ranges from assault to having no light on your bicycle and the published court statistics do not distinguish between these very different offences. So for our purposes here we confine our attention to indictable offences.

A number of points can be made from Table 7.1. The figures indicate substantial increases in the case-loads of the courts and associated with this a rise in the backlog of cases. Overall there has been a 176 per cent increase in the number of proceedings started in the courts, though this increase is considerably smaller than the corresponding increase in crime. The increase has been most pronounced in the district court where proceedings rose from 9,202 in 1961 to 25,944 in 1991.

Table 7.1 Indictable offences: proceedings against the person, 1961–1991

	1961	1971	1981	1991
A: District Court	7,662	13,432	10,331	6,702
Convicted/order proved	487	1,061	658	508
Adjourned/other	216	315	259	114
Pending	837	2,574	17,587	18,620
Total	9,202	17,282	28,835	25,944
B: Jury Courts				
Convicted/order proved	249	672	845	536
Acquitted/withdrawn	102	131	66	52
Adjourned/other	2	14	26	8
Pending	221	540	381	532
Total	574	1,357	1,318	1,128
C: Totals (A+B)				
Convicted	7,911	14,104	11,176	7,238
Acquitted	589	1,192	724	560
Adjourned/other	218	329	285	122
Pending	1,058	3,114	17,969	19,152
Total:	9,776	18,739	30,153	27,072

Source: *Statistical Abstracts of Ireland*, various years. Excludes those for which information was refused.

By contrast, while the case-load of the jury courts rose from 574 in 1961 to 1,357 in 1971, it fell back to 1,128 in 1991.

The backlog of cases has also increased, measured that is by the number of cases begun in one year and still pending at the end of it. In 1961 11 per cent of cases fell into the pending category; in 1991 71 per cent did. The backlog is most significant in the district courts where 72 per cent of cases in 1991 were still pending at the end of the year. The reasons for the backlog are not clear. It may be due to an increase in the complexity of the cases that are being dealt with or to the failure to increase the number of court personnel in line with the increase in court business. The size of the backlog suggests that justice is not particularly swift and indeed that it is getting slower. The figures for convictions however suggest that it is sure. The conviction rate in the courts is very high and has remained so over the years. In 1961, 91 per cent of all proceedings in which a decision was made ended in a conviction. In 1991 the corresponding figure was 92 per cent. The conviction rate in jury courts has always been slightly lower than for the district courts but it has grown from 72 per cent in 1961 to 92 per cent in 1991.[1]

These figures do not give us much insight into the reasons for the high conviction rate. It is possible that it is a product of the way the statistics are collected. The cases that are dealt with in any year may be the ones in which the evidence is clear, unambiguous and not contested by the accused. By contrast those cases that are more difficult may be more likely to be deferred by the courts and hence show up in the statistics as 'pending'. The results of these cases are not included in the statistics for the following year as the annual statistics show only figures for cases which commenced in the particular year. A case which began, for example, in 1991 but in which the court's decision was reached in 1992 is included in the figures for 1991 under the heading of 'pending' and it is not included in the 1992 figures. Thus the manner in which the statistics are compiled may inflate the size of the conviction rate.

The attempt to explain the seemingly high conviction rate is also hampered by the absence of comprehensive information on the numbers who plead guilty. The conviction rate may be high because a significant proportion of defendants plead guilty. Research shows that the 'single most important feature of criminal procedure (both in England and in the United States) is its fundamental dependence on the guilty plea . . . almost 90 per cent of all defendants charged with serious criminal offences plead guilty' (Baldwin and McConville, 1981: 7). The information available on the guilty plea in Ireland is limited to two studies. These suggest that while the rate of guilty pleas is not as high as it is in the English or the American systems it is still very important. Michael Needham's study of the operation of the district court in Galway over the period 1978 to 1981 showed that 69 per cent of a random sample of defendants pleaded guilty. Rottman and Tormey (1985: 150) studied the operation of the Dublin Circuit Court. This deals primarily with the more serious indictable offences. They found that the majority of defendants (74 per cent) pleaded guilty.

It is generally recognised that the courts could not function in any reasonable way if all or even a significant number of defendants were to exercise their right to trial by jury or to plead not guilty and require the state to present the relevant evidence against them. Yet, if so many plead guilty it raises the question of why? The obvious answer is because they are. The less obvious but equally important one is that there may be strong pressures on defendants to plead guilty.

Research in other jurisdictions indicates that these pressures include the belief or the promise from the police or from prosecutors that a guilty plea will make it easier to get bail, that the agreement to plead guilty will lead to a lesser charge or that the police or the prosecutor will put in a good word for defendants or present the details of the case against them in a manner which reflects favourably on them (see Saunders, 1994). These kinds of pressures are central to what is called the 'plea-bargaining process', where a defendant agrees to plead guilty in return for favourable treatment from the courts. This process has its origins in administrative expediency but it can also be driven by a desire to protect witnesses from the trauma of giving evidence under cross-examination. Thus a guilty plea to a charge of indecent assault rather than rape may be agreed on to save the victim the humiliation of a court appearance.

It is impossible to ascertain the extent to which plea-bargaining is a practice in the Irish courts. However Rottman and Tormey (1984) argue that implicit rather than explicit bargaining is present in the Irish system. This does not require face-to-face negotiations between prosecutor and defender but it emerges from a set of shared understandings of how the courts have dealt with similar offences in the past or from what the response of particular judges and indeed particular juries is likely to be to the specific kind of evidence being offered. These form the basis from which prosecutors may agree to a plea to a lesser charge or on which defending solicitors will advise their clients on whether to plead guilty or not.

Kevin Boyle (1984: 208) has also argued that there is a form of 'statutory plea-bargaining' in operation in Ireland. This comes from the way in which 'sentence discount' operates here. There is, for example, an inducement to opt for trial before a district court because the maximum sentence the court can impose is two years' imprisonment whereas the next court up the legal hierarchy, the circuit criminal court, can impose significantly longer sentences. There is also an inducement to plead guilty because if a defendant pleads not-guilty and the subsequent trial establishes guilt then the sentence imposed is likely to be considerably longer.

The majority of defendants plead guilty but what happens to those who plead not-guilty? The information we have here is limited. But the study of the Dublin Circuit Court (Rottman and Tormey, 1985: 151) established that a defendant who opts for trial has a strong probability of being acquitted. Less than three out of every ten in their study who opted for a trial were found guilty. When we ally this to another finding – that a substantial proportion (13 per cent) of cases were dropped by the prosecution before the trial began – it suggests that there may be problems with the way in which decisions are made on the prosecution of offenders. This view is supported by the finding that the majority of acquittals are at the direction of judges and not because of decisions of juries. On this basis Rottman and Tormey (1984) argue that there is a need for the reform of the prosecution process. Their suggestions include the restriction of the gardaí's role as prosecutors to minor offences and the involvement of the Director of Public Prosecutions at an earlier stage in the prosecution process. An equally important though somewhat under-emphasised issue which this data also leads to is the possibility that there are shortcomings in the ability of the gardaí to assemble the quality of evidence that will meet the requirements of the courts.

Stage Three – Punishing Offenders

Given that a substantial proportion of cases in the Irish courts are settled by a guilty plea, it means that, as Shapiro (1981: 53) has remarked about American courts, 'their time is spent disposing of the bodies of those who plead guilty'. However it is not possible to establish from published court statistics how the Irish courts dispose of the bodies before them. The statistics do not tell us the frequency with which particular sanctions or punishments are imposed or what sanctions are imposed for what offences.

The only guide we have to these issues is again the research conducted by Rottman and Tormey (1985). They looked at the sanctions imposed by the district courts over a four-week period in 1984. They found that the courts were restrained in their use of prison. Fines were the most common sanction (imposed on 47 per cent of those found guilty), followed by prison (20 per cent) and the use of the Probation Act (18 per cent). However we need to be cautious in interpreting these figures. Because they do not distinguish between indictable and non-indictable offences we cannot determine whether 'serious' offences are more likely to receive prison sentences though there is some suggestion that this may be the case. Thus while 72 per cent of offences under the Road Traffic Act and 46 per cent of assaults resulted in fines, only 17 per cent of convictions for burglary did. Where the 'unauthorised taking of motor vehicles' was concerned the spread was somewhat more even with 41 per cent of offenders fined and 36 per cent imprisoned.

The study also looked at the Dublin Circuit Criminal Court. It is here that the more serious criminal cases are dealt with and where the most frequently used sanction is imprisonment. Just under half of those convicted were given a prison sentence with an additional 38 per cent receiving a suspended sentence. 'Most sentences', according to Rottman and Tormey (1985: 229), 'fall within a band of one to five years, with two years the most frequently imposed sentence length.' Fines were used on only 4 per cent of those convicted in this court. These findings suggest that the further up the court system defendants go and the more serious the criminal offence they face, the more likely they are to receive a prison sentence.

Consistency in Sentencing

The difficulty with such aggregate figures is that they may conceal more than they reveal. In particular they may hide the level of inconsistencies with which sentences are imposed. This issue has been a matter of special concern in cases of violence against women and children where the apparent leniency and inconsistency of the courts in sentencing offenders has been commented on (see Shanahan, 1992: 31–9) and in turn it has provoked a call for mandatory sentences for these offences. The problem is in fact a more widespread one and relates to the general unpredictability of judicial sentencing (see O'Mahony, 1993: 221). Ireland, according to O'Malley (1990), 'enters the 1990s with the most unstructured and outdated sentencing system in the western world'. What this suggests is a need to add structure to the system, something which can be more easily said than done.

It is difficult to devise a sentencing or, more accurately, a punishment policy. The major problem is that such a policy must have a certain purpose to it. We must be clear about what we are trying to achieve when we inflict punishment on offenders. This is discussed in more detail below but it is useful to point out here that the demand for consistent sentencing is based on a justice model which argues that the punishment is fair when it is proportional to the crime and when those convicted of similar crimes earn similar punishments. An alternative argument is that sentencing is fair when it is tailored to the needs of the offender rather than to the offence committed. This means that judicial discretion is essential in sentencing policy if these needs are to be taken into account. There is no clear statement in Ireland of which, if either, of these rationales punishment should have. As a result it could be argued that the actual practice in the Irish courts is a reflection of the different priorities and the different balances struck by individual judges between the competing claims of justice and offenders' needs.

If it is difficult to arrive at some level of agreement on the purpose of punishment and it is equally difficult to achieve consensus on the relationship between the severity of sentence and the seriousness of the offence. In Ireland the current practice seems to be that legislation to increase sentence length is introduced in a piecemeal way and in an atmosphere of public disquiet over particular crimes. The intent behind the legislation is to respond to the immediate sense of outrage in the community rather than to devise a system in which there is a clear relationship between offence and sentence (Fennell, 1993). The creation of such a system that will have public support, however, requires at the very least some knowledge of how the public evaluates the seriousness of particular offences and of the level of agreement between the public's evaluations and judicial ones. This kind of information is not available in Ireland.

The final problem is that a policy to introduce more consistency in sentencing through clearly stated sentencing guidelines may be very difficult to enforce. Research shows that it can be hard to get sentencers to change their established pattern of using prison and to follow new guidelines. In England, for example, Elizabeth Burney (1985) found that where statutory procedures were introduced in magistrates courts to require them to use custody as a last resort they simply did not follow them. They also showed considerable skill in interpreting the new legal justifications for custody in ways that allowed them to continue with their previous pattern of sentencing. In the United States, Michael Tonry (1993) has shown how the new Sentencing Commission's guidelines have failed to reduce sentencing disparities in the federal courts. In both cases a major factor was the resistance of sentencers to any move that they interpreted as an attempt to control their discretion and independence in sentencing.

The Courts – Centrepiece of the System?

The conventional wisdom is that the courts are the centre of the criminal justice system and that they constitute the central institution in which guilt or innocence is determined. However our analysis suggests that this is not the case. The bulk of the work of the courts is not concerned with the establishment of guilt or innocence but with the processing of those who plead guilty and with deciding on the appropriate sanctions to be used against them. By contrast the data would suggest that it is the gardaí who are at the centre of the system.

It is the gardaí who decide who to arrest. They decide who will be prosecuted. They decide the precise nature of the charges that many offenders will face. They initiate and handle most of the prosecutions in court. Most of these are settled by guilty pleas based on confessions made to them and they are the main witnesses in court cases. Indeed in the study of the Galway district court, the only witness in the majority of cases was a garda (Boyle, 1984). This is particularly problematic given that there is considerable room for the operation of discretion in much of the work that the gardaí do. But despite its central role we know little about how this discretion is used. Many people ask whether the balance in the criminal justice system has swung too far in favour of the defendant. A more appropriate question might be whether it has swung too far in favour of the police?

If it has, then it raises other issues. In particular it suggests that much of the concern with the rights enjoyed by defendants at the trial stage may be misplaced. We should be more concerned about the pre-trial rights of defendants and most notably their access to legal counsel. As we have seen in the previous chapter, the right to silence is a right that exists more in theory than in practice. Its effective exercise requires the access to and the availability of legal advice at the time of arrest. As the system operates in Ireland, many of those charged with criminal offences are entitled to legal aid. But as the relevant law stands they are informed of this at the *trial* stage. By this time they may have admitted guilt and the role of the legal representation is reduced to that of arguing for a lenient sentence.

II The Prison System[2]

In this section we turn our attention to the prison system. It could be argued that it does not merit such extensive treatment. Imprisonment may be an important sanction of the court but as we have seen above it is not the principal or indeed the most frequently used one. However it does have a more profound significance that justifies its closer scrutiny. Since the elimination of the death penalty, deprivation of physical liberty is now the most severe sanction that is available in our society. Moreover it is the ultimate guarantor for all of the other sanctions that are available for the punishment of offenders. The incentive to accept the conditions of sanctions such as probation, fines and community service, is the threat of a prison sentence.

The features of the prison system that we consider here include:

- the numbers of inmates in the system and what they are committed for,
- the significance of remand prisoners,
- the increases in the use of prison and in the severity of prison sentences,
- international comparison on the use of prison and its effectiveness,
- suicides in prison, and
- the issue of invisible decision-making in penal institutions.

Finally we discuss the nature of the relationship between the use of prison and the level of crime.

Increased Numbers

Table 7.2 shows the changes in the numbers sent to prison under sentence for selected years from 1961 to 1991. While the numbers fluctuate somewhat from year to year the underlying trend has been inexorably upwards. In 1961, 1,828 people (1,495 males, 194 females and 139 juvenile males) were committed under sentence. The number first broke the 3,000 mark in 1971; in 1983 it broke the 4,000 mark. The highest prison population in the history of the state, 5,106 prisoners, was recorded in 1987. In 1991 it had fallen back somewhat to 4,435. In effect then over the period 1961 to 1991 the percentage increase in the numbers committed to prison under sentence was 143 per cent, again considerably lower than the corresponding increase in crime.

These figures aggregate the numbers of adult males, females and juvenile males.[3] When we break these figures down into the various categories, there are significant differences between the groups. The percentage increase in adult males from 1961 to 1991 was 117 per cent, representing a pattern of small but steady annual increases. By contrast the number of female prisoners in 1991 was down on that in 1961 and their number fluctuated much more than was the case with adult male prisoners. It rose throughout the 1960s reaching a high point in 1971. It declined somewhat in the 1970s, rose again towards the end of the 1980s and then fell in 1989, 1990 and 1991. It is among male juveniles that the most substantial increases have been recorded, though here also the figures have fluctuated considerably. The number rose steadily from 139 in 1961 to reach 815 by 1970. It fell through the 1970s though never to its 1961 level. From there it rose steadily to reach a high point of 1,057 in 1985. Since then, it has fallen somewhat and has stabilised around 950 male juveniles per annum. The percentage increase between 1961 and 1991 was just under 600 per cent.

As we have seen in chapter four the fluctuations in the numbers of women prisoners may be interpretable in terms of changes in the legal treatment of prostitution. However we are unable to tell from these figures or from any available research why the most significant increases in prison numbers have been among juvenile males.

Types of Committal: Why Are They There?

Prison statistics give three categories of reception of adults into prison under sentence: under sentence without the option of a fine; in default of a fine i.e. failure to pay a fine and in default of sureties, failure to pay debts or for contempt of court. Juveniles, by contrast, are simply recorded as committed under sentence. While the majority of adults sent to prison has always been those committed under sentence without the option of a fine, the size of this majority has fluctuated. It was 79 per cent of committals in 1961, 84 per cent in 1971, 78 per cent in 1981 and in 1991 it was 72 per cent.

Table 7.2 Committals to prison (under sentence/or on conviction) 1961–1991

Year	(i) Committed under sentence (adult prisons)						(ii) Committed on conviction	Total (i + ii)
	Without option of fine		In default of fine		In default of sureties		Total		Juvenile males	
	M	F	M	F	M	F	M	F		
1961	1221	120	178	69	96	5	1495	194	139	1828
1971	1971	186	255	62	100	5	2326	253	767	3346
1981	1679	91	331	19	136	1	2146	111	641	2898
1991	2361	146	743	26	187	9	3291	181	963	4435

Source: *Annual Report on Prisons and Places of Detention* for the various years

In effect, these figures mean that around a quarter of those being committed to prison at present are defaulting on the payment of fines or debts. O'Mahony (1993: 105) argues they do not spend a long time in prison but the fact remains that fine-default appears to be widespread. The Committee of Inquiry into the Penal System (1985) suggested that the reason for this was the poor system of enforcement. In 1991 almost 80 per cent of fine-defaulters were released on payment of the fine, so a 'taste' of prison may simply be the final stage in a poor enforcement process.

Remand Prisoners

The numbers in prison are not exhausted by the consideration of those committed under sentence. Remand prisoners constitute a substantial part of the prison population. These are prisoners who are awaiting trial or who are awaiting sentence. Their number has always been reasonably high in comparison to the numbers committed on conviction. In 1961, 1,240 were remanded in custody and 1,828 were committed on conviction, a ratio of remand to sentenced of 1:1.47. By 1991 the number of remand prisoners had grown to 3,517 and the number of convicted ones to 4,435, but the ratio had fallen somewhat to 1:1.26. Another indication of the high number of remand prisoners is that they made up 42 per cent of the numbers committed to prison in 1991. This means that almost half of those sent to prison in that year may not have been convicted of any crime.

It is not possible to tell from official statistics how long these prisoners spent on remand but their numbers should be a matter of concern. O'Mahony (1993: 103) has estimated that the average length of stay of remand prisoners is ten days yet during that time they share essentially the same prison regime as those who are convicted, with the exceptions of different visiting rights and the right to wear their own clothes. A more comprehensive assessment of the effects of remand must take account of its consequences for the prisoner's family and employment and its effects on the outcome of the subsequent court appearance. Some research suggests that 'the prejudice created by the defendant's appearance in court in the custody of police or prison officers' (Bottomley, 1973: 92) may have an influence on the eventual outcome of the trial. What is clear is that a remand in custody makes the preparation of a defence more difficult and it can undermine the resolve to maintain a 'not-guilty' plea (see the discussion in Mc Cullagh, 1990: 276).

The Growth of a Punitive Society?

The increases in the numbers of committals to prison under sentence, in the number of fine-defaulters being imprisoned and in the size of the remand population suggests that Irish society is becoming a more punitive one. This view is supported by one other change in the prison system. This is the strong upward trend in comparatively long sentences and the significant decline in shorter ones. In 1961 6 per cent of committals to prison on conviction were for periods of one year or more. In 1991 this had risen to 32 per cent. At the other end of the spectrum, in 1961 93 per cent of sentences were for less than one year. In 1991 the comparable figure was 68 per cent. A particularly significant decline has been in sentences of under three months. In 1961 these represented 55 per cent of the total. In 1991 they were 32 per cent of the total.

International Comparisons: A Perspective on Irish Prisons

How does the Irish use of prison compare to that of other countries? As is always the case, such comparisons are difficult to make. Countries differ in the ways in which they count their prison populations and in the policies that they use for particular groups of offenders. The Danes, for example, operate a queueing system for short sentences: you have to wait until there is a place vacant for you. In 1981 the number on the prison waiting list was four times the size of the prison population (see Rottman, 1984: 160–4). With these limitations in mind we can consider the results of the comparative data collected by the Council of Europe in 1983 and 1986 (see National Association for the Care and Resettlement of Offenders Briefing, March 1987).

Two different statistics are important here. The first is the detention rate. This is the number held in prison on any one day, i.e. the daily average prison population, expressed as a ratio of the population. Information on this is available for twenty-one European countries. In 1987 the European average was 78 per 100,000. A rate of 56 per 100,000 of the population put the Irish figure well below this. Only four countries had lower detention rates. The second statistic is the imprisonment rate. This is the number sent to prison in any one year expressed per 100,000 of the population. Information is available on this for fifteen countries. Here the Irish rate – at 206 per 100,000 – was well above the European average of 186. Ten of the fifteen countries had lower rates. This may appear at first sight to be a contradiction. Our detention rate is low but our imprisonment rate is high. The anomaly is resolved by the fact that while we imprison a higher percentage of our population than other European countries we keep them there for shorter periods of time. So the average length of sentence in Ireland in 1987 was 3.2 months compared, for example, to that in West Germany (as it was in 1987) of 6.5 months and Greece of 12 months. This may not continue to be the case as these figures also confirm the growing punitiveness in Irish society. Ireland was one of the seven European Community countries in which the annual numbers imprisoned between 1982 and 1985 increased, though the increase was below the average. In four countries – Italy, West Germany, Luxembourg and Belgium – the annual numbers imprisoned fell.

These changes suggest that Rottman's (1984: 164) conclusion that Ireland has a moderate use of imprisonment must be modified. The percentage of the population being imprisoned increased during the 1980s. However his other conclusion still remains valid. Considered in a European context there is a tendency in Ireland to use imprisonment for shorter sentences. Unfortunately international statistics do not allow us to determine if this reflects a more lenient judiciary in Ireland or the presence in other European countries of a greater range of alternative sanctions to be used in lieu of short prison sentences.

What is perhaps the most crucial aspect of the Irish penal system from a comparative perspective is our treatment of juveniles. The detention rate for juveniles (i.e. those aged under twenty-one) is, according to the 1987 figures, highest in England, followed by Ireland with 16 per 100,000. In France, by comparison, the figure is just under 10 per 100,000 and in Spain just under 6 per 100,000 (figures are from O'Mahony, 1993: 107). But it is at this point that statistical issues become crucial. This trend may reflect the fact that we deal with juveniles more harshly than other countries do. Alternatively it may be that other countries use different ways of dealing with juveniles offenders. These may be as coercive and as punitive as those used in Ireland but if they are not run by justice departments of the relevant states they may not show up in these kinds of comparisons.

Prison Overcrowding

The most obvious consequence of all of these changes has been, and continues to be, prison overcrowding. The system simply cannot accommodate the increase in the number of juveniles being imprisoned, the increase in remand prisoners and the tendency of the courts to give longer sentences. It has responded in a number of ways. The most significant is the use of early release through which prisoners are freed before their sentences are complete. This is the so-called 'revolving door' syndrome and it is dealt with in more detail below.

The other response has been to increase the amount of prison accommodation. This has been done through the building of the first purpose-built prison in the history of the state – Wheatfield Prison in Dublin – and through the refurbishment of existing facilities. However much of this involves spending of money on what are already outdated and unsuitable Victorian buildings. Moreover it appears that despite this expenditure overcrowding is likely to continue. The Department of Justice recently expressed a desire to keep the prison population at around the 2,300 mark. The necessary space would be provided though further refurbishments of existing prisons (Department of Justice, 1994: 7). Yet the estimates made by Paul O'Mahony (1993: 109) suggest that the real 'demand' for prison places in 1993 was in the region of 2,900, making a shortfall of 600 places.

The Revolving Door: Invisible Decision-Making

The 'revolving door' is the name by which the system of early release is more popularly known. Under section 2 of the Criminal Justice Act 1960, the Minister for Justice can give early release to prisoners, the most common form of which is 'full temporary release'. This is also known as 'shedding'. The original rationale behind this was to aid the re-integration of offenders into the community. However since the late 1970s it has been used as a method of relieving overcrowding in the system and making space available for newly sentenced prisoners.

As a route out of prison full temporary release has increased enormously in significance. In 1973 when the number committed to prison on conviction was 3,246, 64 prisoners were given temporary release. By 1981 the number committed was 2,898 and the number granted early release was 1,296. It reached its highest point in 1984 when 2,604 prisoners were released but following public controversy its use was curbed. Since then the number involved has begun to rise again. In 1991 the number committed was 4,435 and the number granted early release was 1,619. In practice then, full temporary release has grown from having a marginal role to being a central element in the management of the prison system. It is now a major strategy through which prison overcrowding is dealt with.

Any vestige of rehabilitative intention has been dropped as the vast majority of those given temporary release have no further contact with any state service (including the probation and welfare one). Their only requirement is to sign on in prison once a week. It is therefore relevant to ask on what basis are offenders selected for early release? There is evidence to suggest that it is an arbitrary process. One might anticipate that length of sentence and previous criminal history would be relevant factors in that they might be crude indicators of a propensity towards further crime. But as they do not appear to be factors in the granting of other forms of temporary release (O'Mahony, 1993: 188), we have no guarantee that they are used in these circumstances. The main point however is that the criteria for which offenders are sent to prison have at least the benefit of being publicly available through media coverage. Those criteria for which people are granted 'full temporary release' are not.

The Cost of Prison

International comparisons of prisons reveal two other characteristics of the Irish system. The first is the level of staffing and the second is its high cost. About 80 per cent of those employed in the prison service are prison officers. Their number has grown from 194 in 1961 to 2,161 in 1991. This increase cannot be explained simply in terms of the increases in the number of inmates. In 1961 there was one prison officer to just under every three prisoners.[4] By 1991 this had reached parity, with one prison officer for every prisoner. This ratio is high by international standards. According to the Council of Europe figures for 1987, the ratio in most European countries was one officer to at least two prisoners (see O'Mahony, 1993: 95).

It also cannot be explained in terms of the security needs of dealing with political prisoners. The number of those imprisoned in the maximum security prison in Portlaoise has not increased in any significant way since the mid-1970s and is now beginning to decline. A certain portion of it might be explained in terms of the antiquated nature of prisons such as Mountjoy and Portlaoise. This makes the supervision of prisoners fairly labour intensive. But Victorian buildings are not unique to the Irish prison system. They are a feature we share in common with the British system. It is more likely that the high level of staffing is a reflection of political rather than penal requirements. These relate to the central role of government expenditure in stimulating economic activity and in attempting to reduce unemployment.

The high level of staffing contributes to what is a very expensive penal system. The average cost of keeping a prisoner in prison for a year in 1991 was just under £36,000.[5] When appropriate adjustments are made for the differing levels of wealth of the countries in the Council of Europe 'each prisoner costs about 3.5 times each Irish citizen's share of the national annual GDP [Gross Domestic Product]' (O'Mahony, 1993: 98). France and Germany by contrast spend about a seventh of the Irish figure. These costs could perhaps be justified if the Irish system was efficient in meeting its penal purpose but the argument of the next section is that it is not.

Does Prison Work?

Any discussion of the effectiveness of prison must begin with some specification of what the purposes of prison are as it is only then that we can decide if it achieves them. Traditionally three justifications have been offered for the use of prison. The first is the symbolic or expressive one of indicating social disapproval of certain kinds of behaviour. The second justification is that of discouraging others from doing what people get put into prison for. This is referred to as the 'general deterrence effect.' The third is the individual effect of ensuring that imprisoned individuals do not re-offend or, to put it more positively, are rehabilitated by the experience of prison.

Arguments about social disapproval and general deterrence raise similar issues. They divorce the issue of punishment from the fact that the prison population is predominantly a marginal working-class one. In effect, the process of imprisonment is a differential one, singling out the members of one class and punishing them. This raises questions of whose disapproval is being expressed through the use of prison and if we punish some people in order to deter others do we, as Mathiesen (1990: 72) suggests, 'sacrifice poor and stigmatized people in order to keep others on the narrow path', a position which he argues is morally problematic. The other difficulty is an empirical one. The symbolic disapproval argument cannot be assessed in terms of effectiveness in deterring or preventing crime as the effect it intends punishment to have is purely symbolic. General deterrence has been assessed but the relevant research shows only modest effects (Mathiesen, 1990: 77).

It is at the level of individual deterrence that it should be possible to be more definitive. The standard measure of such deterrence is the rate of recidivism, that is the previous criminal involvement of those currently in prison. If this is low then prison is a successful deterrent. If it is high it is not. However there are particular difficulties in establishing what this is in the Irish context. The annual reports on prisons give data on the number of prison sentences served by those currently in prison. In 1991 51 per cent of those in prison had been there before. However this is only a fairly crude indicator of recidivism (see Rottman, 1984: 160). The tables do not show the number of previous convictions of those who are now in prison. This makes it impossible to say whether those imprisoned for the first time in 1991, for example, had been involved in and convicted of crimes prior to the ones that earned them their first prison sentence. If they had been then it is possible that they were sent to prison not because it would rehabilitate them but because the judiciary had run out of alternatives. A more direct objection is given by O'Mahony (1993: 177) who claims that the figures for recidivism in the prison reports are simply inaccurate. His own survey of a sample of prisoners in Mountjoy prison in 1986 would appear to confirm this. Ninety per cent of these had been in prison before. This figure is significantly higher than the official one. Just under 50 per cent had six or more previous sentences while a remarkable 14 per cent had more than twenty previous prison sentences. This suggests that prison had little of no effect on the willingness of convicted criminals to get involved in further crime.

A Role for Prisons in Crime Reduction?

This information provides the context within which we can consider whether prison has a role to play in crime reduction. For many, a significant element in the crime problem is the way in which prison is currently being used: sentences are too short and the 'revolving door' means that there is no relationship between the sentence imposed and the sentence served. Holders of this view believe that the solution is the provision of more prison spaces and the imposition of more and longer prison sentences.

However before going on to consider this it is useful to point out that this position is not universally shared. The Committee of Inquiry into the Penal System (called here for convenience the Whitaker Report, 1985) argued that this option was too expensive and unlikely to be successful. The report called for the opposite: 'fewer committals, shorter sentences and shorter periods in custody'. These were to be achieved through the more extensive use of non-custodial sanctions, 'a liberal approach to conditional releases' (Whitaker Report, 1985: 72) and increases in remission for good behaviour. The effects of these measures would be to bring about a reduction in prison overcrowding and create the circumstances in which the possibilities for rehabilitation could be increased.

The analysis and recommendations of the Whitaker Report have been challenged, particularly the belief that alternative non-custodial sanctions are successful in reducing the use of prison (Mc Cullagh, 1988a) and the assumption that there are people currently in prison who would qualify for non-custodial sentences (O'Mahony, 1993: 217). However to a large extent these issues are academic because while there is a broad commitment to implement the recommendations of the Whitaker Report, on closer examination this does not translate into a pledge to reduce the prison population. The recently published *Management of Offenders Plan* (Department of Justice, 1994) lists how the department, for example, introduced a new non-custodial sanction, Intensive Supervision, in 1991. But the key point is that while the plan discusses the need to ensure that the prison population does not move above 2,300 places, significantly, it says nothing about its reduction. Moreover in the years since the publication of the Whitaker Report there have been a number of moves to expand the capacity of the prison system. Perhaps the most significant is the experience of Spike Island. The Committee of Inquiry (1985: 113) stated that it 'should not be envisaged as permanent accommodation for any class of prisoner'. By 1991 it had to all intents and purposes become this (*The Irish Times*, 4 May, 1991). In practice the real commitment seems to be to a controlled expansion of the prison system rather than to its reduction.

The increase in the use of prison is often justified by the assumption that there is public support for tougher sentences and by a style of economistic reasoning which says that 'people commit crimes so long as they are willing to pay the prices society charges' (Reynolds, 1990: 263). If prison as it is currently operated is not reducing crime then it follows that the price it is charging is not high enough. The solution is to increase the price of prison by increasing its use and in particular by increasing the length of prison sentences. We will examine each of these suggestions in turn.

In Ireland we have no systematic evidence on public attitudes to sentencing. However if there is public demand for longer sentences then it can only be given serious consideration if the public's knowledge of the sentencing system that they perceived to be lenient is accurate. In general, researchers find that people over-estimate the leniency of the courts (see, for example, Dobbs and Roberts, 1988). But interestingly when they are presented with hypothetical cases and asked to pass sentence and when these sentences are compared to actual court practice there is a fair degree of agreement between the two, particularly in relation to the use of prison (Hough and Moxon, 1985). This suggests that while opinion polls may show the public to be in favour of harsher sentences, the sentences they would pass themselves would be fairly similar to current court practices.

There are also problems with the effectiveness of more severe penalties. We have seen already how prison has little rehabilitative effect but it can be said to deter crime in the obvious sense that while offenders are in prison they are not free to commit crime. However it may not be legitimate to extend this into an argument that the longer they are in prison the more the crime that is prevented. Harsher sentences may have a number of unintended consequences. They may lead more defendants to contest their cases and may make juries more reluctant to convict (see Greenberg, 1990, for an example of this). Longer sentences may also mean that while offenders will take longer to graduate from prisons (which have been described as universities of crime), they will eventually come out with higher qualifications and possibly a greater commitment to using them. As a result they may lengthen their criminal careers or get involved in far more serious kinds of crime than they were previously involved in. 'Enhancements of this sort' can, according to Greenberg (1990: 60), 'negate much of the crime reduction that incapacitation achieves.' Another drawback with regard to longer sentences is that those who propose them also assume that if one offender is put away the effect is to deter others from taking his or her place. The extent to which this is true for many serious crimes is open to question. Alfred Blumstein, for example, has argued that the imprisonment of drug-dealers causes only momentary disruption to the drugs trade. If there is sufficient demand and easy profits, removing one drug-dealer simply means that a new one moves in. 'It may take some time for recruitment and training, but experience shows that the amount of time is rarely more than a few days' (Blumstein, quoted in Hagan, 1994: 164).

From this it would seem that both the reformative and the incapacatitive capabilities of prison are somewhat over-rated. In particular, the kinds of changes in sentencing policies that would lead to more people being sent to prison and to longer sentences may have unintended consequences that negate whatever their crime preventative effects might be.

Why Does Prison Fail?

It is by no means clear why the experience of prison fails to rehabilitate so many offenders. One suggestion has been that the sub-culture created among prison inmates functions as a form of defence against the institution and as a means through which prisoners can maintain their sense of self-esteem. At its most basic it provides a set of values that show prisoners how to adapt to prison life and how to serve their time. The central values are loyalty and solidarity with other prisoners and the maintenance of distance from the authorities. These have been summarised as: 'don't inform', 'don't whine' and 'don't talk to screws' (see Mathiesen, 1990). 'In effect', as McCorkle and Korn (1954:88) put it, the culture 'permits the inmate to reject his rejectors rather than himself'.

While there is some agreement that such a culture exists to a greater or lesser extent in prisons, there are differences between criminologists on what the sources of the culture are (see Morgan, 1994). For some, particularly those who have studied long-term prisoners in the United States, it is a response to the deprivations and indignities of prison. For others it is simply an extension into a prison setting of particular values that are part of the social environment that the typical prisoner comes from. Either way the effect of the culture is to cushion prisoners against attempts to reform them.

It is important to know if such a sub-culture exists in Irish prisons. Some of the conditions of prison life here, such as the relatively short sentences served by most prisoners, mitigate against its formation. The range of positive ties that prisoners can maintain with the outside world has been found in other systems to reduce the hold of the culture but this presumes that the nature of the communication between the prisoners and families challenges the norms of the inmate culture and the attitudes to authority that are contained within it. This may not be the case. Some would also argue that the availability of drugs in prisons is an important impediment to reform. However it is useful to point out that the high rates of recidivism predate the current drug problem. Rates of recidivism were as high in the 1970s as they are now.

A second factor which also has clear implications for recidivism in the ability of offenders to 'go straight' after a term of imprisonment is getting and keeping a job. Yet a period in prison puts ex-prisoners at a significant disadvantage in attempts to re-enter the world of legitimate employment. They are, for example, disqualified from employment in the public service in Ireland. They may also be seen as posing a potential risk for an employer and in the current tight labour markets, there is little incentive to employ them. The time they spend in prison also dates whatever legitimate job skills they may have had and cuts them off from whatever networks of contact they had to conventional lawful employment. Moreover involvement in the prison sub-culture encourages attitudes such as toughness and a distrust for authority which may be functional in prison but are a significant disadvantage outside it. For these reasons many ex-prisoners are, in effect, unemployable. This makes re-involvement in criminal networks not only more likely but in many cases unavoidable.

The Issue of Prison Suicide

The role of the inmate culture in allowing prisoners to reject their rejectors may be effective for large numbers in the Irish system but there is a significant and growing number for whom it offers inadequate protection. These are prisoners who make successful or unsuccessful attempts to kill themselves. The suicide rate in Irish prisons is sixteen times that in the general population and over twice the rate in the British prison system (Advisory Group on Prison Deaths, 1991: 11–23). There were twenty-three suicides in Irish prisons between 1975 and 1990. Over half of these were in Mountjoy prison and most were committed by prisoners under twenty-five years of age. All but one were by males and 70 per cent of prisoners who had committed suicide were classified as either having psychiatric or drug abuse problems. It is also a problem that seems to be increasing in intensity. There have been, according to O'Mahony (1993: 194), an average of four deaths per year in the late 1980s and early 1990s.

What these deaths raise is the question of whether they are caused by the level of stress experienced in prison or by the psychiatric problems that prisoners bring with them into prison? If prior psychiatric problems are the cause then it raises questions of why such people end up in prisons where there are inadequate facilities to deal with the problems they have. If, on the other hand, these suicides are caused by the level of stress of prison life brought on by overcrowding, lack of suitable activity and antiquated conditions then it casts doubts on the degree to which the prison service has succeeded in 'treating those in custody with care, justice, dignity and respect' (Department of Justice, 1994: 22). Either way, the answers to these questions cannot be said to constitute a defence of the prison system.

The Growth of the Prison Population: An Explanation?

In this section we have reviewed a number of key issues relating to prisons in Ireland. What is perhaps the most striking of these has been the growth in the prison population. The question we now wish to address is how this growth might be explained. The most obvious starting point is to suggest that the increases in the numbers in prison can be explained in terms of the increase in the level of crime. However Paul O'Mahony's (1993: 116) analysis of Irish crime and prison statistics shows the 'independence of the growth of the prison system from the growth of crime'. So if it is not the increase in crime that is responsible, what is it?

An alternative answer is provided by a particular tradition of research in the sociological study of punishment. This suggests that the relevant relationship is not between imprisonment and crime but between imprisonment and other social conditions such as rising unemployment and the level of welfare dependence (Rusche and Kirscheimer, 1968). A number of studies have looked specifically at the relationship between the level of unemployment and the use of imprisonment in different countries (for a summary see Mc Cullagh, 1992). Most have come to a similar conclusion. As unemployment in a society rises so too does the number imprisoned. This has been interpreted as indicating that one of the functions of prison is to control and contain what are seen as the dangerous classes, the unemployed (see Christie, 1994: 59–80).

This explanation has considerable rhetorical attractions but it also has the shortcomings which are common to conspiracy theories (see Jankovic, 1980). It assumes that power élites control the criminal justice system yet it cannot explain satisfactorily how this control is organised and how it operates. An alternative and more sophisticated explanation for these kinds of results is offered by the Italian sociologist, Dario Melossi (1985). He argues that to understand this relationship, we need to understand what he calls the 'vocabulary of motives', or what we might call the 'moral climate', that is present in society at particular times. This vocabulary is the dominant perspective in terms of which a society explains issues to itself. Where crime is concerned if the terms in which it is understood change then this has important implications for the manner in which crime is responded to. This, according to Melossi, is what happens in a recession. The vocabulary shifts 'toward verbalisations which become motives for more severe punitive action among agents of social control' (Melossi, 1985: 178). These shifts are produced, he argues, by the way in which recessions alter the balance of power in society and change the ability of different groups to shape its moral climate. As a result offenders are more likely to be sent to prison and for longer periods of time than would be the case in times of economic growth.

Melossi goes on to argue that while such verbalisations may be found at all levels of a society the most significant and socially relevant ones are those found 'among individual actors who are able to control the usage of punishment' (Melossi, 1985: 186), in particular those found among the judiciary. This means that the relationship between imprisonment and unemployment can be understood through examining the way in which a society conceptualises crime and in particular the way in which judges do. If their understanding of it changes in a time of recession to see those who commit crime as a major threat to social order then this will be reflected in changes in their sentencing practices and particularly in the more extensive use of imprisonment.

This relationship has been examined in an Irish context using data for the years 1951 to 1988 (Mc Cullagh, 1992). The necessary statistical controls were used to ensure that factors like the level and seriousness of crime were not confusing any potential relationships. The analysis indicated that while there was a relationship between unemployment and imprisonment it was a more nuanced one than had been found for other countries. There was no strong direct relationship between unemployment and imprisonment over the period 1951 to 1988 but to the extent that such a relationship exists it is only for the period 1980 to 1988 and it only holds true for male offenders. If we wish to use Melossi's argument to explain this particular relationship then we have to establish two things. One is to show that the 'vocabulary of motives' used by judges changed in the recession of the 1980s as it is only in this period that the relationship arises. The other is to establish that they have the level of discretion through which such changes can find direct reflection in changes in their sentencing policies.

To establish if the vocabularies of Irish judges have changed requires us to ask how their vocabularies and 'world-view' are constructed. The argument is that, like most world-views in a complex and increasingly differentiated society, these are socially constructed from two elements. One is their own immediate social experience and social background. These appear to be fairly limited, if one looks, for example, at the schools Irish judges have attended and the areas in which they live. According to the Institute of Public Administration yearbook for 1988 – the last one to publish the addresses of individual judges – none of the Dublin metropolitan judges lives in either north Dublin, or west Dublin or the inner city. This suggests that their social circles are unlikely to contain many people from the backgrounds that many of the offenders who appear before them come from. By contrast, it is likely to contain people – such as those in the business community – whose concerns and opinions about crime may be more punitive and whose views tend to get more publicity in times of recession.

The other source of judges' world-view is likely to be the mass media. As society becomes more complex, people depend more on the mass media for access to what is happening in the wider society and access to what 'public opinion' on issues and events might be. Judges are no exception to this. This makes it important to examine how crime is dealt with in the Irish media. It has always been presented as a male phenomenon and while this has remained constant there was a significant shift in the late 1970s and early 1980s in important aspects of the way in which the media presented the crime problem (see Mc Cullagh, 1986b; Kerrigan and Shaw, 1985). It ceased to be a routine news story. Increasingly it came to be presented as a problem that was out of control and to which the only 'obvious' solution was imprisonment. This form of presentation had only tenuous links to the reality of crime. But if judges feel they must take public opinion and public anxieties into account in their response to crime and if their major source of access to the nature of 'public opinion' is the media then in the late 1970s and early 1980s an increasingly punitive attitude was likely to be part of the vocabulary with which they approached the issue.

However if judges became more punitive-minded, do they have the kind of discretion that would allow it to have a real impact on sentencing? The answer is yes. Without such discretion the issue of inconsistencies in sentencing practices could not arise. The scope for discretion has also been widened by the provisions of the Criminal Justice Act 1984, which increased the maximum sentence at district court level, where the bulk of criminal cases are dealt with, from one to two years. Moreover the separation of the sentencing function from any administrative role in the running of, or responsibility for, prisons means that in practice judges do not have any formal information available to them about the capacity of the prisons and so can make their sentencing decisions without reference to this as a criterion. In this way changes in their understanding of the crime problem or in the 'vocabulary of motives' they use can have very direct effects on the numbers of people sentenced to imprisonment. The empirical substantiation of this argument requires further study, particularly of what their 'vocabulary of motives' might have been prior to the recession of the 1980s. However the implications of the perspective presented here are significant. They suggest that it is the increased punitiveness of the Irish judiciary rather than the increase in crime that is responsible for the increases in the prison population and for the consequent overcrowding in the prisons. This means that prison overcrowding cannot be resolved simply by increasing prison space. It also requires some limitations on the sentencing discretion of judges. The irony is that the kind of public opinion that the judges refer to in justifying their increased punitiveness is exactly the same one that makes it politically impossible to place any restraints on their sentencing powers.

Conclusion

In this chapter we have reviewed the operations of two central elements of the criminal justice system in Ireland – the courts and the prisons. We have identified significant features of each of these. These include the reliance of the courts on guilty pleas and on plea-bargaining for their effective operation. In effect these mean that the courts have been displaced from their role of assessing the guilt of defendants and are primarily involved in sentencing them. The key features of prison include the level of overcrowding, the increase in the number of prison suicides and the continuing failure of prison to rehabilitate offenders. Finally we documented and attempted to explain what appears to be an increasing punitiveness in our responses to crime. What is perhaps the most significant point in this chapter (and in the previous one) is the suggestion that there are clear limits to what policies based exclusively on policing and prisons can do to reduce crime. What this means for effective policies to cut crime levels is discussed in the next and final chapter.

Notes

1. These figures are taken from the court data in *Statistical Abstracts* for the relevant years.
2. Unless otherwise indicated the data on prisons used in this section is taken from the *Annual Reports on Prisons and Places of Detention* for the relevant years.
3. As we have seen in chapter four there is no separate prison for juvenile females. Those that are sent to prison are incarcerated with adult women.
4. This is calculated by comparing the number of officers to the daily average number of prisoners, i.e. adults and juveniles.
5. This is calculated by dividing the total current expenditure (i.e. pay and non-pay running costs) of the prison system by the daily average prison population.

CONCLUSION: HOW TO REDUCE CRIME

In the last two chapters we reviewed the state of policing and prisons in Ireland and we looked in particular at the role which they can play in crime reduction. We concluded that, while specific forms of policing may be successful against particular types of crime, overall the police are not, as Reiner (1994: 755) puts it, 'realistically a vehicle for reducing crime substantially'. Equally whatever about the usefulness of prison in keeping criminals off the streets, it is not particularly successful at rehabilitating them or deterring them from further criminal involvement. Indeed there are some indications that longer prison sentences may have consequences that those who propose them do not anticipate. These include the involvement of ex-prisoners in more serious and more successful criminal enterprises.

This is not to suggest that the police and the prisons are irrelevant. They play a significant role in providing the sense of public reassurance and security on which organised social life depends. It is, for example, important that the gardaí can respond rapidly to calls for help from the public. It is also important that prison space is provided for those offenders who pose particular dangers for society and that it should be the 'ultimate penalty for those who, violently or otherwise, commit grievous offences' (Whitaker Report, 1985: 7). However there is no guarantee that tinkering with either policing or prisons will have a substantial pay-off in terms of the reduction of crime. This realisation is increasingly beginning to permeate official thinking on the crime problem as can be seen from the new kinds of defensiveness with which both the gardaí and the prisons now present themselves.

The Retreat from Crime Reduction

We can see a retreat from crime reduction in a number of ways. One is the manner in which the institutions with a major role in crime prevention and crime reduction are beginning to argue that these are not their specific responsibility but that of the wider community. Another is the way in which the language of crime policy is moving increasingly from that of prevention and reduction towards that of management and control.

A diffusion of responsibility can be seen in the article which the garda commissioner wrote for *The Irish Times* (19 September, 1994). Here he argues that the maintenance of law and order should not be seen exclusively as a matter for the gardaí. It must be seen, he says, 'as a communal responsibility' though he does not indicate quite how the community is supposed to exercise its responsibility in this area. It can also be seen in the corporate strategy document produced by the gardaí in 1993 (Garda Síochána, 1993). This is in many ways a progressive document in that, for example, it includes 'to seek, identify and eliminate the causes of crime' as part of what it calls the 'mission statement' of the gardaí. But when the document goes on to discuss the means through which the 'mission' is to be achieved, this specific goal is re-defined as being about the reduction of 'the incidence of *police preventable crime*' (italics added). However as this term is not defined at any point in the document, it means in effect that the success of the gardaí in dealing with crime cannot be the subject of independent assessment. An increase in the crime rate may not necessarily be an indication of police failure as the increase may not be in 'police preventable crime' and hence not the responsibility of the gardaí.

The policy document produced by the Department of Justice (1994), which is intended to set out prison policy for the next five years has many of the same defensive characteristics. It promotes many important and progressive additions to the prison service but is silent or at least fairly quiet on others. It argues that the major problem in the prison system is not, as one might anticipate, that it is not particularly effective. The main one is overcrowding and the solution to this is the provision of more prison places. The document also sets out goals for the prison service but these are predominantly about efficiency and ensuring that those who are sent to prison by the courts will be kept in 'appropriate security' (1994: 22) and treated with 'care, justice, dignity and respect' (Department of Justice, 1994: 22). To the extent that there is an emphasis on rehabilitation it is a qualified one. It sees one of the aims of prison 'as preparing those in custody, *as far as it is practicable to do so* [italics added], to resume on release a constructive place in the community' (Department of Justice, 1994: 22). The report is also significant for the manner in which it suggests that the success of prison is to be judged. This is not in terms of its degree of success in deterring or rehabilitating offenders but in terms of the degree to which it lives up to the standards set out in the European Prison Rules (Department of Justice, 1994: 22). This change of emphasis in official thinking is perhaps best captured by the title given to the policy document. It is called 'The management of offenders' not, one will note, their rehabilitation.

This attitude to prisons is very much in line with the notion of 'humane containment' advocated by the Whitaker Report (1985) and mentioned again in the Department of Justice's policy document (1994: 98). Its central feature is the containment of a limited number of prisoners in clearly specified and measurable standards of accommodation and in circumstances that do not increase the level of punishment already implicit in the deprivation of liberty. What is significant is that this model has its origins in the so-called 'just-deserts' theory of punishment and so it makes no claims for its effectiveness in terms of crime reduction and indeed argues that this is not a relevant criterion in terms of which punishment should be judged. It lays a stress on the rights of prisoners to be well treated, to be confined under clean and hygienic conditions and to be allowed to exercise their rights as prisoners. But it also argues that as prison exists to deliver justice its success at rehabilitating offenders is not one of the terms in which it should be judged (see, for example, Stern, 1987: 64).

In these ways then the failure of the police and prisons to reduce crime has led to attempts to deflect responsibility for this away from them or more typically it has led to a retreat from the aims of crime reduction to those of having well-managed and well-run organisations. The crime problem is no longer seen as something that can be solved but as something that can be managed. The surface manifestations of the problem can be dealt with, public concerns can be responded to through more legislation and, if necessary, more police officers and longer sentences, and the indicators of success will be the degree to which organisations meet their self-imposed targets, none of which have much to do with the reduction of crime.

However these kinds of solutions have a limited life span. Perceptions of the crime problem can be managed or suppressed for long periods of time but crime always outruns the ability to manage it. Spectacular or horrific crimes or a sudden burst of media attention blow the cover and the problem is revealed, momentarily at least, to be still unresolved. In this sense the root causes of the crime problem can be evaded for long periods of time but eventually they will return to haunt us. This means that if there is to be a serious commitment to crime reduction then at some point these causes must be focused on and addressed. In the end, as the AGSI (1982: 10) recognised, 'crime can only be prevented by a determined

attack on the type of social, environmental and recreational
conditions that encourage the development of criminal tenden-
cies in the first place'. The real issue for public policy on crime
is the form that such an attack should take.

The Road Back? The Creation of an Inclusive Society

The solution to crime is to address the nature of crime-
producing conditions in the society. As has been suggested in
chapter five, these lie chiefly in the problem of marginalisation.
Societies with high levels of marginalisation have high levels of
crime; societies with low levels of marginalisation have low
levels of crime. However the problem of marginalisation in
Ireland has two dimensions to it. One is the marginalisation of
significant sectors of the working class from full participation
in economic and social development and the other is the
marginalisation of significant sectors of the middle class from
the control of the state and the legal system. Attempts to
address the crime problem must address both of these issues.

The marginalisation of sectors of the working class can be
addressed through programmes and policies that, in John
Hagan's (1994: 168) words, represent 'forms of capital investment in . . . distressed and low-income communities'. These
are investments in job-creation schemes, job-training, the up-
grading and restoration of job skills, improved quality of
education, the provision of recreational facilities, community
centres and adequate housing. The items on the list, and the
failure to provide them, is depressingly familiar. In a very
important sense these go beyond the recommendations of the
Inter-Departmental Group on Urban Crime and Disorder
(1992). The focus there was on offenders. What we are suggesting here is that the focus should be on communities in which
poverty and its attendant problems of marginalisation have
become concentrated.

However any policy that remains solely at that level will not work. The effects of marginalisation are manifested at a community level but the problem is not caused there. Community-based strategies cannot solve the problem by themselves. They must be accompanied by societal-level change also. The problem with community schemes is that if left by themselves they may exacerbate rather than diminish the problem. They raise expectations that they cannot fulfil, their success at job-creation is strictly limited and they may solve a problem in one community by displacing it to another. There is little point in using resources to increase the level of attachment of individuals in one community to the labour market if, as a result, they take the jobs of people in other communities. Community-based and community-oriented strategies have also a major disadvantage if they are the main policy instrument in the fight against crime. Their failure can displace responsibility for the problem from the central institutions in the society to local communities, thus increasing the negative labelling to which such communities are already vulnerable.

Accordingly, such schemes must be supplemented by economic development strategies that utilise the skill levels of those involved and that produce real alternatives to the financial attractiveness of many forms of crime. In this sense there is little point in a response to the de-industrialisation of inner cities that replaces the old industries with new high technology ones which have no use for the skills available in the community. How many local people are employed, for example, in the Financial Services Centre in inner-city Dublin?

The other problem of marginalisation is that of sectors of the middle class and of corporate groups from the control of the state and the legal system. It is an issue that is increasingly recognised in sociology (see, for example, Braithwaite, 1993) but there is little consensus on how it should be responded to. Based on the analysis presented in chapter three it is clear that there are three issues that initially at least need to be addressed.

The first is that of law. As we have seen, the criminal label is distributed in an uneven way in that it does not encompass the full range of what might be regarded as socially harmful behaviour. We need to examine this and look at the extent to which the use of the criminal label is pervaded by class bias. We need also to consider the degree to which it should be extended to include certain kinds of behaviour and the degree to which it should be withdrawn from other kinds of behaviour. An example of the former is the criminalisation of pollution offences and an example of the latter is the decriminalisation of many forms of recreational drug-use.

The second issue is the manner of enforcement of existing legislation and the level and kind of resources devoted to it. We need to consider whether the level of policing of offences is commensurate to their threat and cost to society. Fraud is the most obvious example of a disproportion between the resources devoted to investigation and the cost to society, but there are other areas such as health and safety legislation, tax law and pollution control that would repay investigation. We also need to consider the ways in which these are policed. Is the middle class more likely to be policed by administrators and the working class by the uniformed police force? The kinds of behaviour that are policed by administrators do not have the same level of stigma attached to them as those that are policed by the gardaí.

The third issue is the punishment of offenders. The kinds of offences committed by middle-class offenders are not the ones that are likely to be punished by prison sentences; those committed by offenders from working-class backgrounds are. How can this class bias be eliminated in order to underpin our system of punishment with some basis in equity? This does not require an increase in our use of prison against middle-class offenders. There is after all little reason to expect it will be any more successful against them as it is against other kinds of offenders, though this is currently an issue of controversy in criminology (see Cullen and Dubeck,

1985). But it does suggest that we need to apply the same level of ingenuity to keeping working-class offenders out of prison as we now apply to middle-class ones.

Concluding Considerations

We have suggested here that a rational crime reduction policy must eventually address the underlying causes of crime. These are located in the 'double' marginalisation produced by the process of economic and social development in Ireland over the past thirty years. This is the marginalisation of significant sectors of the working class from the benefits of development and the marginalisation of sectors of the middle class from state regulation generally and from regulation by the legal system specifically. We have in addition proposed a number of ways in which these problems can be responded to.

There are three final points to be considered about these kinds of solutions. The first is the emergence in recent years of a new set of crimes – the sale and use of illegal drugs, in particular heroin and cocaine – which for many has changed the nature of the crime problem and invalidated the explanations and solutions that we have outlined here.[1] The increase in crimes of all sorts, including assault and other crimes of violence, it is argued, can be attributed to the increased availability and consumption of such drugs. When significant levels of addiction emerge in a community, addicts become so desperate for the drug that they are forced to get involved in crime to feed their habit. In a departure from 'traditional' criminal practice they commit crimes against people in their own communities and neighbourhoods and their desperation is reflected in the use of significant levels of violence. In this way a drug problem has emerged in which the profits are accruing to a small number of large dealers and the consequences are visited on inner-city communities in the form of a general decline in the quality of life. Thus for many a war on drugs must take precedence over a war on crime.

It is undoubtedly the case that drug offences are new – many were created by the Misuse of Drugs Act 1977 – and although we do not have accurate data on them they also appear to be extensive in certain areas of our major cities at least. Garda crime statistics in 1993 record just over 4,000 offences under the Misuse of Drugs Act 1977, almost three out of every four of which are for possession rather than for intent to supply. It is unlikely that these figures give a very accurate indication of the amount of drugs in circulation or the numbers involved in their sale as offences in this area do not come to the attention of the police in the normal way that most crimes such as burglary and robbery do. That is through victim complaint. Victims, in this case drug-dealers and users, have little incentive to report their own criminal activities to the police. Drug offences are generally uncovered by proactive policing, that is by the police targeting a type of crime and devoting resources to its detection and to its control. Thus the number of recorded drug offences is not so much an indication of the level of such offences as it is of police activity against them.

The difficulty in responding to the drugs problem is that it is actually two problems and these have tended to become separated. There is the problem of supply and the problem of demand. Most resources are targeted at the problem of supply in the belief that if the importation of drugs can be contained or eliminated then the problem can be resolved. The concern is to get the drug suppliers off the streets, a task which is currently proving enormously difficult. The drugs industry is organised with considerable sophistication and, as many of the major dealers do not directly handle the drugs themselves they are difficult to tie to the offences. The current strategy is to pursue them through the investigation of the means through which they dispose of their considerable profits, a strategy which has had some success in dealing with the problem of organised crime in the United States.

However it should be noted that it is often the case that removing one major dealer increases the level of violence in the industry as the others compete for the vacant position of control and for an increased share of the profits. Moreover as Fagan (quoted in Skolnick, 1995: 11–12) argues about the drug economy in the United States, as long as demand for drugs remains high and as long as there are profits to be made from them, however small, the incentive to participate in the drugs economy is difficult to neutralise.

This suggests that a strategy aimed at the supply must also be accompanied by strategies aimed at reducing demand. The high profits and the scale of the drugs industry are dependent on the ready availability of groups of people who need the kinds of effects that the drugs produce. Even if we make due allowance for the fact that the addictive nature of the drugs may to some extent create the demand, what we are dealing with is social situations that generate the need for the kinds of escapism that drugs offer. This means that policies which succeed in reducing supplies but which do not reduce addict demand have counter-productive effects. They increase the price of the remaining drugs thus forcing addicts to make extra income to buy their supply. They can only do this through intensifying their involvement in crime either through increasing their drug-pushing activities or through greater involvement in property crime.

As a result, a successful drugs policy must also address the issue of addict-demand and the complexities of how to reduce it. Where these policies need to begin is from a detailed knowledge of the kinds of people who are addicted. The limited information we have about them is depressingly familiar. As reports from the Medico-Social Research Board (1983, 1984) indicate, their background is one of lack of employment, education or occupational skill. In other words they are part of the group whom we identified in chapter five as being marginalised by the recent development of the Irish economy. In that sense the response to both drugs and to many forms of crime is the same. We need to consider the ways in which we can create a society in which such marginalisation is reduced or ended.

The second problem with the solutions proposed here is that they are not instant ones. They will not necessarily have an immediate effect on the present generation of marginalised middle-class and marginalised working-class communities. Their success will have to be judged by their ability to end marginalisation and to prevent the crime of the next genera-tion. There will, in effect, be a significant time lag between the policies and their success. This should not surprise us. It took thirty years for Irish society to develop its current crime problem. We need to be prepared to commit a realistic portion of time to its reduction.

This makes the final problem most important. This is the question of who will support, promote and defend these pol-icies. They can be justified on the grounds of rationality, justice and efficiency but these are not a sufficient guarantee that they will become part of public policy. The history of policy-making shows that particular policies are not implemented because of their inherent rationality, they are implemented because they are supported by significant groups inside and outside the government. It is not clear who will support and promote the kinds of solutions being proposed here. Though they are not particularly new they have as yet not found much active support among political parties or among other particip-ants in the politics of criminal justice. In the end the issue of crime control and crime reduction cannot be separated from the issues of social and distributive justice. These kinds of justice can only be achieved through the curtailment of the privileges of some in order to make opportunities available to others. There is little indication that the privileged are willing to make this concession or that any political party is overly anxious to ask them to. Because of this, the problem of rising crime in Ireland is likely to be with us for some time to come.

Notes

1. A more extended discussion of drugs would need to distinguish between drugs like heroin and cocaine and those of what might be termed a more recreational nature such as ecstasy and marijuana. While the importation and sale of all of these is illegal, their ability to create addiction and their effects in terms of user-related crime may be different. While many are prepared to argue that much serious crime is caused by heroin addicts trying to finance their habit, there have been few similar claims about the users of ecstasy. This may reflect class differences in the users of the different drugs. If those who use ecstasy are mainly middle class then they may well have access to the legitimate resources from which they can fund their drug purchases.

BIBLIOGRAPHY

Adler, Freda, 1975. *Sisters in Crime: The Rise of the New Female Offender*, New York: McGraw-Hill.

Adler, Freda, 1983. *Nations Not Obsessed with Crime*, Littleton, Colo.: Fred B. Rothman.

Advisory Committee on Fraud, 1992. *Report*, Dublin: Stationery Office.

Advisory Group on Prison Deaths, 1991. *Report*, Dublin: Stationery Office.

Allen, Robert and Tara Jones, 1990. *Guests of a Nation: People of Ireland versus the Multinationals*, London: Earthscan.

Amir, Menachem, 1971. *Patterns in Forcible Rape*, Chicago: University of Chicago Press.

Annual Report on Crime, various years, Dublin: Stationery Office.

Annual Report on Prisons and Places of Detention, various years. Dublin: Stationery Office.

Arthur, John A., 1991. 'Development and Crime in Africa: A Test of Modernization Theory', *Journal of Criminal Justice*, Vol. 19, No. 6, pp. 499–513.

Arthur, John A., 1992. 'Social Change and Crime Rates in Puerto Rico', *International Journal of Offender Therapy and Comparative Criminology*, Vol. 36, No. 2, pp. 103–119.

Association of Garda Sergeants and Inspectors (AGSI), 1982. *A Discussion Document containing Proposals for a System of Community Policing*, Dublin: AGSI.

Baldwin, John and Michael Mc Conville, 1981. *Courts, Prosecution and Conviction*, Oxford: Clarendon Press.

Baldwin, Robert and Richard Kinsey, 1982. *Police Powers and Politics*, London: Quartet.

Bannon, Michael, J. Eustace and M. O'Neill, 1981. *Urbanisation: Problems of Growth and Decay in Dublin*, National Economic and Social Council Report No. 55, Dublin: Stationery Office.

Becker, Howard, 1963. *Outsiders*, Glencoe: Free Press.

Beirne, Piers and James Messerschmidt, 1991. *Criminology*, New York: Harcourt Brace Jovanovich.

Bennett, Don, 1988. 'Are They Always Right? Investigation and Proof in a Citizen Anti-Heroin Movement', in Mike Tomlinson, Tony Varley and Ciaran Mc Cullagh (eds.), *Whose Law and Order*, Belfast: Sociological Association of Ireland, pp. 21–40.

Bennett, Richard R., 1991. 'Development and Crime: A Cross-National, Time-Series Analysis of Competing Models', *Sociological Quarterly*, Vol. 32, No. 3, pp. 343–363.

Benyon, John, 1986. 'Policing in the Limelight: Citizens, constables and controversy', in John Benyon and Colin Bourn (eds.), *The Police: Powers, Procedures and Proprieties*, London: Pergamon Press, pp. 3–42.

Bernard, Thomas J., 1990. 'Twenty Years of Testing Theories: What Have We Learned and Why', *Journal of Research in Crime and Delinquency*, Vol. 27, No. 4, pp. 325–347.

Bittner, Egon, 1981. *The Functions of the Police in Modern Society*, Massachusetts: Oelgeschlager, Gunn and Hain.

Bohan, P. and D. Yorke, 1987. 'Law Enforcement Marketing: Perceptions of a Police Force', *Irish Marketing Review*, Vol. 2, pp. 72–86.

Bottomley, A.K., 1973. *Decisions in the Penal Process*, London: Martin Robertson.

Box, Steven, 1981. *Deviance, Reality and Society*, London: Holt, Rinehart and Winston, 2nd edition.

Box, Steven, 1983. *Crime, Power and Mystification*, London: Tavistock.

Box-Grainger, Jill, 1986. 'Sentencing Rapists', in R. Matthews and J. Young (eds.), *Confronting Crime*, London: Sage, pp. 31–52.

Boyle, Kevin, 1984. 'The Galway District Court Study', in *The Criminal Justice System: Policy and Performance*, National Economic and Social Council, Dublin: Stationery Office, pp. 206–209.

Braiden, Olive, 1992. 'The Lonely Journey to Justice', in *Safety for Women Conference*, Dublin: Government Publications, pp. 21–23.

Braithwaite, John, 1984. *Corporate Crime in the Pharmaceutical Industry*, London: Routledge and Kegan Paul.

Braithwaite, John, 1993. 'Crime and the Average American', *Law and Society Review*, Vol. 27. No. 1, pp. 215–231.

Breathnach, Séamus, n.d. *An Inquiry into the Criminal Justice System in the Republic of Ireland*, unpublished paper.

Breen, Richard, 1984. 'Status Attainment or Job Attainment? The Effects of sex and class on youth unemployment', *British Journal of Sociology*, Vol. 35, No. 4, pp. 363–386.

Breen, Richard and David Rottman, 1983. 'Counting Crime', *Social Studies*, Vol. 7, No. 4, pp. 271–281.

Breen, Richard and David Rottman, 1985. *Crime Victimisation in the Republic of Ireland*, Dublin: Economic and Social Research Institute (ESRI), paper No. 121.

Breen, Richard, Damian F. Hannan, David B. Rottman and Christopher T. Whelan, 1990. *Understanding Contemporary Ireland*, London: Macmillan.

Brogden, Mike, 1994. 'An Agenda for Post-Troubles Policing in Northern Ireland – The South African Precedent', unpublished paper.

Burney, Elizabeth, 1985. *Sentencing Young People: What Went Wrong with the Criminal Justice Act*, Aldershot: Gower.

Burke, Helen, Claire Carney and Geoffrey Cook (eds.), 1981. *Youth and Justice: Young Offenders in Ireland*, Dublin: Turroe Press.

Callan, Tim, 1994. 'Poverty and Gender Inequality', in Brian Nolan and Tim Callan (eds.), *Poverty and Policy in Ireland*, Dublin: Gill and Macmillan, pp. 178–192.

Cardoso, F. H., 1973. 'Associated Dependent Development', in A. Stepan (ed.), *Authoritarian Brazil*, New Haven: Yale University Press, pp. 142–175.

Cardoso, F. H. and Enzo F., 1979. *Dependency and Development in Latin America*, Berkley; University of California Press.

Carlen, Pat, 1988. *Women, Crime and Poverty*, Milton Keynes: Open University Press.

Carty, Michael, 1991. 'How Professional Are We?, *Garda Review*, Vol. 19, No. 4, pp. 16–17.

Charleton, Peter, 1992. *Offences Against the Person*, Dublin: Round Hall Press,

Christie, Nils, 1994. *Crime Control as Industry*, London: Routledge, 2nd enlarged edition.

Clarke, Michael, 1990. *Business Crime*, Oxford: Polity Press.

Clinard, Marshall, (ed.), 1964. *Anomie and Deviant Behaviour*, Glencoe: Free Press.

Clinard, Marshall and Daniel J. Abbott, 1973. *Crime in Developing Nations*, New York: John Wiley.

Collins, Anthony, 1990. 'The Irish Dimension – the Companies (No. 2) Bill, 1987', in Irish Centre for European Law (eds.), *Insider Dealing* Dublin: Trinity College, pp. 31–38.

Commission on the Garda Síochána, 1970. *Report on Remuneration and Conditions of Service*, Dublin: Stationery Office (also known as the Conroy Report).

Commission on Taxation, 1985. *Fourth Report*, Dublin: Government Publications.

Committee of Inquiry into the Penal System, 1985. *Report* (also known as the Whitaker Report). Dublin: Stationary Office.

Corcoran, T., J. J. Sexton and D. O'Donoghue, 1992. *A Review of Trends in the Occupational Pattern of Employment in Ireland 1971–1990*, Dublin: FAS/ESRI.

Costello, Judge Declan, 1980. *Report of Tribunal of Inquiry into Disaster at Whiddy Island*, Dublin: Government Publications.

Council of Europe, 1983. *Prison Management*, Strasbourg.

Council for Social Welfare, 1983. *The Prison System*, Dublin: Council for Social Welfare.

Cullen, Barry, 1989. 'Community Action in the Eighties: A Case Study', in Combat Poverty Agency (eds.), *Community Work in Ireland: Trends in the 80's, Options for the 90's*, Dublin: Combat Poverty Agency, pp. 271–294.

Cullen, Francis, Gregory Clark, Richard A. Mather and John Cullen, 1983. 'Public Support for Punishing White-Collar Crime, *Journal of Criminal Justice*, Vol. 11, pp. 481–493.

Cullen, Francis T. and Paula J. Dubeck, 1985. 'The Myth of Corporate Immunity to Deterrence: Ideology and the creation of the invincible criminal', *Federal Probation*, Vol. 49, pp. 3–9.

Culligan, Patrick, 1994. 'Maintaining Law and Order should be seen as Community Responsibility', *The Irish Times*, September 19, p. 6.

Currie, Elliott, 1985. *Confronting Crime: An American Challenge*, New York: Random House.

Curtin, Chris and Dan Shields, 1988. 'The Legal Process and the Control of Mining Development in the West of Ireland', in Mike Tomlinson, Tony Varley and Ciaran Mc Cullagh (eds.), *Whose Law and Order?* Belfast: Sociological Association of Ireland, pp. 109–128.

Daly, Mary, 1989. *Women and Poverty*, Dublin: Attic Press.

Deming, Mary Beard and Ali Eppy, 1981. 'The Sociology of Rape', *Sociology and Social Research*, Vol. 65, No. 4, pp. 357–380.

Department of Justice, 1994. *Management of Offenders: A Five Year Plan*, Dublin: Stationery Office.

Dobbs, Anthony and Julian Roberts, 1988. 'Public Punitiveness and Public Knowledge of the Facts: Some Canadian Surveys', in Nigel Walker and Mike Hough (eds.), *Public Attitudes to Sentencing: Surveys from Five Countries*, Aldershot: Gower, pp. 111–33.

Drudy, Sheelagh and Kathleen Lynch, 1993. *Schools and Society in Ireland*, Dublin: Macmillan.

Eaton, Mary, 1986. *Justice for Women: Family, Court and Social Control*, Milton Keynes: Open University.

Einstadter, Werner J., 1984. 'Citizen Patrols: Prevention pr Control', *Crime and Social Justice*, No. 21–22, pp. 200–211.

Eipper, Chris, 1989. *Hostage to Fortune*, Newfoundland: Institute of Social and Economic Research.

Elliott, D. S. and D. Huizinga, 1983. 'Social Class and Delinquent Behaviour in a National Youth Panel: 1976–1980', *Criminology*, Vol. 21, No. 2, pp. 149–177.

Fennell, Caroline, 1993. *Crime and Crisis in Ireland: Justice By Illusion*, Cork: University Press.

Fielding, Nigel and Jane Fielding, 1991. 'Police Attitudes to Crime and Punishment: Certainties and Dilemmas', *British Journal of Criminology*, Vol. 31, No. 1, pp. 39–53.

Flynn, Sean and Padraig Yeates, 1985. *Smack*, Dublin: Gill and Macmillan.

Frank, André G., 1967. *Capitalism and Underdevelopment in Latin America*, New York: Monthly Review.

Freeman, John R., 1982. 'State Entrepreneurship and Dependent Development', *American Journal of Political Science*, Vol. 26, No. 1, pp. 90–112.

Garda Síochána, 1994. *Corporate Strategy Policy Document 1993–1997*.

Gobert, James, 1994. 'Corporate Criminality: New Crimes for the Times', *Criminal Law Review*, pp. 722–734.

Gottfredson, Michael and Travis Hirschi, 1990. *A General Theory of Crime*, Stanford: University Press.

Greenberg, David F., 1990. 'The Cost–Benefit Analysis of Imprisonment', *Social Justice*, Vol. 17, No. 4, pp. 49–75.

Hagan, John, 1994. *Crime and Disrepute*, California: Pine Forge Press.

Hardiman, Niamh and Christoper T. Whelan, 1994. 'Politics and Democratic Values', in Christopher T. Whelan (ed.), *Values and Social Change in Ireland*, Dublin; Gill and Macmillan, pp. 100–135.

Harper, R. R., 1991. 'The Computer Game: Detectives, Suspects, and Technology', *British Journal of Criminology*, Vol. 31, No. 3, pp. 292–307.

Harris, William C., 1988. *Policing in Ireland: the Role of the Gardaí*, unpublished masters thesis, University College Cork (UCC).

Harvey, L., R. W. Burnham, K. Kendall and K. Pease, 1992. 'Gender Differences in Criminal Justice: An International Perspective', *British Journal of Criminology*, Vol. 32, No. 2, pp. 208–217.

Healy, John, 1968. *Death of an Irish Town*, Cork: Mercier.

Heidensohn, Frances, 1985. *Women and Crime*, Basingstoke: Macmillan.

Heiland, Hans-Gunther, Louise I. Shelley and Hisao Katoh (eds.), 1992. *Crime and Control in Comparative Perspective*, Berlin: Walter de Gruyter.

Henderson, Paul and Tom Nichols, 1992. 'Offending while on Bail', *Research Bulletin*, London: Home Office, pp. 23–27.

Hindelang, Michael, Travis Hirschi and Joseph Weis, 1979. 'Correlates of Delinquency: The Illusion of Discrepancy between Self-Report and Official Measures', *American Sociological Review*, Vol. 44, No. 6, pp. 995–1014.

Hirschi, Travis, 1969. *Causes of Delinquency*, Berkley: California University Press.

Hoogvelt, Ankie, M. M., 1983. *The Third World in Global Development*, London: Macmillan.

Hough, Mike, 1980. 'Managing with Less Technology', *British Journal of Criminology*, Vol. 20, No. 4, pp. 344–357.

Hough, Mike and Pat Mayhew, 1983. *The British Crime Survey: first report*, Home Office Research Study No. 76, London: Her Majesty's Stationery Office (HMSO).

Hough, Mike and David Moxon, 1985. 'Dealing with Offenders: Popular Opinion and the Views of Victims', *Howard Journal*, Vol. 24, No. 3, pp. 160–175.

Hudson, Barbara A., 1993. *Penal Policy and Social Justice*, London: Macmillan.

Interdepartmental Group on Urban Crime and Disorder, 1992. *Urban Crime and Disorder*, Dublin: Stationery Office.

Jankovic, I., 1980. 'Punishment and Imprisonment', in T. Platt and P. Takagi (eds.), *Punishment and Penal Discipline*, San Francisco: Crime and Social Justice Associates, pp. 93–104.

Jones, Peter, 1990. 'Expanding the Use of Non-Custodial Sentencing Options: An Evaluation of the Kansas Community Corrections Act', *Howard Journal*, pp. 114–129.

Kenny, Austin, 1994. 'Ratio of Police', Letter to the Editor, *The Irish Times*, 23 August.

Keohane, Kieran, 1987. 'Dependent Industrialisation, Crisis and Displacement', unpublished masters thesis, UCC.

Kerrigan, Gene, 1984a. 'The Confession of Christy Lynch', *Magill*, March, pp. 18–34.

Kerrigan, Gene, 1984b. 'The Garda Scandals : The Evidence Noonan Ignores', *Magill*, November, pp. 6–19, 52–54.

Kerrigan, Gene and Helen Shaw, 1985. 'Crime Hysteria', *Magill*, 18 April, pp. 10–21.

Kinsey, Richard, John Lea and Jock Young, 1986. *Losing the Fight Against Crime*, Oxford: Blackwell.

Klein, D., 1981. 'Violence against Women: Some Considerations Regarding Its Causes and Its Elimination', *Crime and Delinquency*, Vol. 27, No. 1, pp. 64–80.

Lampson, L., 1907. *The State of Ireland in the Nineteenth Century*, London: Constable.

Lea, John and Jock Young, 1984. *What Is to be Done about Law and Order*, London: Penguin.

Lee, Joseph, 1984. 'Reflections on the Study of Irish Values', in Michael Fogarty (ed.), *Irish Values and Attitudes – The Irish Report of the European Value System Survey*, Dublin: Dominican Publications, pp. 107–125.

Lee, Joseph, 1989. *Ireland 1912–1985: Politics and Society*, Cambridge: University Press.

Leonard, H. Jeffrey, 1988. *Pollution and the Struggle for the World Market*, Cambridge: University Press.

Lie, John, 1992. 'The Political Economy of South Korean Development', *International Sociology*, Vol. 7, No. 3, pp. 285–300.

Lincenberg, Gary S., 1992. 'Sentencing Environmental Criminals', American Criminal Law Review, Vol. 29, No. 4, pp. 1233–1262.

Lombroso, Cesare, 1913. *Crime: its Causes and Remedies*, Boston: Little Brown.

Lorenz, Walter and Ciaran Mc Cullagh, 1984/85. 'Helping Troublesome Kids: A Hidden Curriculum', *Youth and Policy*, No. 11, pp. 41–46.

Lyons, Ann and Paul Hunt, 1988. 'The Effects of Gender on Sentencing: A Case Study of the Dublin Metropolitan Area District Court', in Tomlinson, Varley and Mc Cullagh, *Whose Law and Order?* Belfast: Sociological Association of Ireland, pp. 129–142.

Madigan, Lee and Nancy Gamble, 1991. *The Second Rape*, Lexington: Lexington Books.

Magee, John, 1988. 'Fraud: Why the war is being Lost', *Business and Finance*, 11 August, pp. 14–17.

Manning, P. K., 1977. *Police Work: The Social Organisation of Policing*, Cambridge, Mass: MIT Press

Mathiesen, Thomas, 1990. *Prison on Trial*, London: Sage.

Matoesin, Geoffrey, 1993. *Reproducing Rape: Domination through Talk in the Courtroom*, Cambridge: Polity Press.

Medico-Social Research Board, 1983. *Drug Misuse in Ireland, 1982–1983*, Dublin: Medico-Social Research Board.

Medico-Social Research Board, 1984. *Characteristics of Heroin and Non-heroin Users in a North-Central Dublin Area*, Dublin: Medico-Social Research Board.

Melossi, Dario, 1985. 'Punishment and Social Action: Changing vocabularies of punitive motive within a political business cycle', *Current Perspectives in Social Theory*, Vol. 6, pp. 169–197.

Merton, Robert, 1968. *Social Theory and Social Structure*, New York: Free Press.

Mirrlees-Black, Catriona and Natalie Aye Maung, 1994. 'Fear of Crime: Findings from the British Crime Survey', *Home Office Research and Statistics Department Research Findings*, No. 9.

Morgan, Rod, 1994. 'Imprisonment', in Mike Maguire, Rod Morgan and Robert Reiner (eds.), *The Oxford Handbook of Criminology*, Oxford: University Press, pp. 889–949.

Morris, Pauline and Ken Heal, 1981. *Crime Control and the Police*, London: HMSO.

Murray, Peter and James Wickham, 1985. 'Women Workers and Bureaucratic Control in Irish Electronics Factories'. in H. Newby (ed.), *Restructuring Capital: Recession and Reorganisation in Industrial Society*, London: Macmillan, pp. 179–99.

McAleese, Mary, 1987. 'Police and People', in William Duncan (ed.), *Some Current Problems in Irish Law*, Dublin: University Law Journal, pp. 45–64.

McCafferty, Nell, 1985. *A Woman to Blame: The Kerry Babies Case*, Dublin: Attic Press.

McCorkle, Lloyd, and Richard Korn, 1954. 'Resocialisation within the Walls', *Annals of the American Academy of Political and Social Science*, Vol. 293, pp. 88–98.

Mc Cullagh, Ciaran, 1983. 'The Limits of Policing', *Social Studies*, Vol. 7, No. 4, pp. 237–247.

Mc Cullagh, Ciaran, 1984. 'Police Powers and the Problem of Crime in Ireland', *Administration*, Vol. 31, No. 4, pp. 412–442.

Mc Cullagh, Ciaran, 1986a. 'Deviance and Crime in the Republic of Ireland', in P. Clancy, S. Drudy, K. Lynch and L. O'Dowd (eds.), *Ireland: A Sociological Profile*, Dublin: Institute of Public Administration, pp. 344–361.

Mc Cullagh, Ciaran, 1986b. 'Crime In Ireland: The Role of the Media', in Tim Chapman (ed.), *Crime in Ireland: Crisis or Manageable Problems*, Belfast: National Association of Probation Officers, pp. 12–17.

Mc Cullagh, Ciaran, 1986c. 'Crime in Ireland: Facts, Figures and Interpretations', *Studies*, Vol. 75, No. 297, pp. 11–20.

Mc Cullagh, Ciaran, 1988a. 'A Crisis in the Penal System? The Case of the Republic of Ireland', in Mike Tomlinson, Tony Varley and Ciaran Mc Cullagh (eds.), *Whose Law and Order*, Belfast: Sociological Association of Ireland, pp. 155–167.

Mc Cullagh, Ciaran, 1988b. 'Is the Force Still with Us? A Review of the Problems of the Garda Síochána', paper read to a conference on policing in University College Cork.

Mc Cullagh, Ciaran, 1990. 'Asking the Wrong Questions? – A Note on the Use of Bail in Irish Courts', *Administration*, Vol. 38, No. 3, pp. 271–279.

Mc Cullagh, Ciaran, 1992. 'Unemployment and Imprisonment: Examining and Interpreting the Relationship in the Republic of Ireland', *Irish Journal of Sociology*, Vol. 2, pp. 1–19.

Mc Cullagh, Ciaran, 1993. 'Explaining Irish (Under)Development', Unit 26, Course Notes for *The Social Context of Information Technology*, Dublin: DCU.

McKeown, Kieran, Teresa Brannick, Siobhan Riordan, Robbie Gilligan, Bridget McGuane and Grace Fitzgerald, 1993. *Child Sexual Abuse in the Eastern Health Board Region of Ireland in 1988*, Dublin: Eastern Health Board.

National Economic and Social Council, 1984. *The Criminal Justice System: Policy and Performance*, Dublin: Stationery Office.

Nelson, Steve and Menachen Amir, 1975. 'The Hitch-hiker Victim of Rape: A Research Report' in I. Drapkin and E. Viano (eds.), *Victimology: A New Focus*, Vol. 5, Mass: Lexington Books, pp. 47–64.

Nolan, Phyllis, 1992. 'The Role of the Gardaí in Crimes against Woman', in proceedings of Safety for Women Conference in Dublin Castle, pp. 43–47.

Oakley, A, 1972. *Sex, Gender, and Society*, New York: Harper and Row.

O'Brien, Joseph V., 1982. *'Dear Dirty Dublin': A city in Distress, 1899–1916* Berkley: University of California Press.

O'Callaghan, Jerry, 1992. *The Red Book*, Dublin: Poolbeg.

O'Connell, Michael and Anthony Whelan, 1994. 'Crime Victimisation in Dublin', *Irish Criminal Law Review*, Vol. 4, pp. 85–112.

O'Donnell, P., 1975. *The Irish Faction Fighters of the 19th Century*, Dublin: Anvil Press.

O'Hearn, D., 1990. 'The Road From Import-Substituting to Export-Led Industrialization in Ireland: Who mixed the Asphalt, Who drove the Machinery, and Who Kept Making Them Change Directions?', *Politics and Society*, Vol. 18, No. 1, pp. 1–39.

O'Mahony, Paul, 1993. *Crime and Punishment in Ireland*, Dublin: Round Hall Press.

O'Malley, Tom, 1990. *Irish Times* article on sentencing, 29 January,

O'Toole, F., 1995. *Meanwhile Bach at the Ranch: The Politics of Irish Beef*, London: Vintage.

Palmer, Stanley H., 1975. 'The Irish Policing Experiment: The beginnings of modern police in the British Isles, 1785–1795', *Social Science Quarterly*, Vol. 56, No. 3, pp. 400–424.

Park, Robert E., 1967. 'Social Change and Social Disorganisation', in Robert E. Park, Ernest W. Burgess and Roderick D. McKenzie (eds.), *The City*, Chicago: University of Chicago Press, pp. 105–110 (originally published 1925).

Pearson, Geoffrey, 1983. *Hooligan: A History of Respectable Fears*, London: Macmillan.

Pollak, Otto, 1961. *The Criminality of Women*, Philadelphia: University of Philadelphia Press.

Punch, Maurice, 1985. *Conduct Unbecoming: The Social Construction of Police Deviance and Control*, London: Tavistock.

Reiner, Robert, 1992. *The Politics of the Police*, 2nd edition, Brighton: Wheatsheaf.

Reiner, Robert, 1994. 'Policing and the Police' in Mike Maguire, Rod Morgan and Robert Reiner (eds.), *The Oxford Handbook of Criminology*, Oxford: University Press, pp. 705–772.

Report of the Tribunal of Inquiry into the Beef Processing Industry, 1994. *Report*, Dublin: Stationery Office.

Reynolds, Morgan O., 1990. 'Crime Pays, But So Does Imprisonment', *Journal of Social, Political and Economic Studies*, Vol. 15, No. 3, pp. 259–300.

Rosenbaum, Dennis P., 1988. 'Community Crime Prevention: A Review and Synthesis of the Literature', *Justice Quarterly*, Vol. 5, No. 3, pp. 323–395.

Rottman, David, 1980. *Crime in the Republic of Ireland: Statistical Trends and their Interpretation*, Dublin; Economic and Social Research Institute.

Rottman, David, 1984. *The Criminal Justice System: Policy and Performance*, Dublin: National Economic and Social Council.

Rottman, David and Phillip Tormey, 1984. 'The System in Criminal Justice' in *Public Social Expenditure – Value for Money?*, Dublin: Economic and Social Research Institute, pp. 129–164.

Rottman, David and Phillip Tormey, 1985. 'Criminal Justice: An Overview' in *Report of the Committee of Inquiry into the Penal System*, Dublin: Stationery Office, pp. 191–240.

Rottman, David and Phillip F. Tormey, 1986. 'Respectable Crime: Occupational and Professional Crime in the Republic of Ireland', *Studies*, Vol. 75, No. 297, pp. 43–55.

Roxborough, Ian, 1979. *Theories of Underdevelopment*, London: Macmillan.

Rusche, George and Otto Kirscheimer, 1968. *Punishment and Social Structure*, New York: Russell and Russell (originally published in 1939).

Russell, Diane, 1984. *Sexual Exploitation*, London: Sage.

Salmon, Trevor C., 1985. 'The Civil Power and Aiding the Civil Power: The Case of Ireland', in John Roach and Jurgen Thomaneck (ed.), *Police and Public Order*, London: Croom Helm, pp. 73–105.

Sanday, Peggy, 1981. 'The Socio-Cultural Context of Rape: A Cross-Cultural Study', *Journal of Social Issues*, Vol. 37, No. 1, pp. 5–27.

Saunders, Andrew, 1994. 'From Suspect to Trial', in Mike Maguire, Rod Morgan and Robert Reiner (eds.), *The Oxford Handbook of Criminology*, Oxford: University Press, pp. 819–860.

Schwendinger, Julia and Herman Schwendinger, 1983. *Rape and Inequality*, London: Sage.

Scully, Diane, 1990. *Understanding Sexual Violence: A Study of Convicted Rapists*, London: Harper-Collins.

Shanahan, Kate, 1992. *Crimes Worse Than Death*, Dublin: Attic Press.

Shapiro, M., 1981. *Courts: A Comparative and Political Analysis*, Chicago: University of Chicago Press.

Shearing, Clifford D. and Philip C. Stenning, 1983. 'Private Security: Implications for Social Control', *Social Problems*, Vol. 30, No. 5, pp. 493–506.

Shelley, Louise I. 1981. *Crime and Modernisation*, Carbondale: Southern Illinois University Press.

Sieber, Ulrich, 1986. *The International Handbook on Computer Crime, Computer-related Crime and the Infringements of Privacy*, Chichester: Wiley.

Simon, Rita, 1975. *Women and Crime*, Lexington: Heath.

Skolnick, Jerome H., 1995. 'What Not To Do About Crime', *Criminology*, Vol. 33, No. 1, pp. 1–15.

Smith, David J. and John Gray, 1983. *Police and People in London*: The PSI Report, London: Policy Studies Institute.

Smith, Lorna, 1989. *Concerns about Rape*, London: HMSO, Research Study No. 106.

Sparks, Richard, 1992. *Television and the Drama of Crime*, Buckingham: Open University Press.

Spitzer, Steven and Andrew Scull, 1977. 'Privatisation and Capitalist Development: The Case of the Private Police', *Social Problems*, Vol. 25, No. 1, pp. 18–29, *Statistical Abstracts*. Various Years, Dublin: Stationery Office.

Stern, Vivien, 1987. *Bricks of Shame: Britain's Prisons*, London: Penguin.

Sutherland, Edwin, 1961. *White Collar Crime*, New York: Holt, Rinehart and Winston (originally published 1949).

Taylor, Ian, Paul Walton, and Jock Young, 1973. *The New Criminology*, London: Routledge and Kegan Paul.

Taylor, Laurie, 1971. *Deviance and Society*, London: Michael Joseph.

Taylor, Maxwell, 1986. 'Police Service and Public Satisfaction', *Police Journal*, pp. 105–118.

Tonry, Michael, 1993. 'The Failure of U.S. Sentencing Commission's Guidelines', *Crime and Delinquency*, Vol. 39, No. 2, pp. 131–149.

Townshend, Charles, 1983. *Political Violence in Ireland*, Oxford: Claredon Press.

Walker, Monica, 1983. 'Self-Reported Crime Studies and the British Crime Survey', *Howard Journal*, Vol. 23, No. 3, pp. 168–176.

Walklate, Sandra, 1995. *Gender and Crime*

Westley, William A., 1970. *Violence and the Police: A Sociological Study of Law custom and Morality*, Massachusetts: MIT Press.

Whelan, Brendan and Miriam Murphy, 1994. 'Public Attitudes to the Gardaí', *Communique: An Garda Síochána Management Journal*, No. 1, pp. 15–18.

Whelan, Christopher T., Richard Breen and Brendan J. Whelan, 1992. 'Industrialisation, Class Formation and Social Mobility in Ireland', in J. H. Goldthorpe and C. T. Whelan (eds.), *The*

Development of Industrial Society in Ireland, Oxford: University Press, pp. 105–128.

Wilson, Harriet, 1974. 'Parenting in Poverty', *British Journal of Social Work*, Vol. 4, No. 3, pp. 241–254.

Wilson, James Q., 1975. *Thinking About Crime*, New York: Vintage Books.

Wilson, James Q., 1986. 'Reply to Currie', Dissent, reprinted in Kevin Stenson and David Cowell (eds.), *The Politics of Crime Control*, London: Sage, pp. 47–61.

Wilson, William, 1991. 'Studying Inner-City Social Dislocation: The Challenge of Public Agenda Research', *American Sociological Review*, Vol. 56, Vol. 1, pp. 1–14.

Young, Jock, 1975. 'Working Class Criminology', in Ian Taylor, Paul Walton and Jock Young (eds.), *Critical Criminology*, London: Routledge and Kegan Paul, pp. 63–91.

Young, Jock, 1986. 'The Failure of Criminology: The Need for a Radical Realism', in Roger Matthews and Jock Young (eds.), *Confronting Crime*, London: Sage, pp. 3–40.

INDEX

Abbott 118, 121
Adler, Freda 54–5, 89, 94
Advisory Committee on Fraud 64, 82
Advisory Group on Prison Deaths 205
AGSI (Association of Garda Sergeants
    and Inspectors) 33, 155, 156,
    164–5, 215
AIDS 170
alcohol 39
Allen, Robert 136
Amir, Menachem 108
Annual Report on Crime 13, 158
*Annual Report on Prisons and Places of
    Detention* 81, 100, 101
arrests 25, 177–9, 187
Arthur, John A. 121
Association of Garda Sergeants and
    Inspectors (AGSI) 33, 155, 156,
    164–5, 215

bail 163–4
Bail Act 1976 (England and Wales) 164
Baldwin, John 182
Baldwin, Robert 157, 162,
Bannon, Michael 139
Becker, Howard 47
Beirne, Piers 26, 27, 53, 61, 94, 106
Bennett, Don 168, 169
Bennett, Richard 121
Benyon, John 151
Bernard, Thomas J. 49
Best, Margaret 78, 79
Best v. Welcome Foundation Ltd 79
Betelgeuse (ship) 67, 68
Bittner, Egon 153
Blueshirts 34

Blumstein, Alfred 203
Boesky, Ivan 76
Bohan, P. 156
Bottomley, A. K. 193
Box, Steven 26, 27, 63, 69, 76, 80, 93,
    106, 109, 110, 111, 112
Box-Grainger, Jill 113
Boyle, Kevin 183, 188
Braiden, Olive 104, 105
Braithwaite, John 60, 79, 217
Brannick, Teresa 16–17
Breathnach, Séamus 20
Breen, Richard 9, 11, 16, 17, 22, 51, 138
British Crime Survey 11, 103, 156
Brogden, Mike 175
Brownmiller, Susan 109
burglaries *see* offences against property
    with violence
Burke, Helen 23
Burney, Elizabeth 187
Burnham, R. W. 89

Cahill, 'General' Martin 13
Callan, Tim 96
capitalism and crime 42–3, 44
car theft 18–19, 36
Cardoso, Fernando 124–6, 131
Carlen, Pat 96
Carney, Claire 23
Carty, Michael 161
Catholic Church 55
Charleton, Peter 107
child abuse 16–17
Christie, Nils 207
Clarke, Michael 63, 78
Clinard, Marshall 42, 118, 121

Collins, Anthony 75, 76
Committee of Inquiry into the Penal
   System *see also* The Whitaker
   Report 64, 66, 192, 201, 212,
   214
Commission on Taxation 82–3
community policing 164–7
Companies Act 1990 76, 82
Concerned Parents against Drugs
   (CPAD) 168–71
Conroy Commission *see* Committee of
   the Garda Síochána
control theories 45–7, 50
convictions, rate of 179–184
Cook, Geoffrey 23
Corcoran, T. 172
corporate crime 57, **61** *see also* white-
   collar crime
Costello, Judge Declan 68–9
Council of Europe 12, 194, 198
Council for Social Welfare 24, 59
courts
   Dublin Circuit Court 182, 183, 185
   Galway district court 188
   gender bias 98–9
   proceedings in 179–80, 187–8
CPAD (Concerned Parents against
   Drugs) 168–71
crime rates
   Ireland low 53–6
   international comparisons 11–12
   structural arguments 35–9
crime reduction 212–19
crime statistics, representativeness 19–21
Crimeline (RTE) 10–11
Criminal Justice Act (1960) 196 (1984)
   163, 178, 209–10 (1985) 168, 178
   (1992) 114
Criminal Justice (Sexual Offences) Act
   1993 87–8
criminal justice system
   confidence in 54
   rape 111–12
   white collar crime 66
   and women **97–103**, 104
   sentencing 185–7
Criminal Law (Rape) Act 1981 107
Criminal Law (Rape) Amendment Act
   1990 105, 107
Cullen, Barry 170–71
Cullen, Francis 80–81, 218–19
Culligan, Patrick 157, 163
Currie, Elliott 50
Curtin, Chris 78

Daly, Mary 95
Dangerous Substances Act 1972 67–8
Data Protection Act 162
de Valera, Eamon 56
Deming, Mary Beard 104
Department of Justice 196, 206, 214–5
dependent development
   and affluence 133–6
   and gender 140–42
   and marginalisation **136–42**, 143,
      216–8, 222
   and opportunities for crime 136–40
   and state weakness 134–6
Desmond, Barry 170
detection rates 2, 4–6, 14, 174
detention rates 194
Dobbs, Anthony 202
Drudy, Sheelagh 137
drugs
   addiction in prisoners 102
   CPAD 168–71
   dealers 203
   economy 38–9, 140
   problems associated with 219–22
Dubeck, Paula J. 218–9
Dublin crime survey 22–3
Dublin Rape Crisis Centre 104
Dworkin, Andrea 109

Eaton, Mary 99
economic development and crime 120–
   21, **127–32**, 217
education and social class 51–2, 138
Einstadter, Werner J. 171
Eipper, Chris 134, 136
Elliott, D. S. 27
embezzlement 76–7
emigration 129–30
empirical research 144
Eppy, Ali 104
European Values Survey 1990 54, 155
Eustace, J. 139

Fagan, J. 221
Faletto, E. 131
fear of crime 9–11, 103
Fennell, Caroline 186
Fielding, Jane 151
Fielding, Nigel 151
Finance Act 1983 74
Finkelhor, David 106–7
firearms *see* guns
Fitzgerald, Grace 16–17

Flynn, Sean 168
Frank, André Gundar 124
fraud 72–4
fraud squad 82
Freeman, John R. 131

Gallagher, Patrick *see* The Gallagher
    Group
The Gallagher Group 69–72
Galway district court 188
Gamble, Nancy 104
Garda Review 20, 148, 154, 161
Garda Síochána
    community involvement 164–7
    confidence in 155–6
    Corporate Strategy Plan 162
    crime reduction 212–19
    deployment 159–60
    discretion 153–5
    historical origins 146–8
    police powers 163–4
    policing levels 158–9
    rape 114
    recruitment 152, 157
    response to crime 17, 89, **157–64**
    role of 148–9, 174
    sub-culture 150–53
    technology 160–64
    training 149, 180
    two-tier policing 175–6
geographical distribution of crime 6–7
Gilligan, Robbie 16–17
Gobert, James 79–80
Goodman Organisation 72
Gottfredson, Michael 45–7, 50
Gray, John 152
Great Britain 125, 142, 187
Greenberg, David F. 202–3
Gulf Oil, Bantry Bay 67–9, 134
guns 8, 37

Hagan, John 15, 62, 63, 81, 139–40, 144,
    203, 216
Haigh 148
Hannan, Damian F. 51
Hanrahan, John 78–9
*Hanrahan v. Merck, Sharpe and Dohme
    (Ireland) Ltd* 78–9
Hardiman, Niamh 54, 155
Harper, R. R. 161
Harris, Liam 148, 149, 152–3
Harvey, L. 88
Hayes, Joanne 90–91
Heal, Ken 161

Healy, John 129
Heidensohn, Frances 89, 91, 93
Henderson, Paul 164
Hindelang, Michael 27
Hirschi, Travis 27, 45, 50
Hoogvelt, Ankie 124
Hough, Mike 156, 202
Huizinga, D. 27
Hunt, Paul 99

IDA (Industrial Development Agency)
    135
imprisonment, rates 194
indictable offences
    categories 4–5
    classification 18
    definition 2
    detection rates 5
    levels 2, 3t, 4
    offences against the person *see*
        offences against the person
    offences against property with
        violence *see* offences against
        property with violence
    offences against property without
        violence *see* offences against
        property without violence
    proceedings 179–84
    recording 178–18, 20
Industrial Development Agency (IDA)
    135
industrial policy 134–6
industrialisation 35, 119, 137
insider dealing 75–6
Inter-Department Group on Urban
    Crime and Disorder 216
international comparisons
    crime rates 11–12
    prisons 193–5
The Irish Victim Survey 9, 16, 17, **22**

Jankovic, I. 207
JLOS (Juvenile Liaison Officer
    Scheme) 178
Jones, Tara 136
judges 98, **208–10**
Juvenile Liaison Officer Scheme
    (JLOS) 178
juvenile offenders 195

Kendall, K. 89
Kenny, Austin 158
Keohane, Kieran 134–5
Kerrigan, Gene 157, 209

Kerry Babies Tribunal 1985 90–91, 157
Kinsey, Richard 157, 162
Kirscheimer, Otto 206
Klein, D. 112
Korn, Richard 204

labelling theories 47–9, 51, 218
Lampson, L. 34
larcenies 5, 6, 72, 88, 96, 99
Lea, John 44, 45
Lee, Joseph 39, 55, 56
legal aid 188
Leonard, H. Jeffrey 82, 134, 135, 136
Levine, Dennis 75–6
Lie, John 131
Limerick Prison 100
Lombroso, Cesare 90
Lorenz, Walter 52
Lynch, Kathleen 137
Lynch, Christie 157
Lyons, Ann 99

Madigan, Lee 104
Magee, John 64–5, 74
Management of Offenders (policy statement) 201, 214–15
Manning, P. K. 153
marginalisation
    development and 136–42, 143, 216–8, 222
    'double' marginalisation 143
    white-collar crime 66–77
    women 140–2
Mathieson, Thomas 199, 204
Matoesin, Geoffrey 105, 110
Maung Natalie Aye 11, 103
Maxwell, Greg 74
Mayhew, Pat 156
McAleese, Mary 168
Mc Cafferty, Nell 91
Mc Conville, Michael 182
Mc Corkle, Lloyd 204
Mc Cullagh, Ciaran 10, 52, 147, 158, 159, 163, 193, 201, 207, 209
McGuane, Bridget 16–17
Mc Keown, Kieran 16–17
Medico-Social Research Board 221
Melossi, Dario 207–8
mens rea 78, 80
Merchant Bank *see* The Gallagher Group
Merton, Robert 40–41, 42–3, 45, 50
Messerschmidt, James 26, 27, 53, 61, 94, 106
middle-class crimes 217–9 *see also* white-collar crimes

migration 122
Mirrlees-Black, Catriona 11, 103
Misuse of Drugs Act 1977 168, 220
Morgan, Rod 204
Morris, Pauline 161
Mountjoy Prison 100, 101, 198, 200, 205
Moxon, David 202
murders 5, 21–22
Murphy, Miriam 17
Murray, Peter 137

National Association for the Care and Resettlement of Offenders (NACRO) 194
National Bureau of Fraud 82
National Economic and Social Council (NESC) 179
Needham, Michael 182
Neighbourhood Watch Schemes 165–7
Nelson, Steve 108
NESC (National Economic and Social Council) 179
new realism theory 43–5, 50
Nichols, Tom 164
Nolan, Phyllis 114
non-indictable offences 2, 18
Northern Ireland, conflict 37–8, 147

Oakley, Ann 92
O'Brien, Joseph V. 33–4
occupational crime 60–61
O'Connell, Michael 16, 22–3
O'Donnell, P. 34
O'Donoghue, D. 172
offences against the person
    definition 4–5
    levels 5, 7–8
    sexual 104
offences against property with violence
    definition 5
    levels 5, 6
    minor 13–14
    professional 13
    stolen property, recovery 9
offences against property without violence
    definitions 4–5
    larcencies 5, 6, 72, 88, 96, 99
    levels 5–6
Offences Against the State Act 1939 178
offenders
    characteristics 23–8, 36–7
    juveniles 195
    prisoners *see* prisoners
    social background 86–7, 140

official crime statistics, limitations 15–19, 57
Official Secrets Act 5
O'Hearn, Denis 129, 130
O'Mahony, Paul 12, 19, 23, 24, 64, 65–6, 102, 158, 162, 185, 192, 196, 197, 198, 200, 201, 205, 206
O'Malley, Tom 185
O'Neill, M. 139
opinion polls 11, 202
O'Toole 133
opportunities for crime see also criminal motivation
    development and 133, 136–140
    women's restricted 97

parental role 32–33, 46–7, 50
Park, Robert E. 32
Pearson, Geoffrey 34
Pease, K. 89
peripheral countries 123–7, 128, 134–6
person, offences against the
    definition 4–5
    levels 5, 7–8
    sexual 104
plea-bargaining 182–3
police see Garda Síochána
policing
    community 164–7
    corporate offences and 218
    Neighbourhood Watch schemes 165–7
    private 171–4
    professional see Garda Síochána
    self-policing 167–71
    two-tier 175–6
political motivation 13
Pollak, Otto 90, 98
Portlaoise maximum security prison 198
prison sentences see also punishment 100, 185–7, 193, 200, 202–3, 209–10
prisoners
    drug addition 102
    early release 196–7
    female 97, 100, 102, 189, 190, 191t
    numbers 189–90, 206–10
    offenders see offenders
    population studies 23–5
    remand 192–3
    sub-culture 203–5
    suicides 205–6
prisons
    cost 198
    effectiveness 199–203, 214–15
    failures 203–5, 215

international comparisons 193–5
    Limerick 100
    Mountjoy 100, 101, 198, 200, 205
    overcrowding 100–101, 195–6, 214
    Shenaganagh open prison 101
    staffing 197–8
    types of commital 190–92
    Wheatfield Prison, Dublin 196
private policing 171–4
prostitution 87–8, 92, 140
Punch, Maurice 155
punishment see also prison sentences
    district courts 184–5
    in Ireland 177–211
    middle-classes 218–9
    purpose 186
    rape 113–15
    white-collar crime 80–83

radical criminology 42–3, 45, 50
rape
    data 104–8
    explanations 109–13
    punishment 113–15
    reporting to police 114
    victim precipitation 108–9
    violence 108, 116
    Rape Act 1990 104
recidivism
    prisons and 199–200, 204–5
    women 102
Reiner, Robert 150, 151, 160, 212
remand prisoners 192–3
Report of the Beef Tribunal 73–4
Report of the Committee of Inquiry into the Penal System 64
reporting incidents 15–16, 20, 89, 114
restricted opportunities theory 93
Reynolds, Morgan O. 202
RIC (Royal Irish Constabulary) 146, 147
right to silence 163–4, 188
risk of crime 9–10, 14
Roberts, Julian 202
Ross, Senator Shane 76
Rottman, D. 9, 11, 16, 17, 21, 22, 23, 24, 32, 34, 45, 39, 51, 75, 76–7, 117, 122, 138, 154, 158, 178, 179, 182, 183, 184, 185, 194, 195, 200
Roxborough, Ian 125, 127
Royal Irish Constabulary (RIC) 146, 147
rural dislocation 122
rural orderliness, myth of 33–4
Rusche, George 206
Russell, Diane 113

Salmon, Trevor 147
Sanday, Peggy 111
Saunders, Andrew 182
Schwendinger, Herman 110
Schwendinger, julia 110
Scull, Andrew 173
Scully, Diane 109
self-policing
    CPAD 168–71
    vigilantes 167–8
self-report studies 26–8
sexist culture 110–12
Sexton, J. J 172
sexual offences
    rape *see* rape
    sexual assault 104
Shanahan, Kate 105, 185
Shenganagh open prison 101
Shapiro, M. 184
Shaw, Helen 209
Shearing, Clifford D. 172
Shelly, Louise I. 55
Shields, Dan 78
shoplifting 89, 90, 96
Sieber, Ulrich 62
Simon, Rita 94
single-parent families *see* child-rearing
Skolnick, Jerome H. 221
Smith, David 152
Smith, Lorna 105, 110
South Korea 131
social background
    offenders 86–7, 140
    victims 22–3
social change and crime **32–5**, 40–41,
    117–18, 120, 216–17
social disadvantage as motivation 50–52,
    136, 139
Spike Island 201
Spitzer, Steven 173
state weakness and development 134–6
Stenning, Philip C. 172
Stern, Vivien 215
Stokes, Kennedy, Crowley (Accountants)
    65
stolen property, recovery 9
suicides, prisoners 102, 205–6
Sutherland, Edwin 60, 81

Tax Amnesty Bill 83
tax evasion 74–5, 82–3
Taylor, Ian 42, 43, 51
Taylor, Maxwell 149

theories
    assessment 49–53
    biological 90
    control theories 45–7, 50
    crime rates 31–9
    criminal motivation 39–49
    definition 30–31
    labelling 47–9, 51, 218
    modernisation 118–23, 132–3
    new realism 43–5, 50
    radical criminology 42–3, 45, 50
    restricted opportunities 93
    structural 35–9
Tonry, Michael 187
Tormey, Philip 75, 76–7, 182, 183, 184,
    185
Townshend, Charles 34

Uganda, white collar crime 121
unemployment *see also* employment
    206–8
urban dislocation 122
urbanisation 119–20

Valera, Eamon de 56
victim surveys
    Dublin crime survey 22–23
    homicide study 21–22
    Irish victim survey 9, 16, 17, 22
victims
    corporate crime 81
    direct 9
    Dublin crime survey 22–23
    financial loss 8–9
    homicide study 21–22
    indirect 9–10
    Irish victim survey 9, 16, 17, 22
    physical harm 7–8
    psychological harm 8
    social background 22–3
    women 103–09
violence 8, 12, 108, 116
Visiting Committee 101

Walklate, Sandra 116
Walton, Paul 42, 43, 51
Weis, Joseph 27
Westley, William A. 150
Wheatfield Prison, Dublin 196
Whelan, Anthony 16, 22–23
Whelan, Brendan 17, 137
Whelan, Christopher 51, 54, 137, 155
Whitaker Report 1985 *see also* Commit-
    tee of Inquiry into the Penal
    System 201, 212, 214

white-collar crime
  cost 64–5
  court decision making 76–7
  definition 60–62
  developing countries 121
  fraud **72–4**, 82
  Ireland 62, 64–6
  law enforcement **72–6**, 82–3
  legal system 66–72
  marginalisation 66–77
  non-reporting 65–6
  perception 63
  punishment 78–83
  tax evasion 74–5, 82–3
Wickham, James 137

Wilson, Harriet 50
Wilson, James Q. 47, 63
Wilson, William 139
women and crime
  biological theories 90–91
  crime rates 86–90
  criminal justice system 97–103
  liberation 95
  offenders 94
  prisons 99–103
  sociological theories 91–7
Yiio, Kersti 106–7
Yeates, Padraig 168
Yorke, D. 156
Young, Jock 42, 43, 44, 45, 51